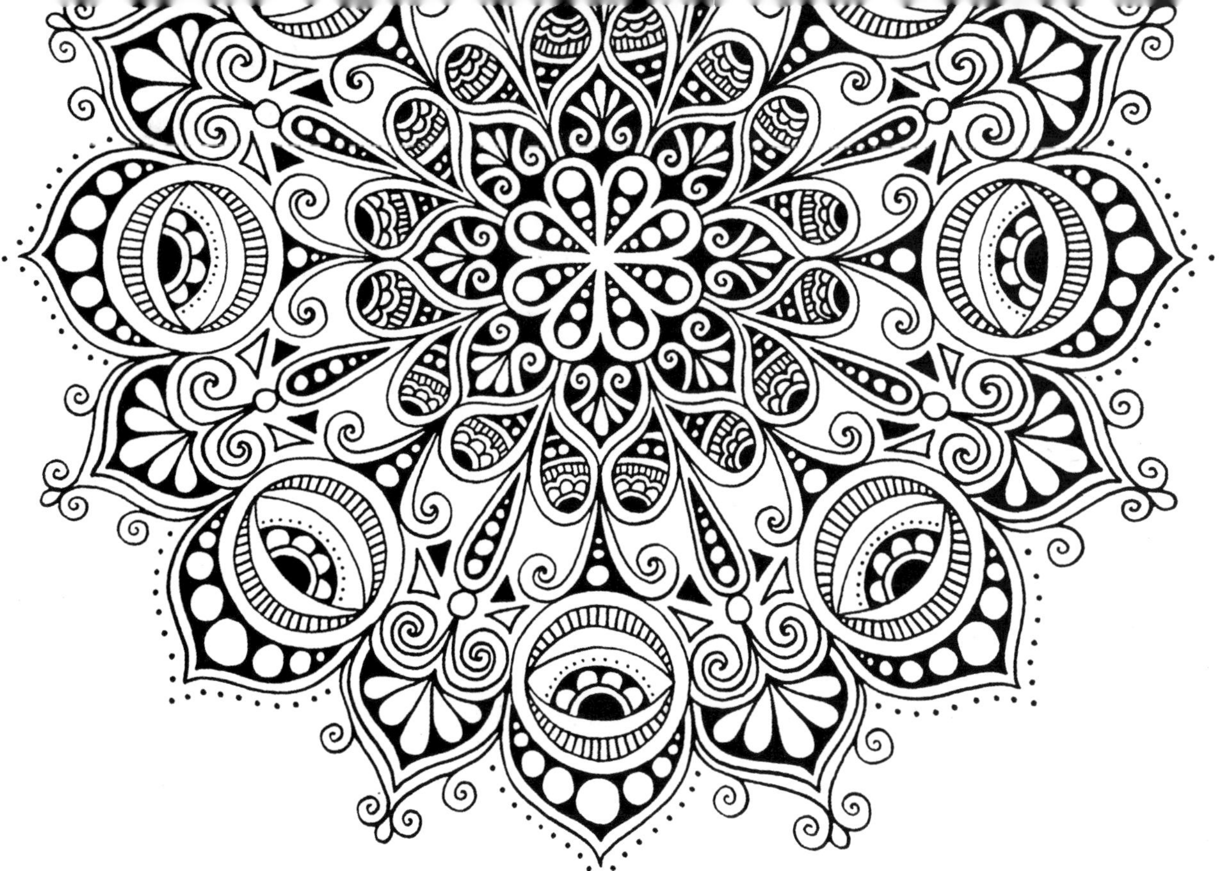

MEDITATIVE DRAWING

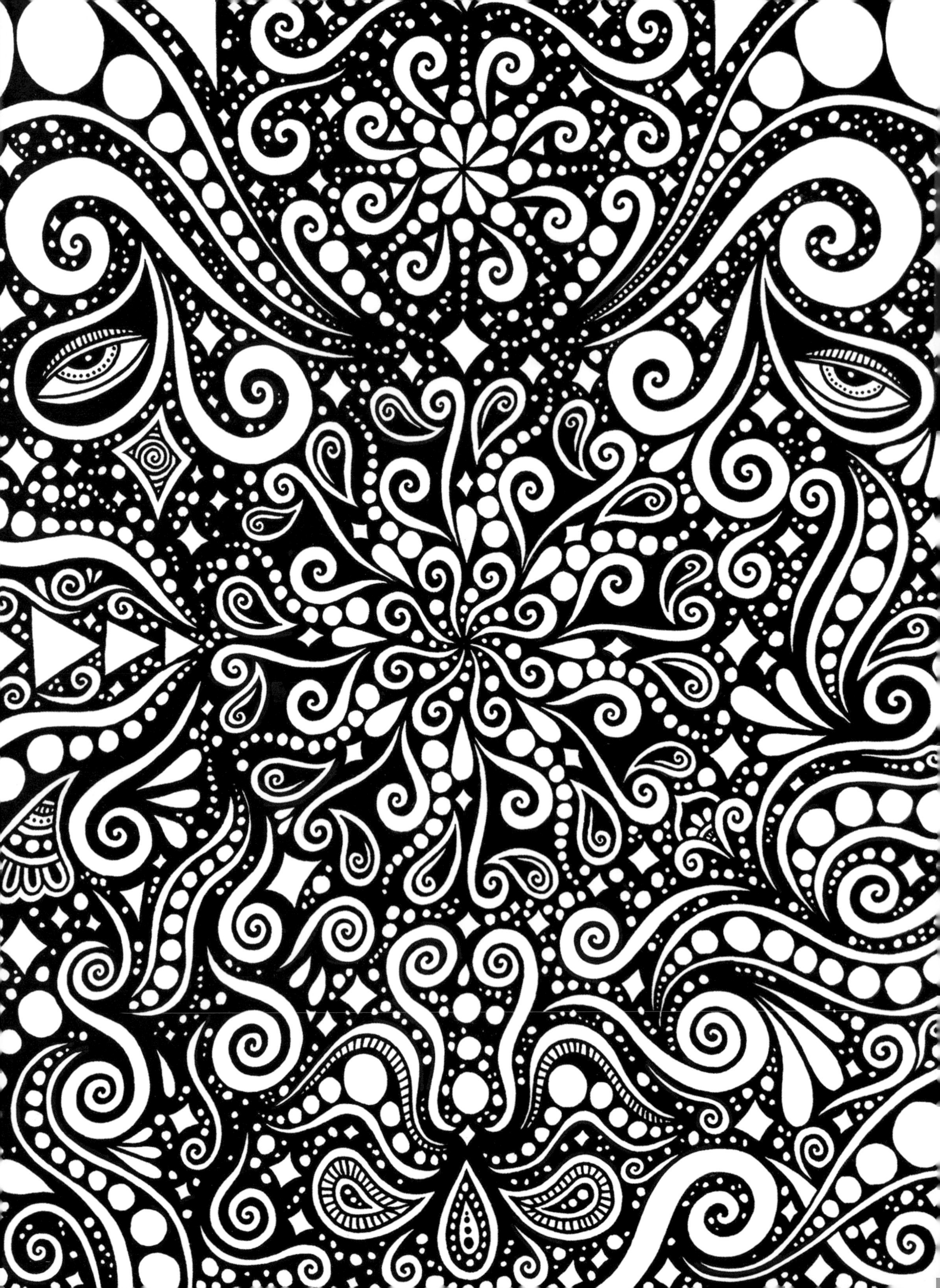

MEDITATIVE DRAWING

LEARN TO DRAW MANDALAS
AND OTHER PATTERNS THAT FOSTER
CALM AND CREATIVITY

Lizzie Snow
fortyonehundred

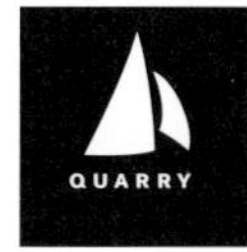

Quarto.com

First Published in 2025 by Quarry Books, an imprint of The Quarto Group, 100 Cummings Center, Suite 265-D, Beverly, MA 01915, USA.
T (978) 282-9590 F (978) 283-2742

29 28 27 26 25   1 2 3 4 5

ISBN: 978-0-7603-9249-2

Digital edition published in 2025
eISBN: 978-0-7603-9250-8

Library of Congress Cataloging-in-Publication Data

Names: Snow, Lizzie, 1995– author.
Title: Meditative drawing : learn to draw mandalas and other patterns that foster calm and creativity / Lizzie Snow, fortyonehundred.
Description: Beverly, MA : Quarry Books, 2025. | Includes index.
Identifiers: LCCN 2024043886 (print) | LCCN 2024043887 (ebook) | ISBN 9780760392492 (trade paperback) | ISBN 9780760392508 (ebook)
Subjects: LCSH: Drawing—Technique. | Drawing—Psychological aspects.
Classification: LCC NC730 .S64 2025 (print) | LCC NC730 (ebook) | DDC 704.9/48--dc23/eng/20241019
LC record available at https://lccn.loc.gov/2024043886
LC ebook record available at https://lccn.loc.gov/2024043887

Design and page layout: Kelley Galbreath

Printed in Malaysia

ABOUT THE AUTHOR

Lizzie Snow is a contemporary visual artist and the creative brand director behind **fortyonehundred**. She has spent the last decade crafting a business and career at the intersection of art and thoughtful study.

With a master's in fine arts and a bachelor's in design, top brand collaborations, a large social media following, and significant media features, she has built a thriving brand by blending marketing acumen with her meditative art practice.

Lizzie has worked with major companies such as Apple®, Lululemon®, and Converse®. Her diverse portfolio includes internationally commissioned murals, original paintings and prints, and product lines ranging from fine jewelry to artist tools. Her online courses on drawing, painting, and creative entrepreneurship, and this book on meditative drawing, reflect her dedication to empowering artists, innovators, and creatives worldwide.

Her artworks are inspired by fractals in nature, with intricate patterns that alternate between free-flowing designs and those built on symmetry, scaling, repetition, and circularity—creating contemporary explorations of the mandala.

Lizzie lives in Auckland, New Zealand.

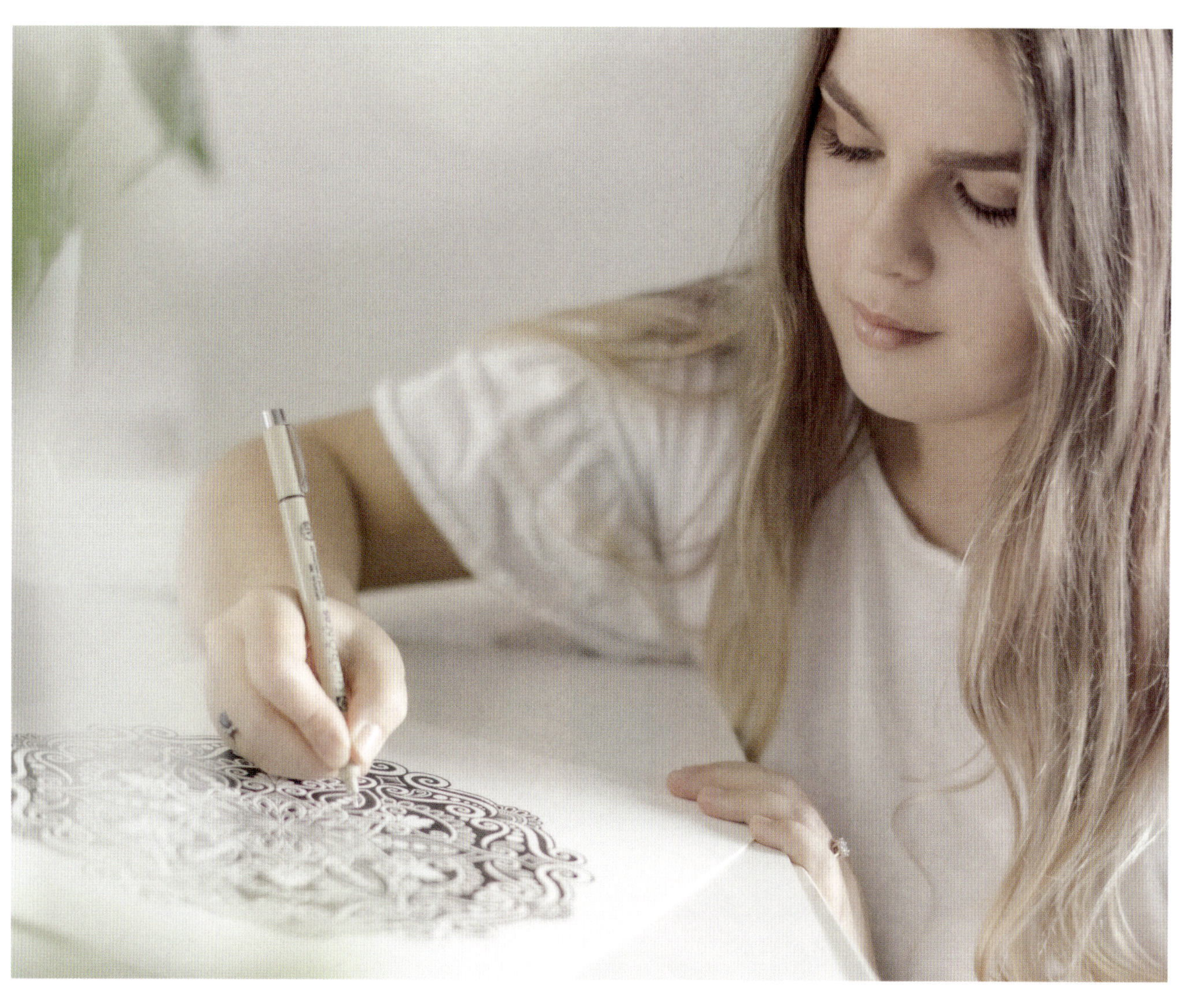

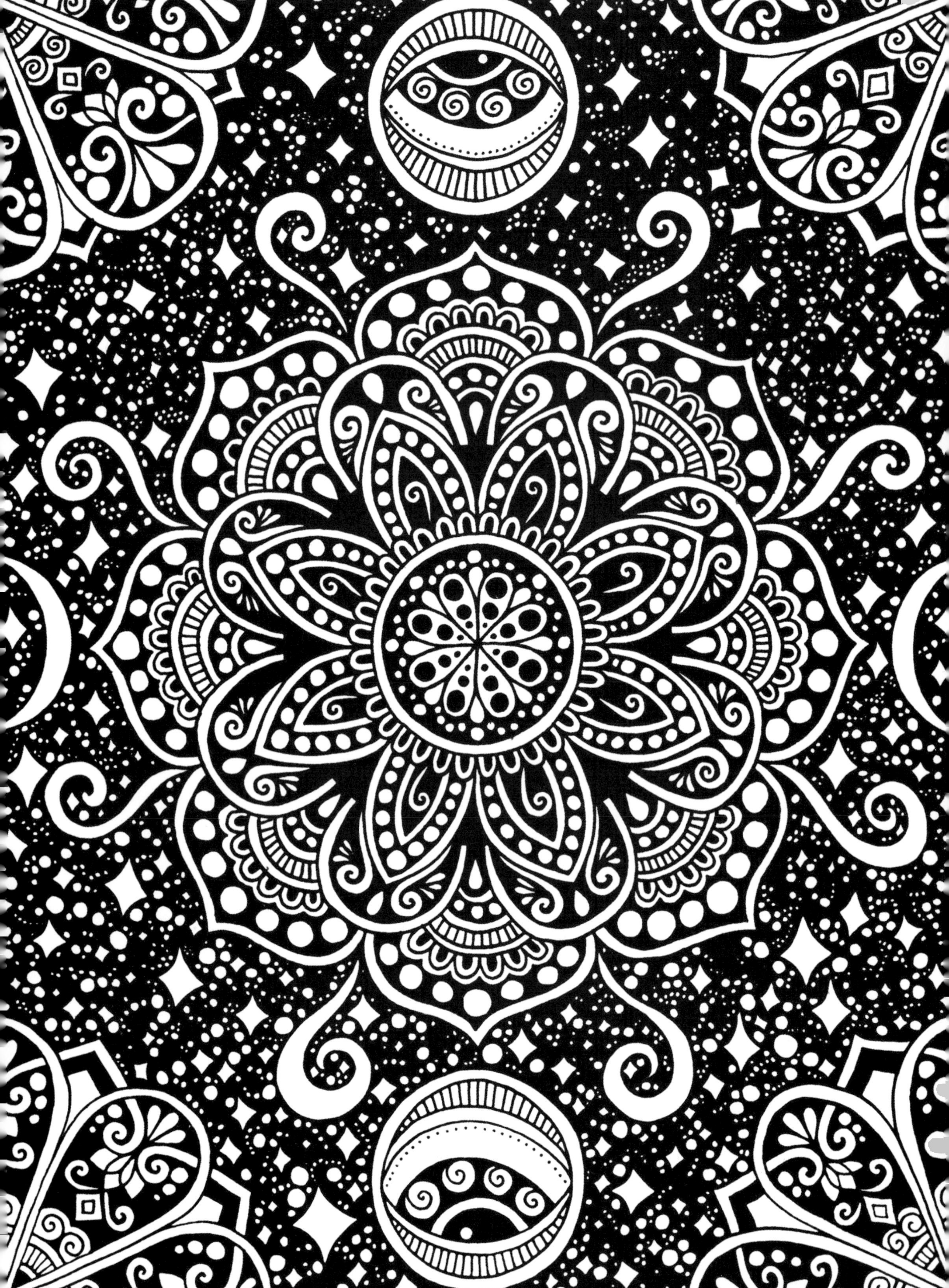

CONTENTS

INTRODUCTION: THE POWER OF A MEDITATIVE ART PRACTICE

EVERYONE HAS THE ABILITY TO DRAW. It can be as instinctive as breathing—if we lean in and allow it. It's a practice like anything else, and we get better through time, attention, and effort.

As children, we draw freely, but somewhere between childhood and our teenage years, many of us decide we "can't draw,"—perhaps influenced by a casual comment that lingers longer than expected, combined with our growing self-awareness and the suppression of self-expression. By adulthood, we've mostly abandoned creating art, yet we may still find ourselves (or our subconscious) sketching intricate patterns while absorbed in a phone call. Creating works like painted portraits or sketched landscapes can feel intimidating, leaving room for self-doubt and the fear of imperfection.

The style of meditative drawing that I'm so passionate about feels free from this emotional roller coaster of self-doubt and judgment. Here's the thing—I know you can draw a dot. Then a line. Then a dot and a line again. Before you know it, a pattern begins to form—the beginning of an artwork. As you progress, you may find yourself exploring more detailed and structured designs. However, the core essence of what I want to inspire is the simple, raw expression of self that pours from the pen when you let it flow—without overthinking it. This is the practice of meditative drawing. When practiced mindfully, drawing can effortlessly deepen our connection with ourselves and the world around us, transforming a simple act of creativity into a profound and playful exploration of life.

Being mindful and focused on the mark being made encourages us to focus on the present moment, allowing each touch of the pen or brush to become an act of meditation. As you immerse yourself in the rhythmic flow of creating, you may find that your mind becomes quieter and other stresses fade away. It's a practice that is accessible, enjoyable, and easy to learn.

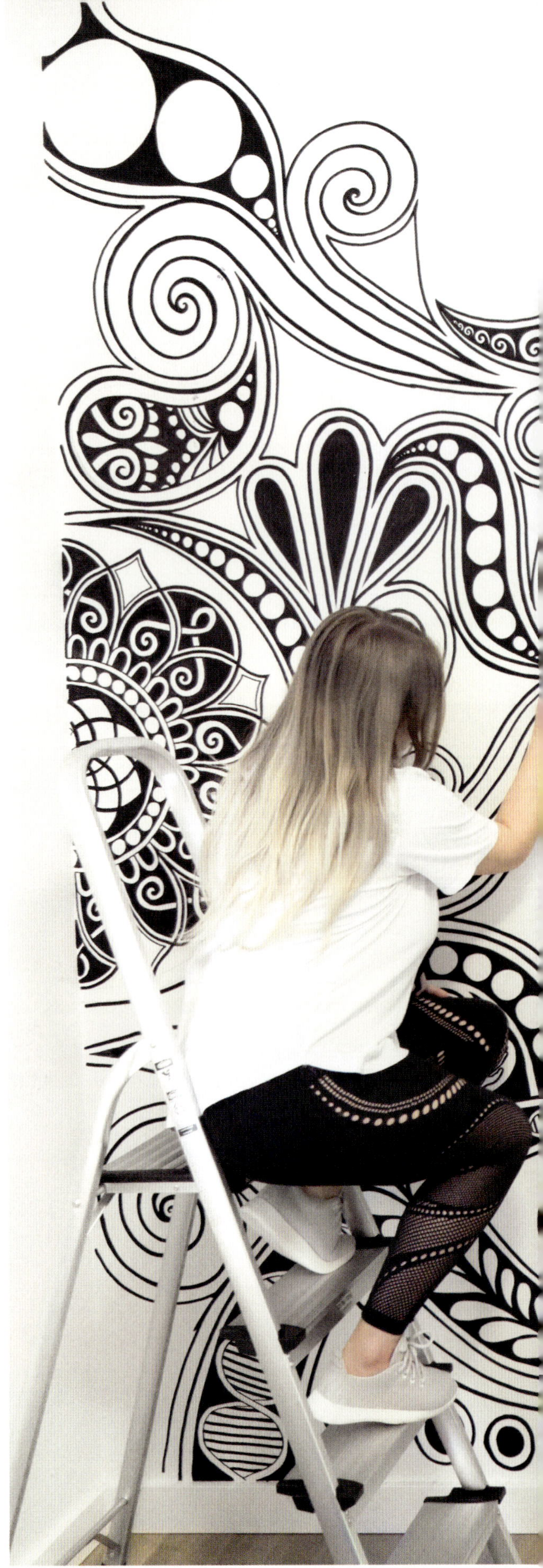

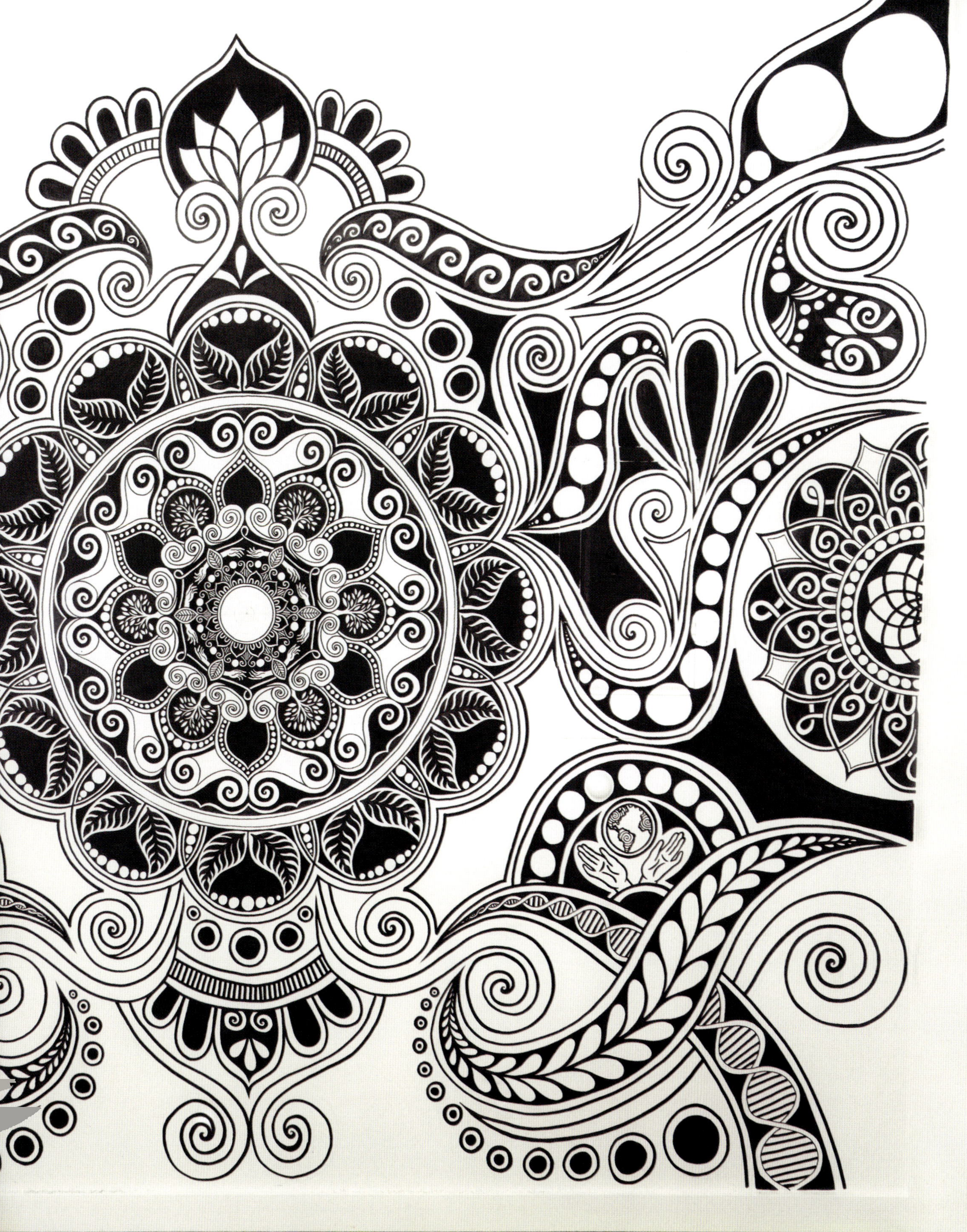

The most important and rewarding aspect I've found in meditative drawing is that the emphasis shifts from the result to the journey itself. The finished product of having a beautiful artwork is simply a bonus. The real beauty lies in the time spent rediscovering stillness and self-awareness through the act of creation.

As you spend more time on this artistic journey, you'll learn how to let go of self-judgment and embrace the process, embarking on a less "performative" path of art creation and finding a more authentic, calming practice. It's a practical technique to foster a deep sense of calm and clarity, especially if the more traditional, seated meditation doesn't work for you (which I struggle with myself).

Meditative drawing offers more than just a creative outlet; it serves as a transformative practice that we can integrate into our lives to teach us more about who we are in any one moment. I'm excited to share some of this knowledge with you and encourage you to think of this style of drawing as an option when you seek the feeling of being grounded.

A lot of us avoid drawing and making art, but I want to encourage you to give yourself permission and freedom to draw, to explore, and to tap into this practice that we have waiting for us at our fingertips.

HOW TO USE THIS BOOK

WHETHER YOU HAVE NEVER DRAWN before or are well experienced in your art practice and perhaps looking for a new perspective, this book was created for you, as you are now.

This book is broken down into steps so that you can learn how to create free-flowing artworks and contemporary explorations of the mandala in a relaxed and straightforward manner. There are lots of options available (for example, you can choose whether to download a completed "mandala grid" or learn how to create it from scratch).

You're welcome to copy the artworks that I've created, but I mostly encourage you to use them as inspiration—to observe the way I've constructed these patterns and then be inspired to create your own. These artworks are like fingerprints, unique to each of us. When we lean in to what evolves naturally from our hands and minds, it's magical seeing what unfolds upon the canvas.

There are no rules in using this book, just an invitation to explore and create. Each chapter builds upon the previous one, offering practical advice, techniques, and exercises to guide you through. You can use it as a step-by-step linear guide, or as a place to return to for encouragement.

This book touches on the aspects of meditative drawing that I find most engaging, and I share my artworks and techniques with you to help you create your own.

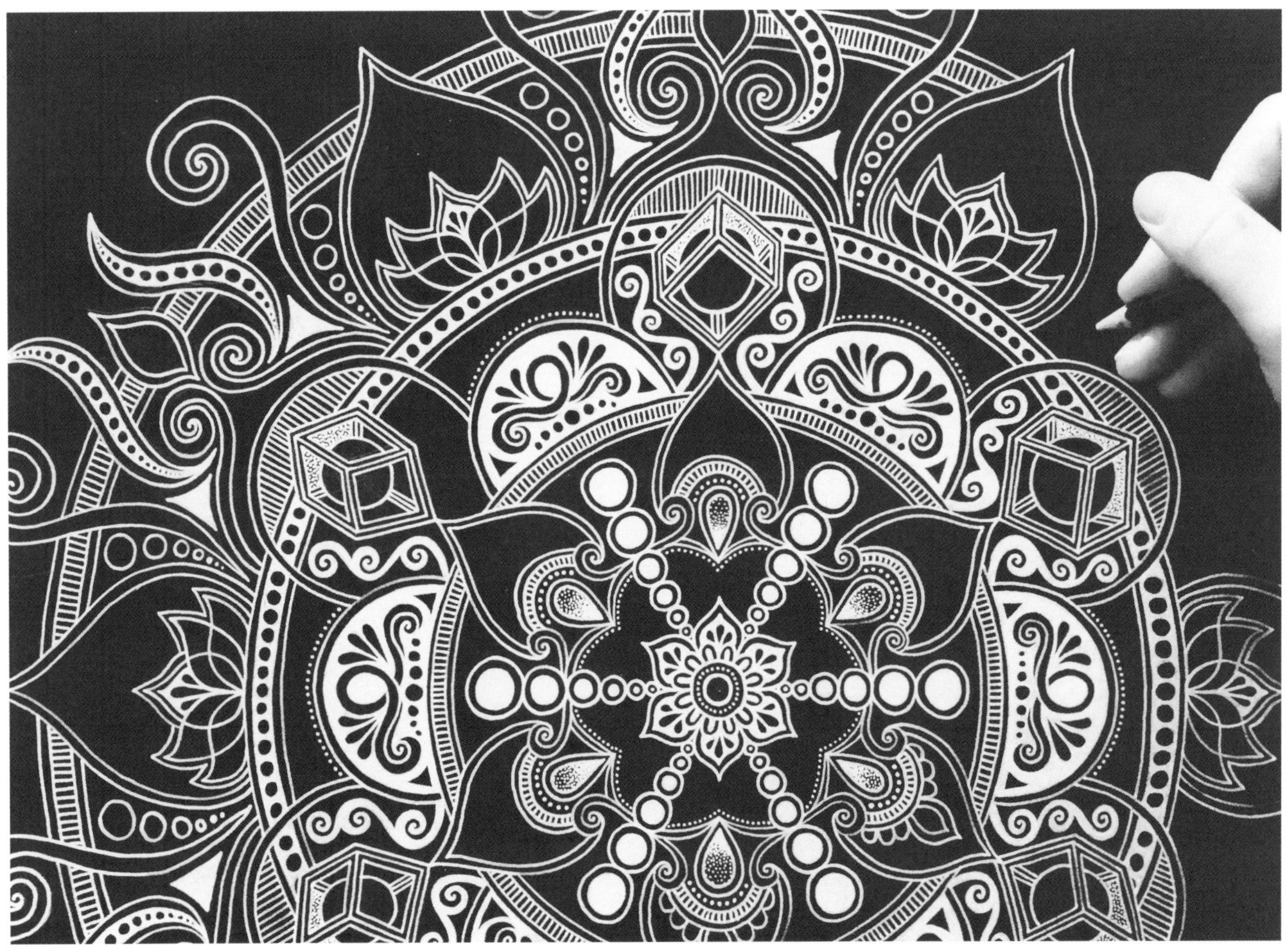

FREE-FLOW VERSUS STRUCTURED DRAWING

The two styles of art that you will learn in this book are free-flow and structured drawing. Free-flow drawing is a spontaneous, intuitive approach that embraces imperfection and creativity, while structured drawing involves meticulous planning and arrangement to achieve aesthetic coherence and order. These art forms are fulfilling and expressive, enabling you to enter a flow state of mind and experience a meditative drawing practice.

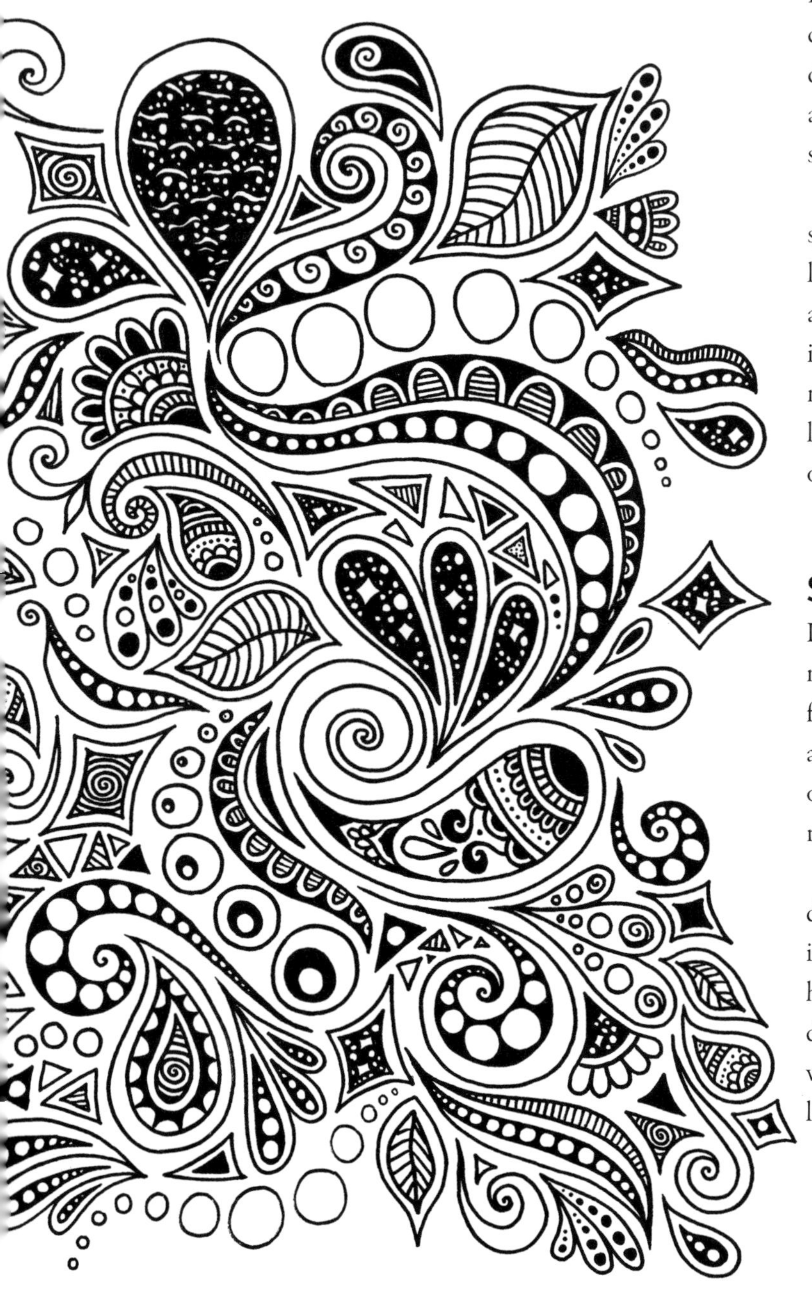

Free-Flow Drawing

Free-flow drawing is a dynamic and organic approach to creative expression, where we unfold a tapestry of intricate designs. In this method, we relinquish any rigid control, allowing the path of the lines and dots and shapes to evolve spontaneously from our pencil or pen.

This style of drawing invites imperfection and celebrates spontaneity. It is a forgiving process, a gentle experience. I like to think of free-flow drawing as a journey, where we as artists surrender to our inner rhythm and let our intuition guide the creativity, rather than having preconceived notions of form or structure or what the artwork "should" look like. The resulting artworks from this technique are often unpredictable and are always different.

Structured Drawing

In contrast, structured drawing offers a deliberate and methodical approach to meditative art, by taking those same free-flowing patterns and then organizing them through arranged frameworks. The structures I am drawn to over and over again are symmetry, circularity, and scaling, which can result in a contemporary exploration of the mandala.

This structured method takes us down a path of detailed preparation, crafting each element with care and intention. Accuracy is the goal here—to achieve visual harmony. Through careful craftsmanship and deliberate design, structured drawing offers a journey through order where beauty emerges from the careful arrangement of lines and shapes. It's a very focused practice.

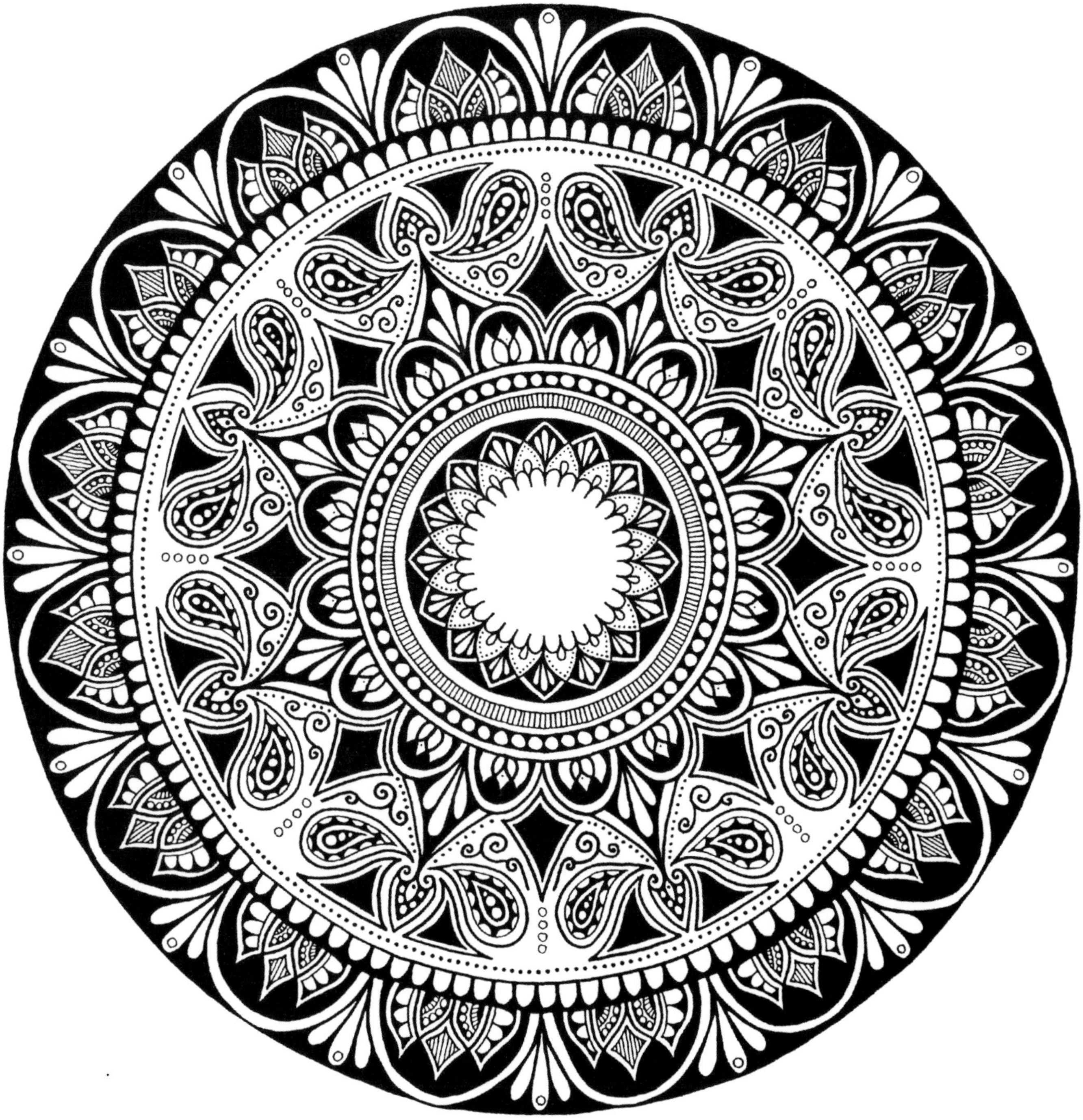

TIP

You can see how shapes and patterns make up these two artworks. The patterns flow freely on the left, and are structured through scale, symmetry, and circularity on the right, creating a contemporary exploration of the mandala.

SCAN TO WATCH A VIDEO in which these two methods are combined: painting a wall mural where I start with a structured artwork in the middle, which then expands outward into free-flowing organic patterns.

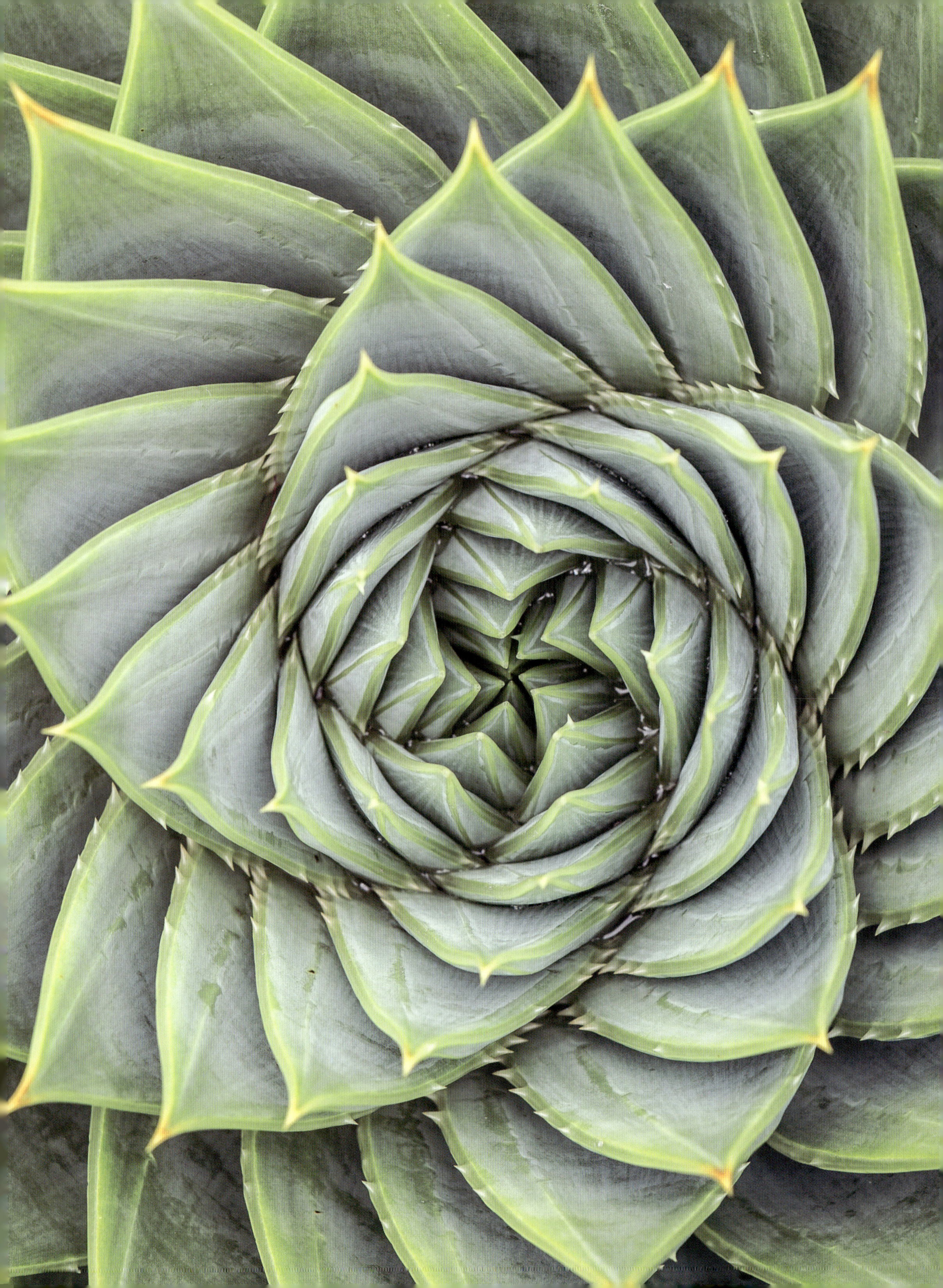

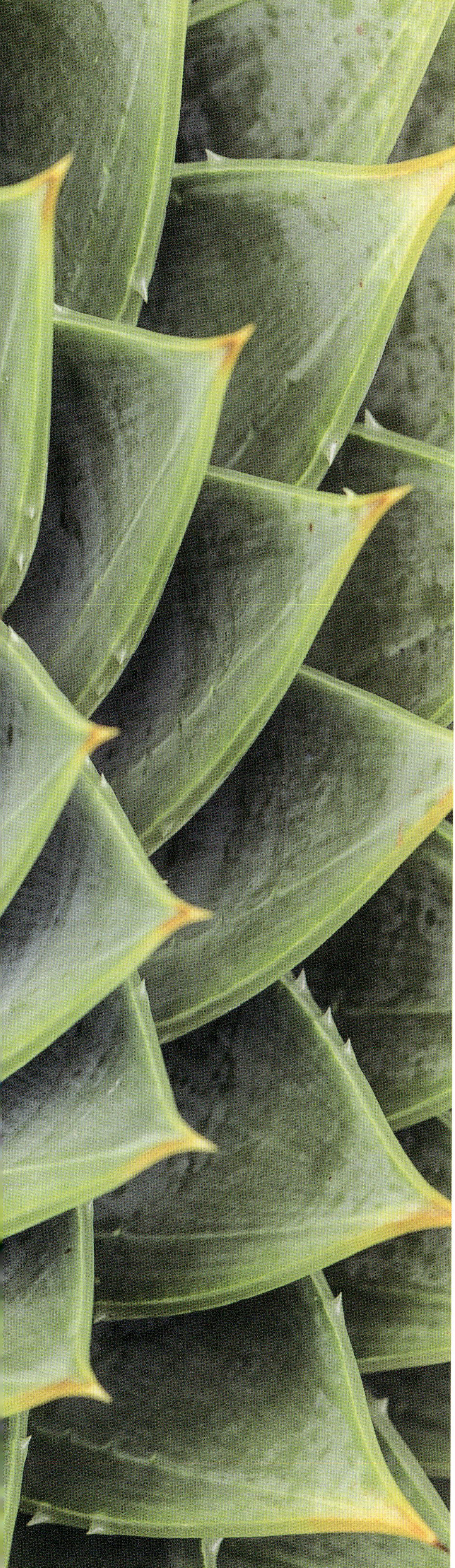

1

ABOUT MANDALAS + FRACTALS

THE MANDALA IS MORE THAN JUST A CIRCLE; it is a symbol of unity, harmony, and interconnectedness that transcends cultures, religions, and time. Found across nature and art, it reflects the intricate balance and order of the universe. This chapter explores the significance of the mandala as a cultural and spiritual symbol, a tool for meditation and self-reflection, and a recurring pattern in the natural world. From ancient traditions to modern interpretations, the mandala continues to captivate and inspire, revealing the profound connection between the inner and outer worlds.

WHAT IS A MANDALA?

A mandala is an intricate orb of organized chaos, an artwork or form based on a circle. The mandala may be one of the most universal symbols in nature, art, architecture, and religious expression from all over the world. Found throughout all civilizations, it isn't unique to one group or area in particular (Slegelis 1987) but is a symbol and form that connects culture and nature together. The mandala can be understood externally as a representation of the universe, and internally as a guide for self-reflection.

The visual themes in a mandala include recurring circles, symbols, symmetry, scaling, and repetition. The history of the mandala extends from its origins in nature, through the evolution of art and architecture over time to the present day. Today, the mandala remains a significant art form, a meditative practice, a cultural artifact, and a tool in art therapy techniques.

Etymology

The word *mandala* is a Sanskrit word that translates to "circle." When broken down, *manda* means "essence," and *la* means "container." This linguistic breakdown unveils the rich symbolism encapsulated within mandalas. They are not merely beautiful shapes or intricate art forms; they are vessels that symbolize the essence of consciousness and the universe.

In Gudran Bühnemann's 2017 research, she delves into the complexity of this ancient term, noting, "Mandala is a polyvalent term, and an attempt to explain the meaning of the word in the different contexts in which it occurs would be an ambitious undertaking." Her words emphasize the multifaceted nature of mandalas, which embody spiritual, artistic, cultural, natural, and psychological dimensions all at once.

Across cultures, the term *mandala* universally signifies a circular artwork. This broad application highlights the mandala's ability to resonate with diverse audiences, serving as a symbol of unity, wholeness, and interconnection between people and with nature.

In modern, Western contexts, mandalas gained awareness through the work of figures such as psychologist Carl G. Jung, who viewed the mandala as a tool for meditation and self-discovery. The mandala is recognized as an aid for meditation, cultural awareness, connection with nature, and a tool for promoting mental calmness and personal insight.

The mandala symbolizes the connection between the vast universe and the individual self, bridging macrocosm and microcosm. Reflecting the structure of vast natural and cosmic systems, from the swirl of galaxies to the orbit of planets, mandalas, at the same time, capture the personal layers within us, symbolizing our journeys and the complexity of consciousness. This duality reminds us that by understanding ourselves, we gain insight into the world around us—illustrating the interconnectedness of all things. Acting as a bridge between inner and outer realms, the mandala's repeating, symmetrical design has a fractal quality, with patterns that echo across scales, reinforcing the link between micro and macro worlds.

On a more personal level, a mandala can serve as a map of the mind, with the self at the center and each layer radiating outward, symbolizing relationships, values, and beliefs. This arrangement illustrates how we relate to the world around us, inviting reflection on our inner priorities and how they align with the outer world.

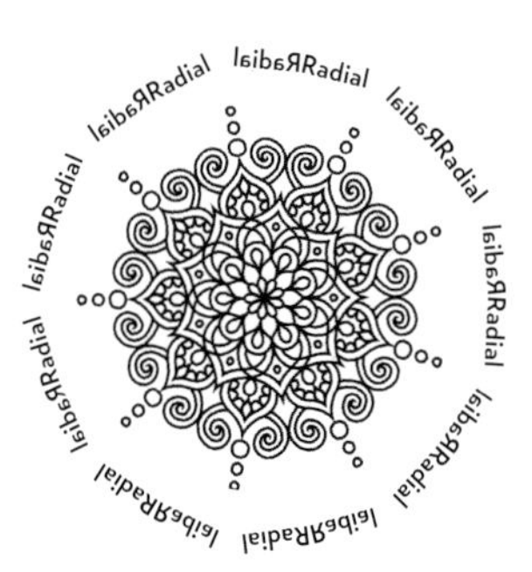

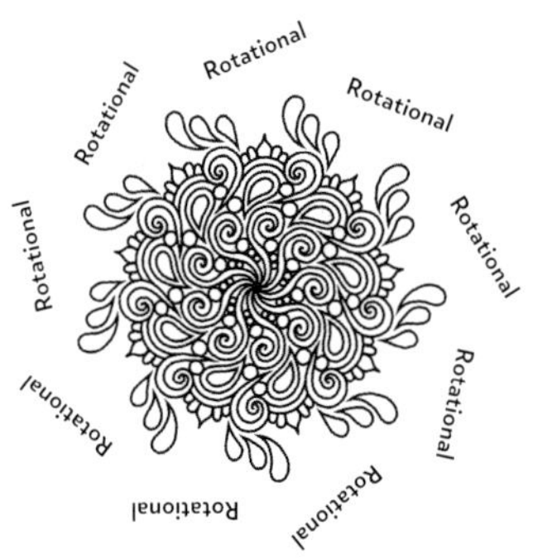

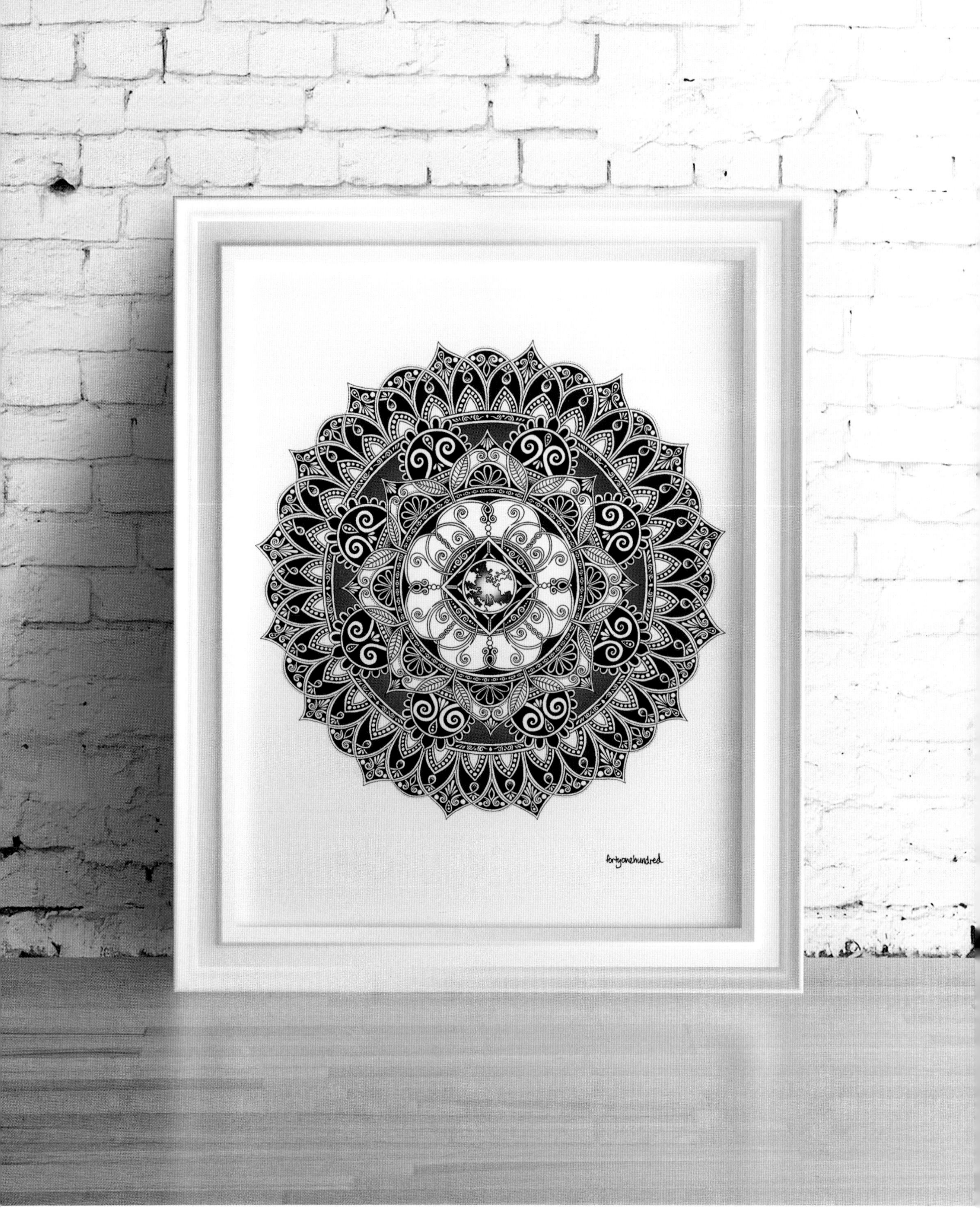
fortyonehundred

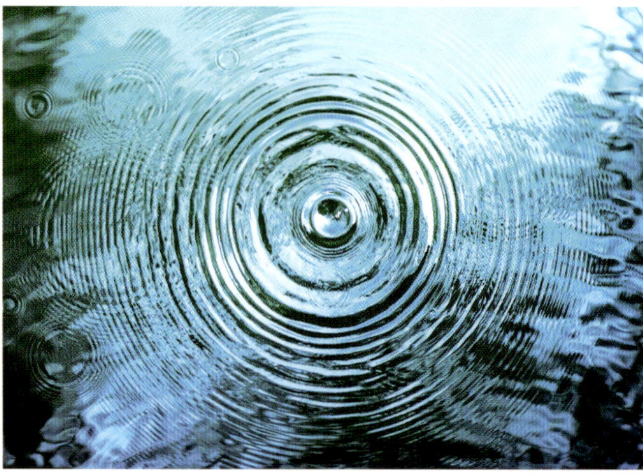
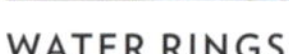
WATER RINGS

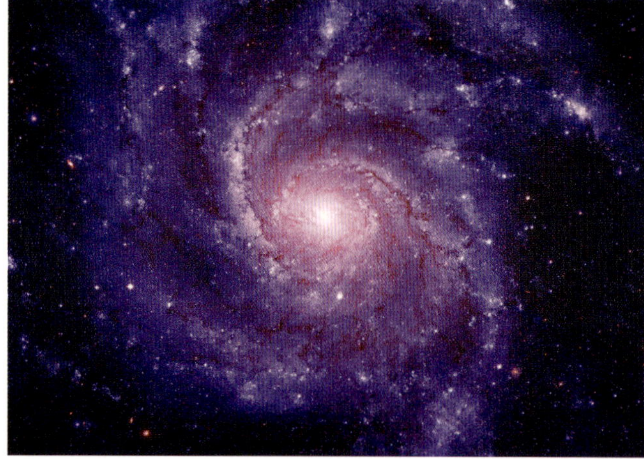
SPIRAL GALAXY

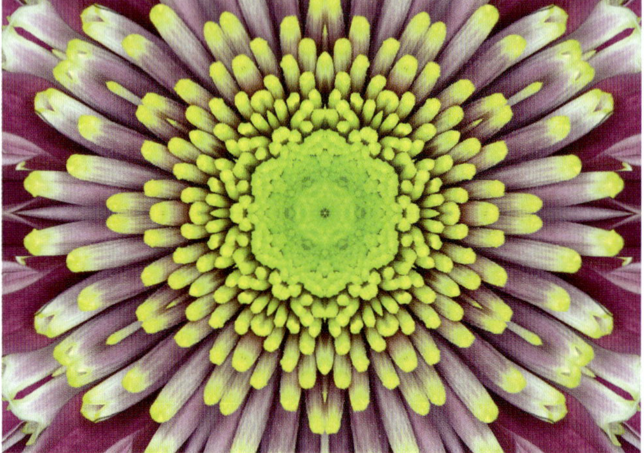
CLOSE-UP OF FLOWER CENTER

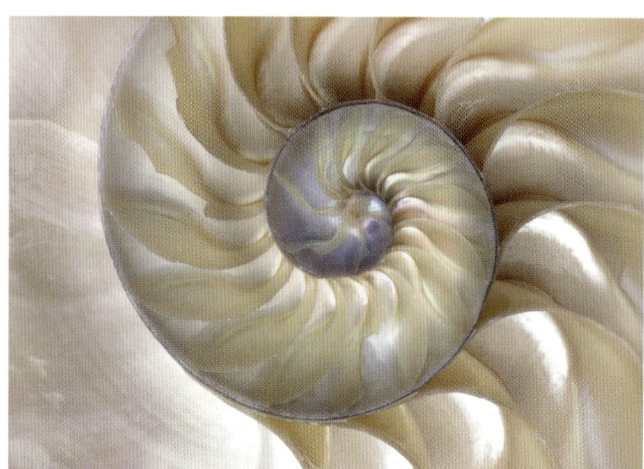
NAUTILUS SHELL

Mandalas in Nature

The universal existence of mandala-like patterns in nature, showcasing intricate and captivating patterns, reflect the interconnectedness of life and the underlying order of the universe. These natural mandalas, with their almost perfect symmetry and balance, have been a source of fascination and inspiration for humans throughout history and demonstrate the fundamental principles of geometry and harmony that shape our existence.

Mandalas can serve as a bridge between the inner and outer realms, offering insights into the unity and continuity of life. Examples of mandalas in nature include:

- **CONCENTRIC RINGS IN WATER:** Ripples formed by raindrops (or impact, like a dropped stone) create captivating expanding circles.

- **HURRICANES AND TORNADOES:** The swirling patterns of weather systems display a natural mandala-like arrangement, created by intense atmospheric forces.

- **FLOWER CENTERS:** Sunflower seeds are arranged in a spiral pattern, reflecting the golden ratio and natural symmetry.

- **THE EYE:** The iris features intricate patterns that are unique to each individual, our portal to personal identity and connection with each other.

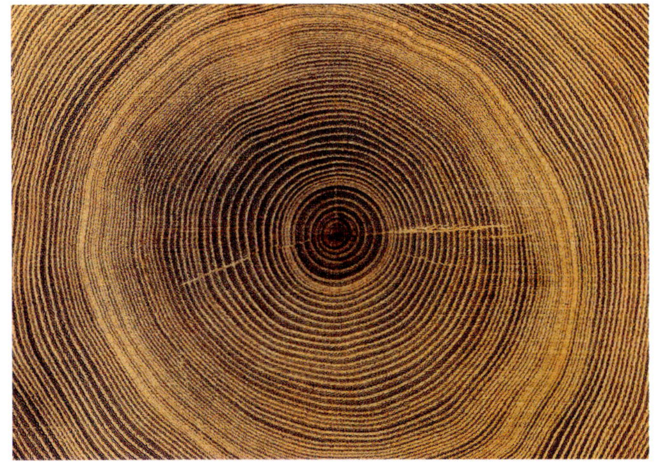

RINGS OF OAK TREE

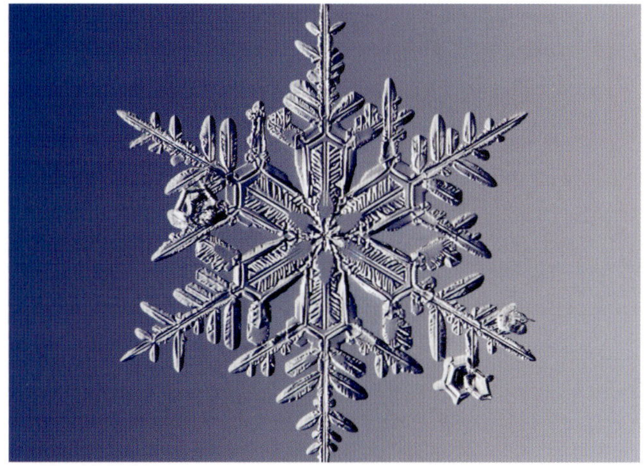

SNOWFLAKE

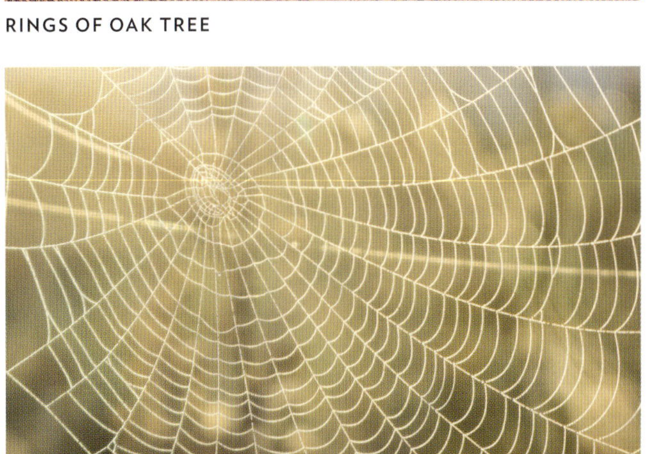

SPIDERWEB

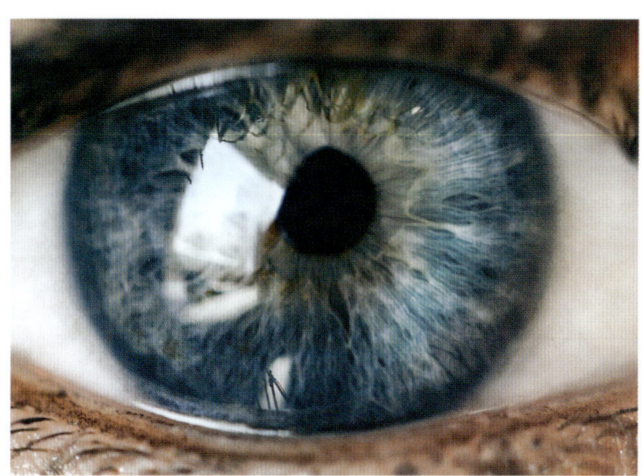

HUMAN EYE

- **CROSS SECTIONS OF FRUIT:** Fruit such as oranges, watermelon, and kiwi display radial symmetry, revealing nature's inherent patterns.

- **SNOWFLAKES:** Each snowflake forms a unique and symmetrical mandala, showcasing the beauty of natural geometry.

- **SEASHELLS:** Spiraling structures in seashells follow the Fibonacci sequence, illustrating mathematical precision in nature.

- **SPIDERWEBS:** These intricate configurations exhibit geometric precision and functionality, serving as clear examples of natural mandalas.

- **BUBBLES:** Spherical bubbles with reflective surfaces create simple yet perfect mandalas.

- **PLANETS AND ORBITS:** The orb-like shape of planets, and their paths and movements in the solar system, take on a very mandala-like formation.

- **TREE TRUNK RINGS:** Growth rings in trees show layered, circular patterns that indicate the passage of time and environmental conditions.

- **PUFFERFISH COURTSHIP RINGS:** Male pufferfish create intricate, circular patterns on the ocean floor as part of their mating ritual, showcasing stunning natural artistry.

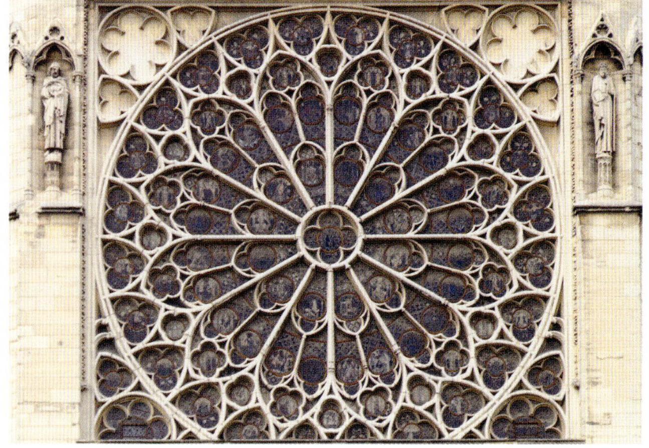
ROSE WINDOW, NOTRE DAME CATHEDRAL, PARIS, FRANCE

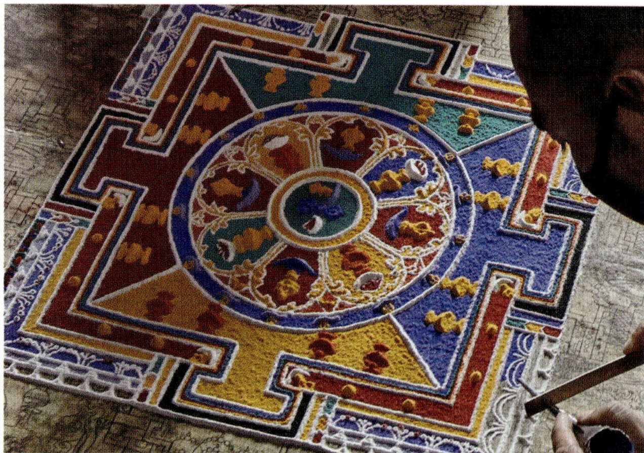
BUDDHIST SAND PAINTING

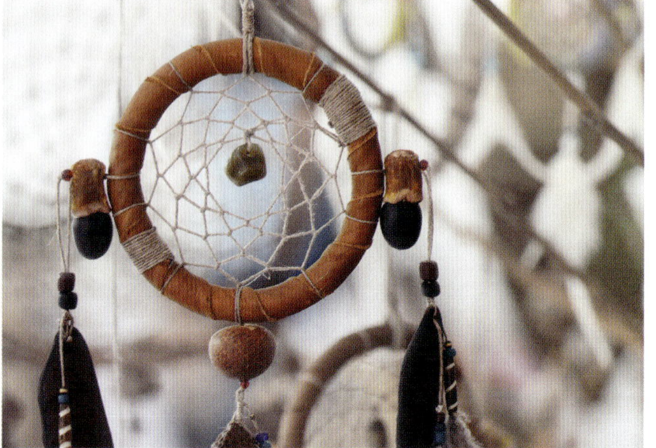
NATIVE AMERICAN DREAM CATCHER

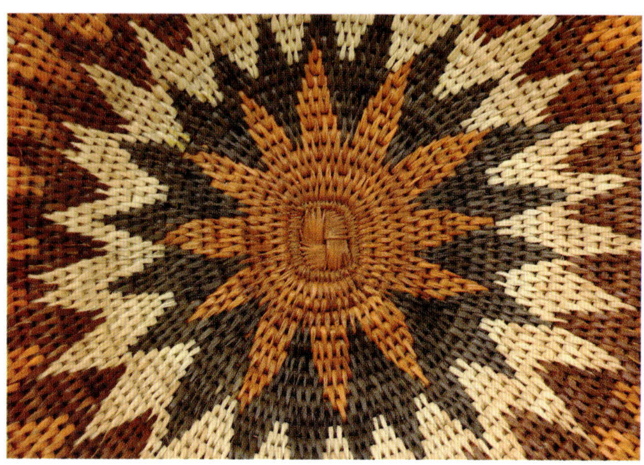
AFRICAN BASKET WEAVING

Mandalas in Art and Culture

A universal symbol found across cultures and time, the mandala transcends geographical and cultural boundaries, appearing in nature, art, architecture, and spiritual practices worldwide. A mandala represents our relationship to infinity, symbolizing that all things in life are interconnected. It embodies the concept of unity and harmony, illustrating the cyclical nature of existence. Cultural examples of the mandala include:

- **CELTIC KNOTS:** These intricate and endless loops used in Celtic art symbolize the interconnectedness of life and eternity.
- **RELIGIOUS ARCHITECTURE:** Intricate patterns tell biblical stories and symbolize the divine order of the universe, often in stained glass or as part of the architecture.
- **THE AZTEC CALENDAR:** A circular stone carving represents the Aztec understanding of time and the cosmos.
- **BUDDHIST SAND PAINTINGS:** Created by monks to represent the universe, sand paintings are meticulously crafted out of colored sand and then destroyed to symbolize the impermanence of life.

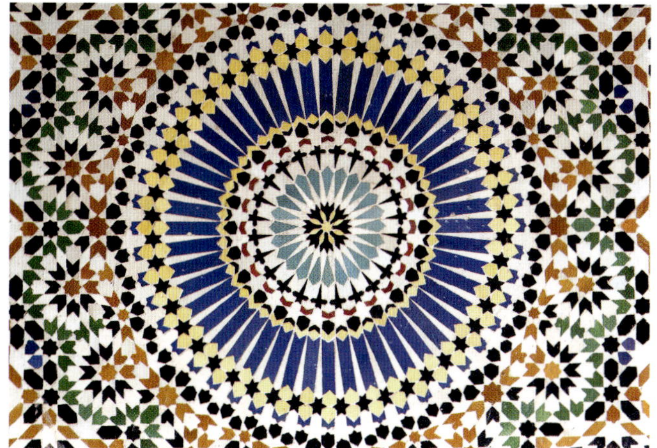

ISLAMIC MOSAICS

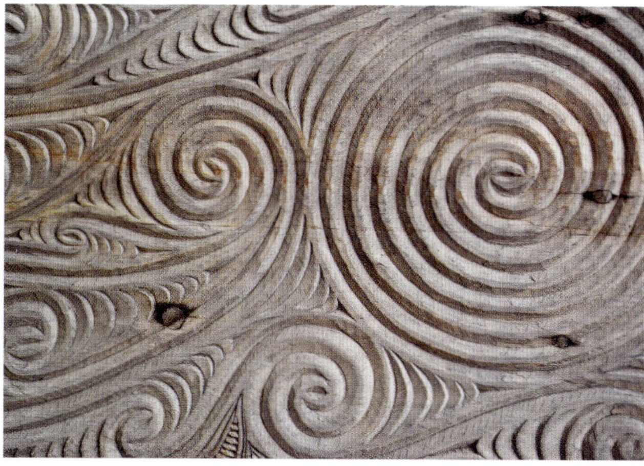

WOODEN MĀORI CARVING, NEW ZEALAND

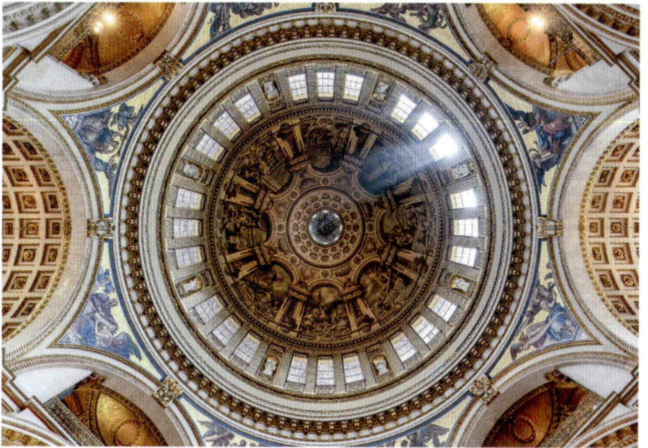

CEILING, ST. PAUL'S CHURCH, LONDON, UNITED KINGDOM

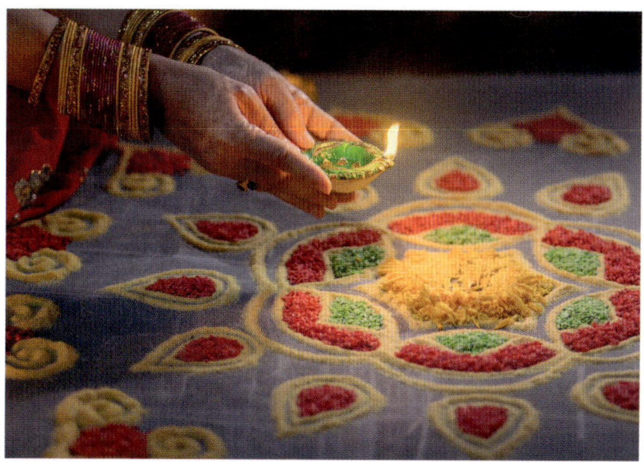

RANGOLI ART, INDIA

- **NATIVE AMERICAN DREAM CATCHERS:** These woven circles protect against negative dreams, symbolizing protection and the cycle of life.

- **INDIAN RANGOLI ART:** Mostly made with colored chalk, rangoli is a decorative art form made on floors, walls, and courtyards during festivals such as Diwali, representing joy, positivity, and sacred geometry.

- **ISLAMIC MOSAICS:** The geometric patterns in Islamic art reflect the interconnectedness of all things and the oneness of God.

- **AFRICAN BASKET WEAVING:** Intricate patterns are woven into baskets that are used daily, representing community, tradition, and the circle of life.

- **LABYRINTH PATHS:** Used in various cultures for meditation and prayer, labyrinths symbolize a journey to the center of the self and back out into the world.

- **TIBETAN THANGKAS:** Painted or embroidered mandalas are used as aids for meditation, rituals, and religious ceremonies.

- **MĀORI AND PACIFIC ISLAND DESIGNS:** Carvings, weavings, tattoos, and paintings from Māori and Pacific Island cultures often feature intricate, symmetrical patterns that tell stories of ancestry, nature, and spirituality.

- **YANTRAS IN HINDUISM:** Geometric diagrams are used in Hindu meditation and worship, representing the universe and the body as a sacred space.

Mandalas in Science

The scientific world provides numerous examples of fractal and mandala-like patterns and symmetries, which reflect the underlying principles of order and structure in natural systems. These patterns, often arising from fundamental laws in physics, biology, and chemistry, offer insights into the organization and dynamics of both microscopic and macroscopic phenomena. The study of these structures highlights the elegance and coherence inherent in the natural world and may also serve as a point of intersection between scientific inquiry and philosophical or spiritual exploration. Examples of mandala-like patterns in science include:

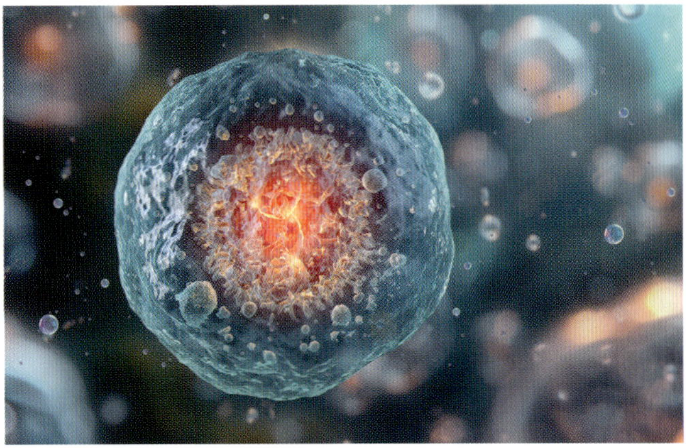

HUMAN EMBRYO CELL

- **CYMATICS:** The study of visible sound and vibration, where sound frequencies create intricate patterns in mediums such as sand, water, or other particles. These patterns, which can resemble Chladni figures, illustrate the relationship between sound and form and often evoke mandala-like symmetry.
- **HUMAN HEARTBEAT PLOTTED:** Sabelli's 2000 study found that when the electrical activity of the human heart is plotted on a graph (such as in an ECG), the repetitive, rhythmic patterns can resemble symmetrical, mandala-like forms, illustrating the intersection of biology and geometry.
- **MAGNETIC FIELD LINES:** The patterns formed by iron filings around a magnet display symmetrical and circular arrangements and are visually similar to mandalas.
- **GALAXY STRUCTURES:** Spiral galaxies, such as the Milky Way, exhibit mandala-like formations with their spiraling arms, showcasing cosmic symmetry and order.
- **ATOMIC AND MOLECULAR STRUCTURES:** The arrangement of atoms in molecules and crystals often forms symmetrical, mandala-like patterns, reflecting the fundamental geometry of matter, such as the hexagonal structure of ice or the cubic arrangement of salt crystals.
- **FRACTALS:** Mathematical sets that exhibit self-similarity across different scales, fractals reveal infinitely complex and repeating patterns. Fractals have been the main inspiration behind my artwork.
- **CHEMICAL REACTIONS:** There are chemical reactions, like the Belousov-Zhabotinsky reaction, that produce repeating, symmetrical patterns similar to mandalas.
- **CARL JUNG'S MANDALA STUDIES:** Jung, a pioneering psychologist, used mandalas in therapy, believing they represented the self and the psyche's wholeness. He saw mandalas as tools for personal transformation and understanding the unconscious mind. We'll explore his work further in the next chapter.

EXPLORING FRACTALS

Fractals are a hypnotizing mathematical construct. They are complex geometric shapes that are characterized by self-similarity at all scales. This means that when you zoom in on a fractal at any one point, you see the same patterns repeating themselves over and over (regardless of the level of magnification). Fractals are found throughout our natural world; think of the similarity between the branching patterns of trees and the structure of our nervous system, the scar of a lightning bolt mirrored in the cracking of mud or concrete, or the jagged silhouettes of mountain ranges reflected on a smaller scale in the shapes that emerge in sand marked by the tide. Fractals allow us to visualize our connection to the infinite—to the largest and smallest thing that exists, and where we are within that continuum—and they suggest that there is no beginning and no end. Once you understand what a fractal looks like, you realize that you already know them and see them everywhere.

Fractals also play a crucial role in science, including chaos theory, computer graphics, and the study of complex systems. In art, fractals have inspired artists to create mesmerizing visualizations and explore the beauty of mathematical patterns. One renowned artist that has famously worked with fractals is Jackson Pollock. When I stood in front of one of his paintings at The Met in New York, during a visit to the city for an art commission, I was struck by how the organized chaos of fractal patterns seemed to come alive through the splattered paint. It felt like being immersed in its rhythm.

Fractals represent a fascinating intersection and interconnection between mathematics, science, art, and culture, offering insights into the underlying order and complexity of the natural world. Fractals provide a tangible window into the infinite diversity of nature's forms. They can be seen as the fundamental design tool behind everything that exists.

Fractals are not only visually captivating but also deeply soothing. One of my favorite studies on fractals is by Robles et al. (2020) from the University of Oregon, which looks into the attraction children have toward fractal patterns.

TIP

One of the most famous examples, and I think the best way of being able to see and visualize fractals, is the Mandelbrot set, named after mathematician Benoit Mandelbrot, who coined the term fractals in the 1970s. It's worth looking up videos on YouTube to see a "Mandelbrot zoom" in action.

INSIGHT

I first discovered fractals alongside my best friend, Claudia. We were on a long walk through native bush in New Zealand and tripping out about how all these beautiful shapes in nature had a similar intrinsic quality, but we couldn't quite figure out the connection. It was fascinating to later discover fractals, and we reveled in the excitement of drawing parallels between the patterns in the mountains and the forest and the natural beauty around us.

My journey with fractals started here—a curiosity that continues to grow. I devoured as many books as I could find, spent countless hours drawing, and even wrote my thesis on them. My fascination with fractals has never stopped, and I still find joy in learning and observing them.

Fractals allow us to visualize our immense interconnection with nature. They've completely changed the way I create and think about art and I hope you will enjoy learning about them too.

The researchers found that by the age of three, children show a remarkable preference for fractal designs over other types of visual stimuli. This suggests that our attraction to fractals might be connected to something fundamental in human cognition, possibly linked to our evolutionary past. After all, fractals are everywhere in nature, so it's no wonder humans are instinctively drawn to them. What's interesting is that this preference doesn't fade with age; it remains a consistent part of our visual processing. The study hints that our affinity for these patterns goes beyond just learning and exposure—they seem to be hardwired into us. This connection shows that fractals are more than just a mathematical curiosity—they are deeply embedded in how our brains process visual information, possibly influencing how we feel and think creatively.

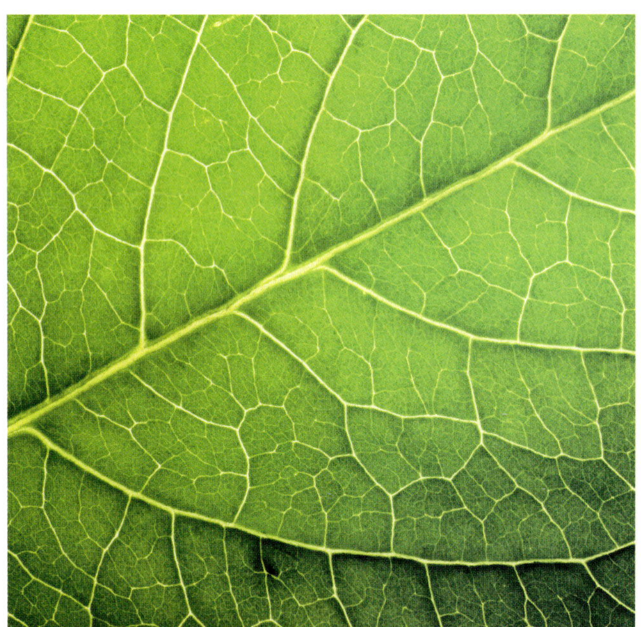

VEIN PATTERNS IN A LEAF

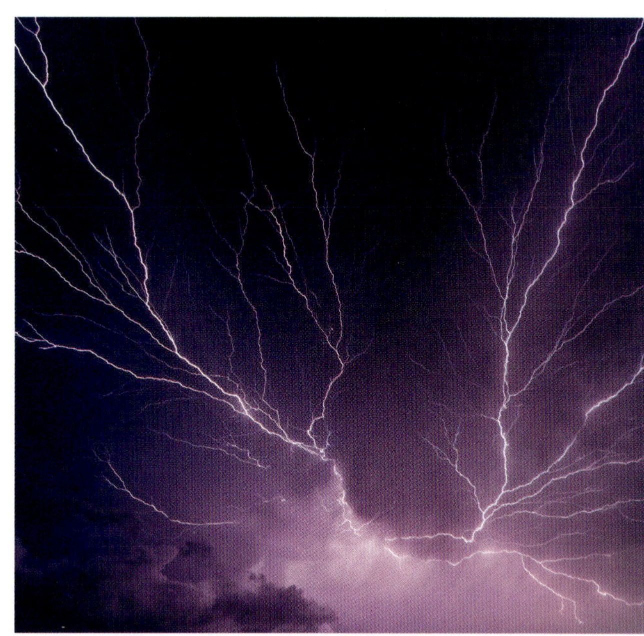

LIGHTNING STORM

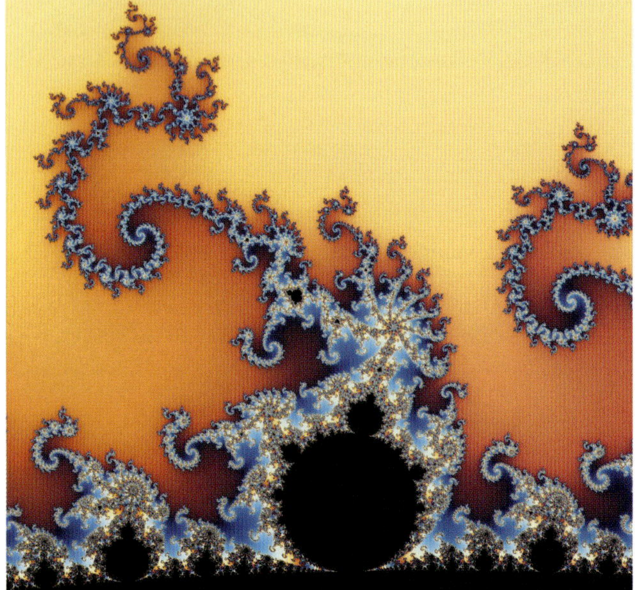

MANDELBROT SET DETAIL

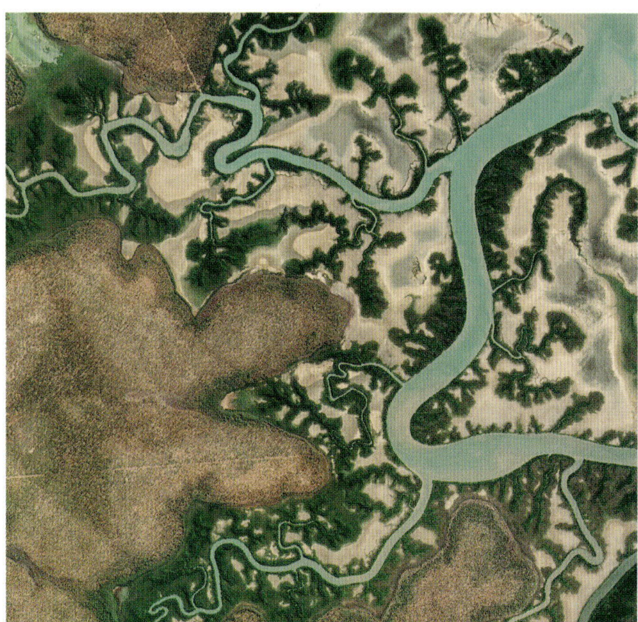

RIVER SYSTEM, AUSTRALIA

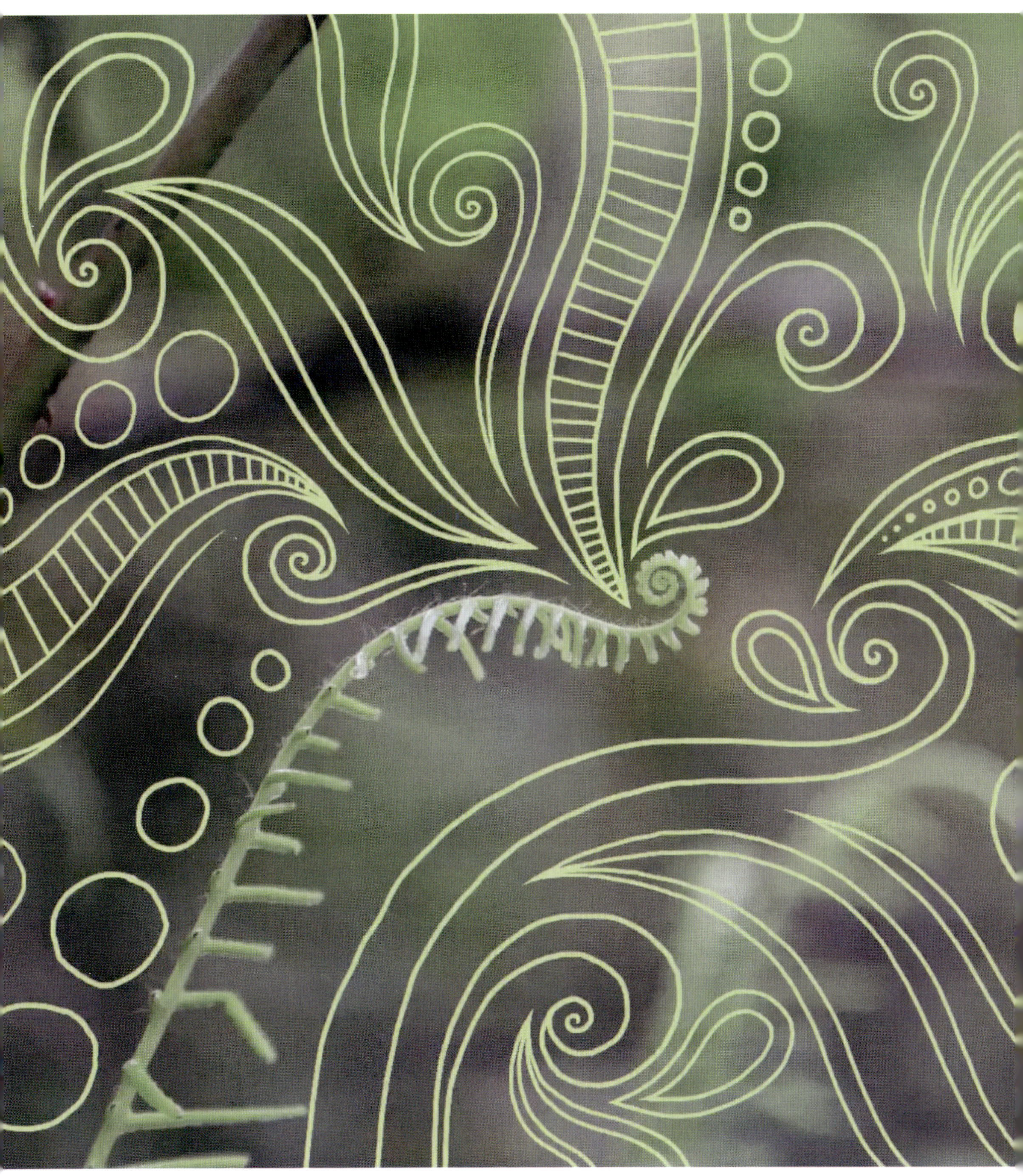

HOW FRACTALS ARE LINKED TO MANDALAS

The relationship between fractals and mandalas lies in their shared structural properties, particularly the concept of self-similarity. Both fractals and mandalas feature a sense of "organized chaos," where complex patterns emerge from simple designs that repeat in various ways. In fractals, this is a mathematical principle, where the same shape repeats infinitely as you zoom in or out. Mandalas achieve this repetition through geometric symmetry, where simple motifs are mirrored or rotated to create a cohesive, complex whole. By incorporating fractal principles into our artwork, we can reflect the complexity of the natural world.

Observing forms in nature—like the veins of leaves or the circular forms of Neptune's necklace on the beach—invites us to engage with fractals both literally, through drawing fractal-based designs, and conceptually, by embracing the idea of self-similarity. These patterns can be structured through repetition and symmetry, resulting in a contemporary exploration of the mandala. Alternatively, we can let these patterns evolve freely, creating fluid, organic designs through free-flow drawing, where shapes evolve without predefined rules. Both approaches—structured and free-flowing—present different methods for meditative drawing, with one emphasizing focus and discipline, the other encouraging spontaneity and freedom.

Inspired by fractals in nature, we can create patterns that expand and evolve on the canvas. Through both fractals and mandalas, we not only observe the beauty of nature's patterns but also explore the universal principles that bind all things together.

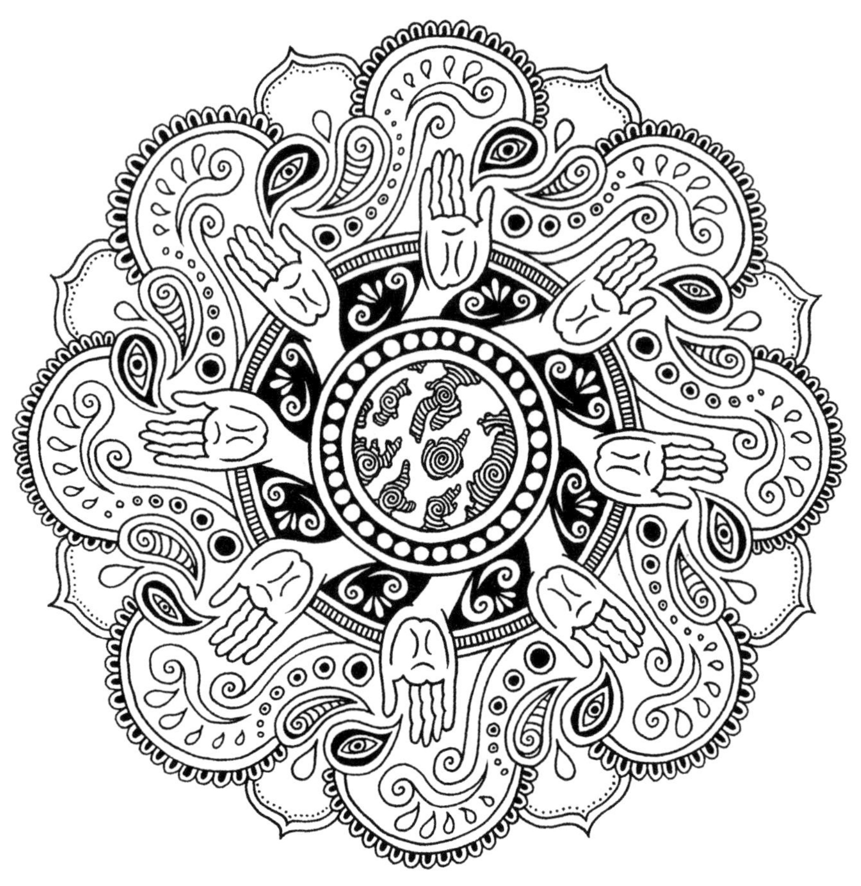

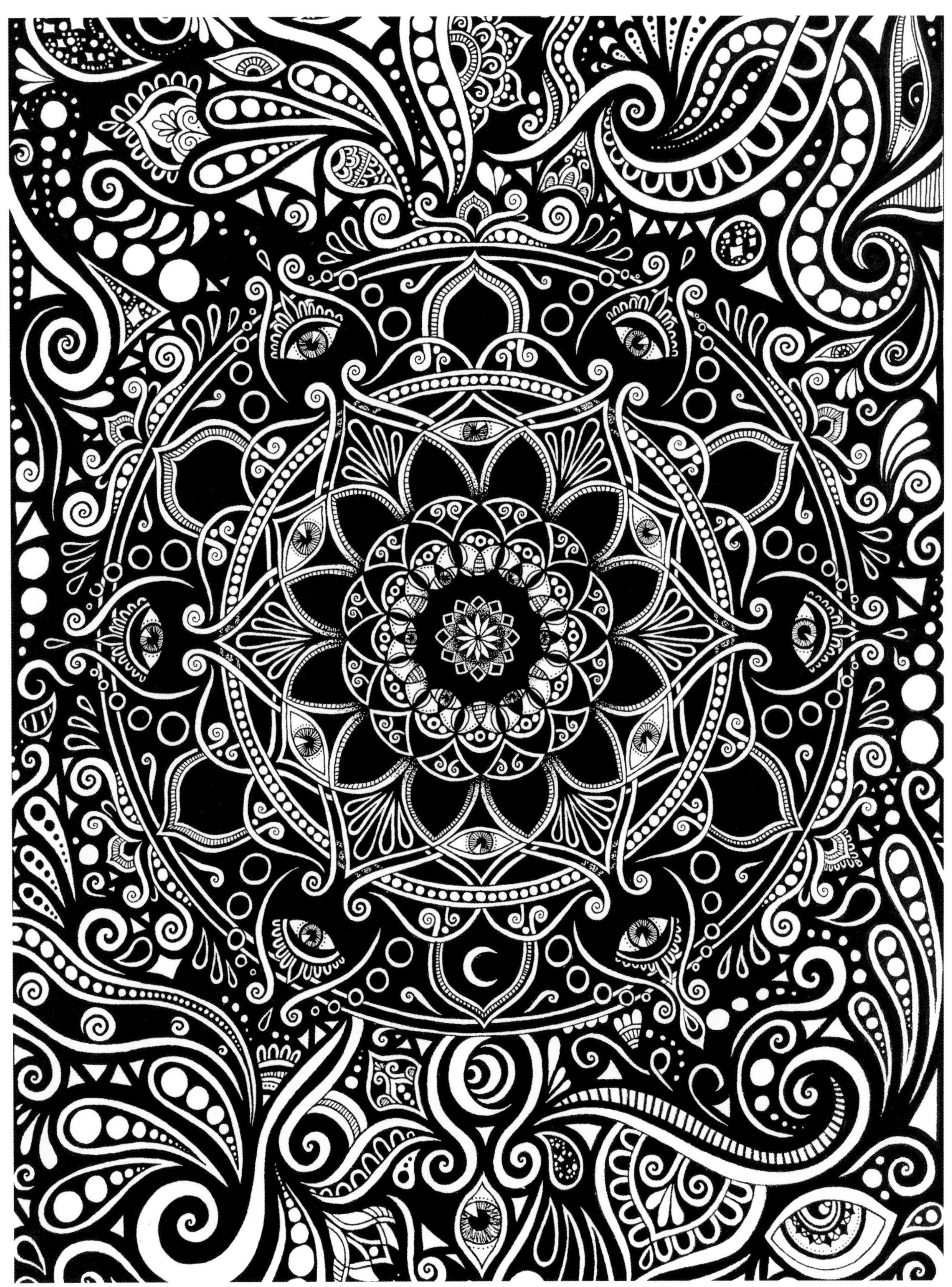

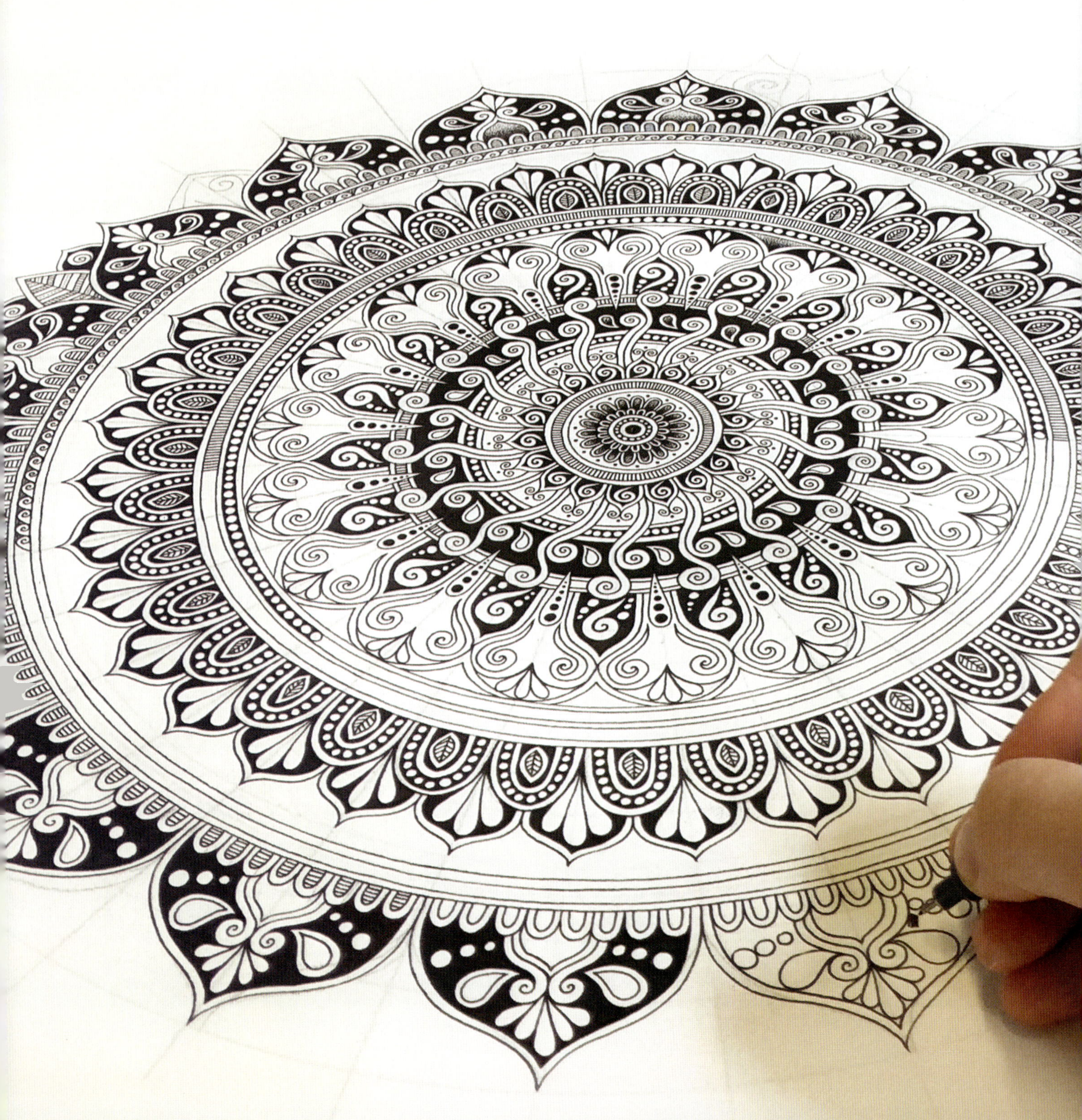

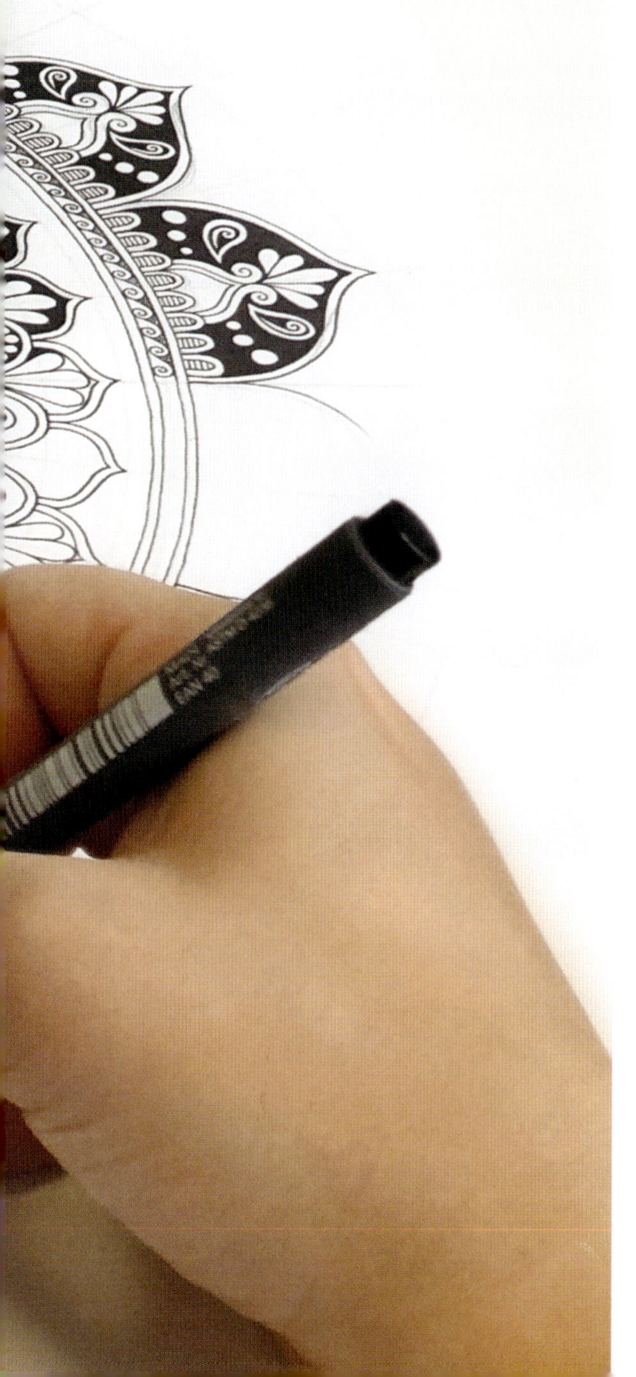

2

MINDFULNESS + DRAWING

MINDFULNESS AND DRAWING OFFER an aligned blend of creativity and self-awareness. This chapter delves into how drawing, when approached mindfully, can become a powerful tool for enhancing mental well-being. By focusing on the act of creation, we can enter a state of flow, where time fades away, and our minds reach a tranquil state. We will explore the psychological foundations of this practice, starting with Carl Jung's famous insights into the mandala as a symbol of the self, extending to modern studies that illustrate the calming, healing effects of mindful drawing.

CARL JUNG

"I saw that everything, all paths I had been following, all steps I had taken, were leading back to a single point—namely, to the mid-point. It became increasingly plain to me that the mandala is the centre. It is the exponent of all paths. It is the path to the centre, to individuation. I knew that in finding the mandala as an expression of the self I had attained what was for me the ultimate."

—C.G. JUNG

Carl Jung was a Swiss psychiatrist born in 1875 whose work has greatly impacted psychology, anthropology, literature, and religious studies. Jung is seen as largely responsible for bringing the mandala into common knowledge in the Western world. He believed there was a shared, or collective, part of the unconscious mind that contains universal memories, symbols, and archetypes—recurring symbols and themes in the human experience.

During Jung's world travels he discovered that the mandala existed in all cultures that he visited. His interest in mandalas developed during this period, when he found that creating and analyzing mandalas helped him understand his own psyche and facilitated psychological healing; he then extended this as a treatment for his patients.

Jung saw mandalas as symbolic representations of the self, reflecting an individual's inner state and journey toward wholeness. He believed that drawing and meditating on mandalas could integrate the conscious and unconscious, promoting self-discovery and mental well-being. Today, his work with mandalas continues to influence art therapy and mindfulness practices.

The vast scope of Jung's work, spread across numerous papers, is extensive. His work on the mandala has been summarized thoughtfully by Slegelis's 1987 paper titled "A Study of Jung's Mandala and Its Relationship to Art Psychotherapy." Jung believed that the mandala was a pictorial statement of the psyche and a key to the process of individuation, a major concept in Jungian theory. To Jung, the mandala was a universal visual symbol, capable of being expressed by all people.

Jung described constructing a mandala as an expression of a self-healing process. He believed that the psyche maintained its own sanity and nurtured its own growth through the process of creating these intricate circular artworks. He said that the mandala was a symbol of the "innermost God-like essence of man." Through the mandala, we can work to unite opposite forces in our life. We essentially make our own personal "Rorschach." (The psychological assessment that uses inkblot images to reveal aspects of an individual's personality and emotional state, named after Hermann Rorschach, a Swiss psychiatrist).

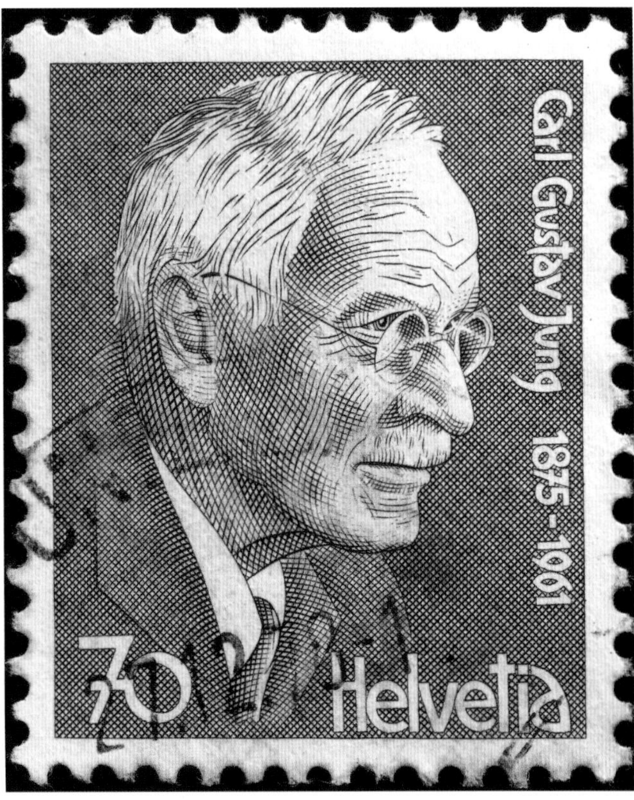

MORE STUDIES

Slegelis also writes about Joan Kellogg, a pioneering art therapist known for her significant contributions to the field of mandala art and its therapeutic applications. She developed a tool called "MARI" (Mandala Assessment Research Instrument). To this day, MARI is still used to assess psychological states and enable self-discovery and healing in some cases. Kellogg's work was inspired by Jung and integrated Jungian psychology, exploring how mandalas could reveal unconscious thoughts and promote personal growth. Her research and methodologies have been influential in art therapy, providing a structured yet deeply intuitive approach to understanding and enhancing mental health through creative expression.

While meditative drawing and its benefits may not qualify as a hard science, scientific studies and theories illustrate how the repetitive, rhythmic movements and visual outcomes involved in this practice might affect our minds and bodies. These findings resonate with the anecdotal experiences shared by many, supporting the idea that practices like meditative drawing, including creating mandalas and geometric patterns, can help reduce anxiety, improve mood, and enhance mindfulness. By engaging with these practices, we tap into our natural attraction to circular shapes and fractal patterns, fostering calmness and emotional well-being.

Some summaries from interesting research are below. The citations can be found at the end of the book, if you're interested in reading and learning more.

- **SANDMIRE ET AL. (2012)** examined the psychological effects of creating art, finding that even brief periods of engagement can significantly reduce a person's state of anxiety.
- **CURRY ET AL. (2005)** found that coloring a reasonably complex geometric pattern may induce a meditative state that benefits individuals suffering from anxiety.
- **CAMPENNI AND HARTMAN (2019)** discovered that multiple types of mandala creation were effective strategies for improving mood, state anxiety, and body mindfulness.
- **TAYLOR AND SPEHAR (2016)** explored why we are drawn to viewing fractal patterns. They are processed easily by our visual system and enhance attention while reducing the stress response.
- **BABOUCHKINA AND ROBBINS (2015)** found that the creation of a mandala (compared with other drawing styles) can reduce negative mood states. The mandala-drawing groups reported significantly greater mood improvement compared to the square-drawing groups. Their results demonstrated that the circular shape of the mandala serves as an "active ingredient" in mood enhancement. We are built to be drawn to circles, as they are all around us. For example, we are drawn to look at the iris of someone's eye for connection. We are naturally drawn to the mandalas of life.

BUILDING A MINDFUL PRACTICE

Mindfulness can be defined as single-minded awareness of the present moment, without thought or reaction (Campenni & Hartman 2019). It is strongly linked to improved psychological well-being and reduced levels of anxiety, negative emotions, and depression. In recent years, interest in self-management techniques for relaxation and stress reduction has grown significantly. Among these, creating mandalas has emerged as a powerful method for fostering calmness and cultivating mindfulness.

In our modern, technology-driven societies, it's undeniable that our minds are constantly overactive. We flit from one activity to another, continuously bombarded by media, traffic, the internet, work, crowds, and our social and family lives. The reality is that, for many of us, moments of silence or peace are rare unless we consciously seek them out. Finding a space to calm and quiet our minds, to simply be, has become more challenging than ever.

DAILY PRACTICE

To build a meditative drawing practice, I highly recommend finding a way to integrate it into your daily, weekly, or monthly habits. You could even simply keep a notepad by your bed and spend a few minutes drawing in the evening after reading. Make a habit of drawing often, and over time, it will become an effortless and rewarding part of your life. These small, intentional steps can transform drawing into a powerful tool for mindfulness and relaxation.

Greenhalgh, in her 2020 book *Mindfulness & the Art of Drawing: A Creative Path to Awareness*, writes about how a mindful practice is about finding a sustained, positive focus. In traditional meditation, this is often achieved by zoning in on the breath—following its path in and out of the body. In mindful drawing, it is the movement of the pen, the hand-eye coordination, and the artwork that slowly unveils. Mindful drawing provides our busy minds with something to rest on, a place to return to when thoughts, worries about the future, reflections on the past, emotions, aversions, or desires try to pull us away from the present moment.

Mindful drawing can serve as a valuable approach to self-reflection, inviting you to turn inward as the creative process unfolds. Immersing yourself in drawing allows your mind to focus entirely on the act of creation, silencing both external distractions and internal chatter. This concentrated attention offers moments of clarity to observe your thoughts—or even pause from them entirely. By engaging this artistic practice over and over again, you open a space for introspection.

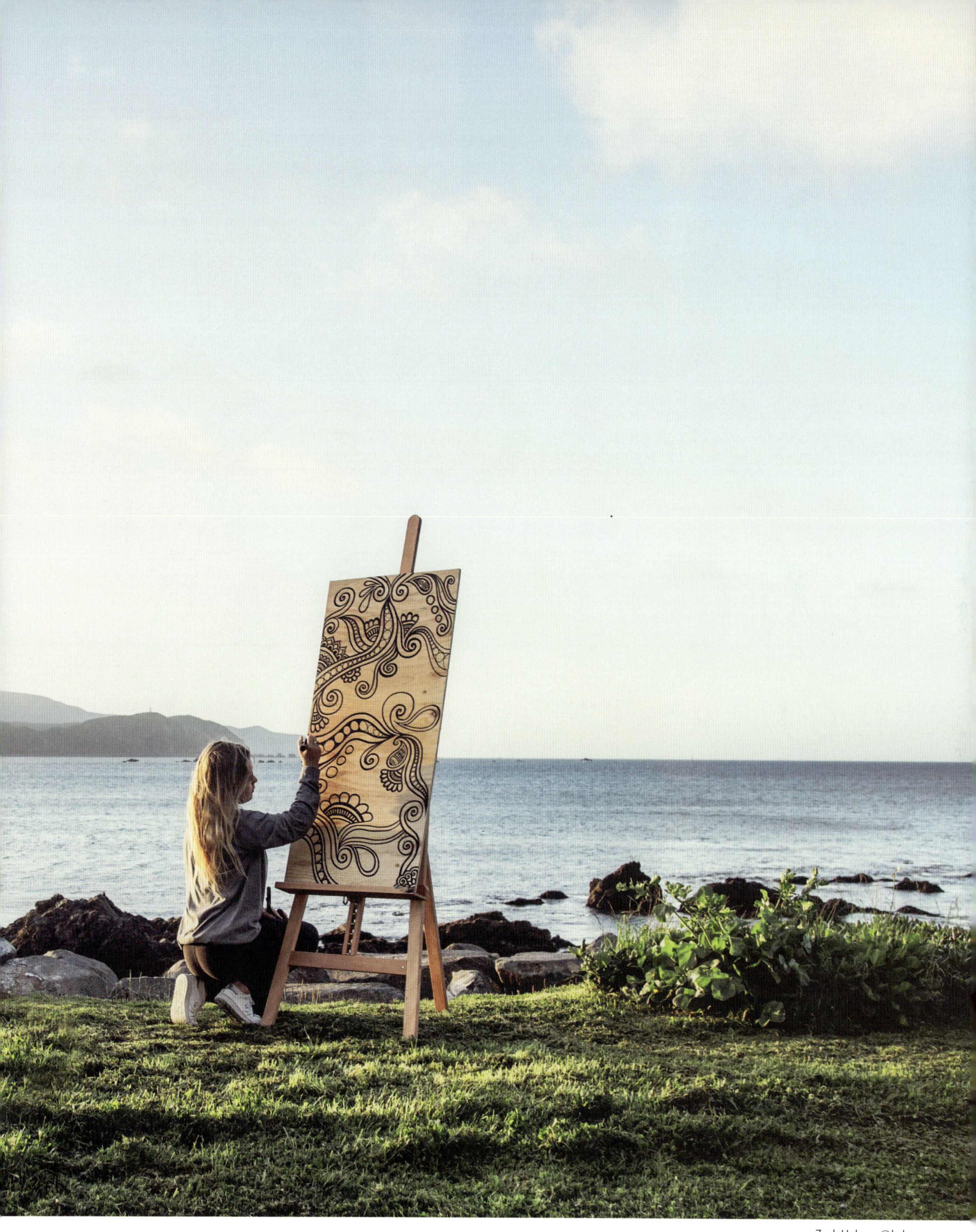

Zach Holmes @hxlmes_

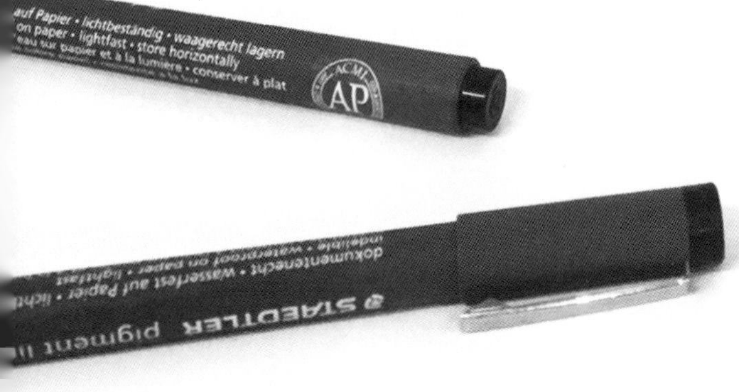
auf Papier · lichtbeständig · waagerecht lagern
on paper · lightfast · store horizontally
conserver à plat
AP
STAEDTLER

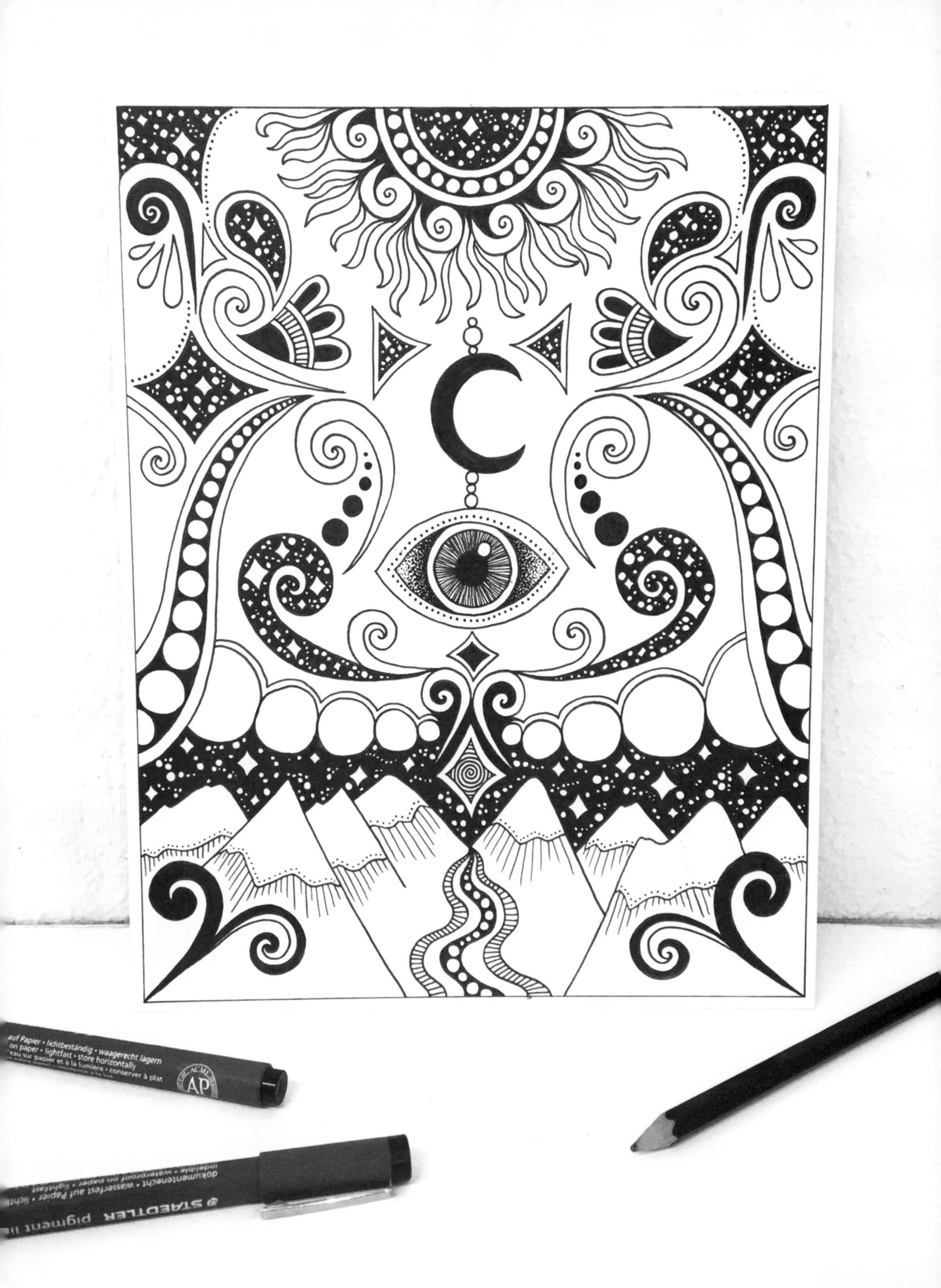

THE "FLOW" STATE OF MIND

Mihaly Csikszentmihalyi, a renowned Hungarian American psychologist, introduced and coined the term and concept of *flow*—when you are fully immersed in an activity, feeling equally energized, focused, and challenged (Csikszentmihalyi 1988). This flow state of mind is characterized by a sense of intense concentration, effortless action, and a loss of self-awareness. Csikszentmihalyi's research on flow has had a significant impact on understanding human motivation, creativity, and well-being.

There's a great chart that shows how flow occurs when the challenges of a task almost match with your skills and abilities. When the level of challenge slightly exceeds your skill level, you become fully engaged and motivated to overcome obstacles and achieve the task at hand, entering the flow state of mind. When the challenge is too low, you might feel bored or apathetic because it's too easy; when the challenge is too high, you might feel anxious or overwhelmed because it seems unachievable.

INSIGHT

I experience the flow state most vividly when I draw and paint. Also, when I'm playing the cello, especially when it's a piece that I haven't quite mastered yet, so I have to really focus to make it sound nice—right on the edge of being able to achieve it, but not quite; it's humbling, motivating, and inspiring. I invite you to think about what activities bring you into the flow state of mind.

From Csikszentmihalyi's research, the five key factors of the flow state include:

1. Intense focus
2. Clear goals and feedback
3. Loss of self-consciousness
4. Sense of control
5. Intrinsic motivation

Experiencing flow is linked to many benefits, including increased creativity, improved performance, and enhanced well-being. When we are engaged in meditative drawing, this is the state of mind we are aiming for.

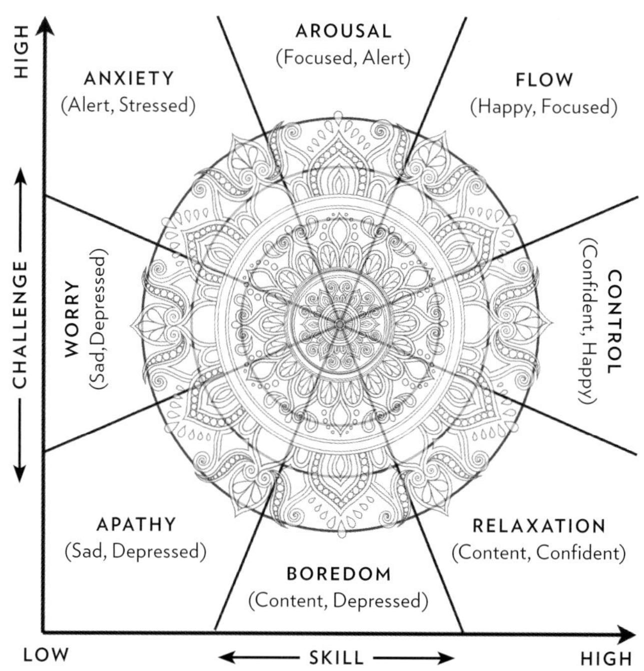

MEDITATIVE DRAWING AND THE FLOW STATE

When you enter the flow state during meditative drawing, it feels as if you're stepping into a realm where time is suspended and all that exists is the liminal space between your mind and what you're drawing. It can last for moments; or sometimes, hours. Each stroke of the pen or brush carries a sense of intention and purpose, driven forward by the motivation and anticipation of the patterns unfolding beneath your hand. Distractions fade into the background and there is a sensation of a seamless flow of ideas and inspiration to manifest. In this state of flow, challenges are embraced rather than avoided. In this way, flow can be a gateway to unlocking your full creative potential—the transformative power of meditative drawing.

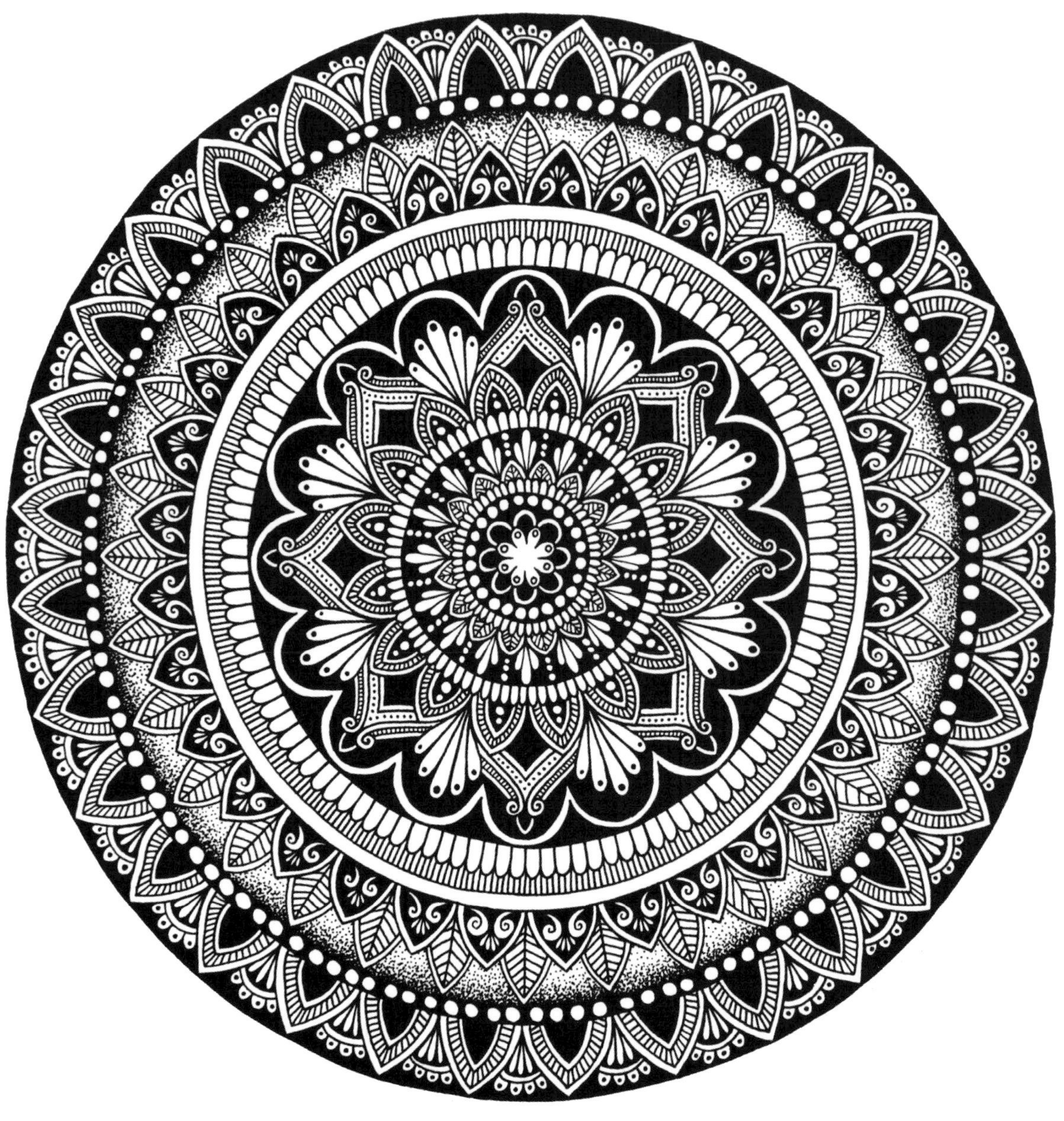

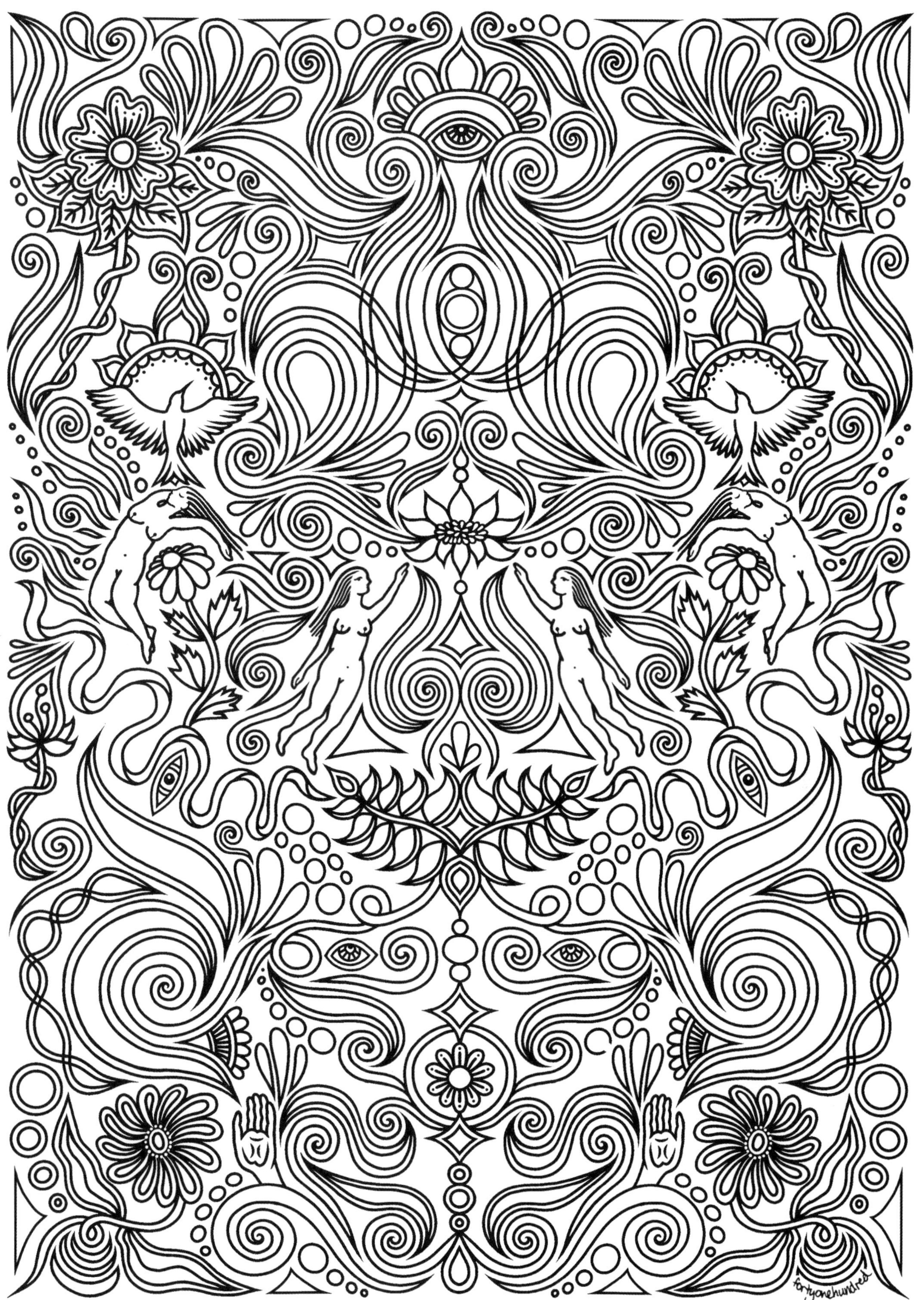
fortyonehundred

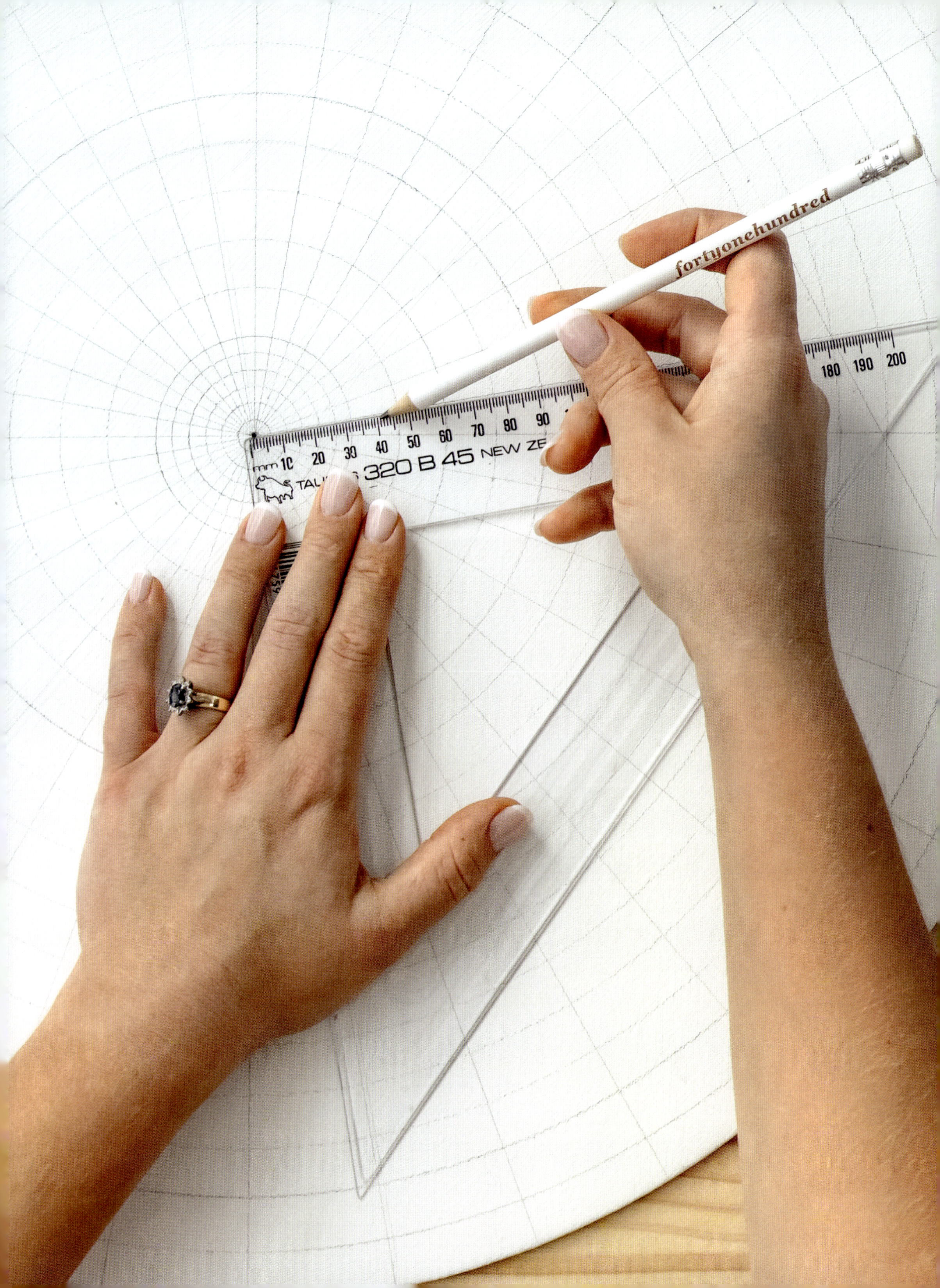
fortyonehundred
320 B 45

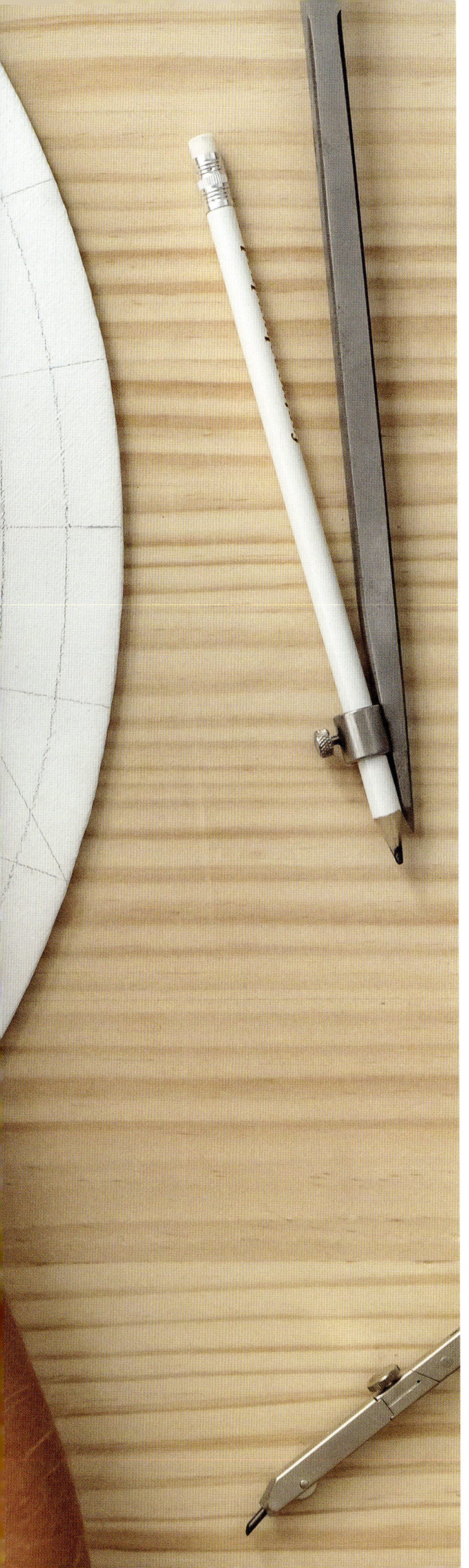

3

GETTING STARTED

EMBARKING ON YOUR MEDITATIVE ART JOURNEY requires only a pen and paper, but as you progress, investing in quality tools can enhance your experience. This chapter is designed to guide you through the essentials, from choosing the right materials to planning your creative process. Whether you're simply sketching on paper or exploring digital mediums, the key is to focus on the the process and joy of drawing in it's pure state, the hand-mind connection. We'll cover everything you need to get started, ensuring your art practice is both enjoyable and fulfilling, regardless of your skill or investment level.

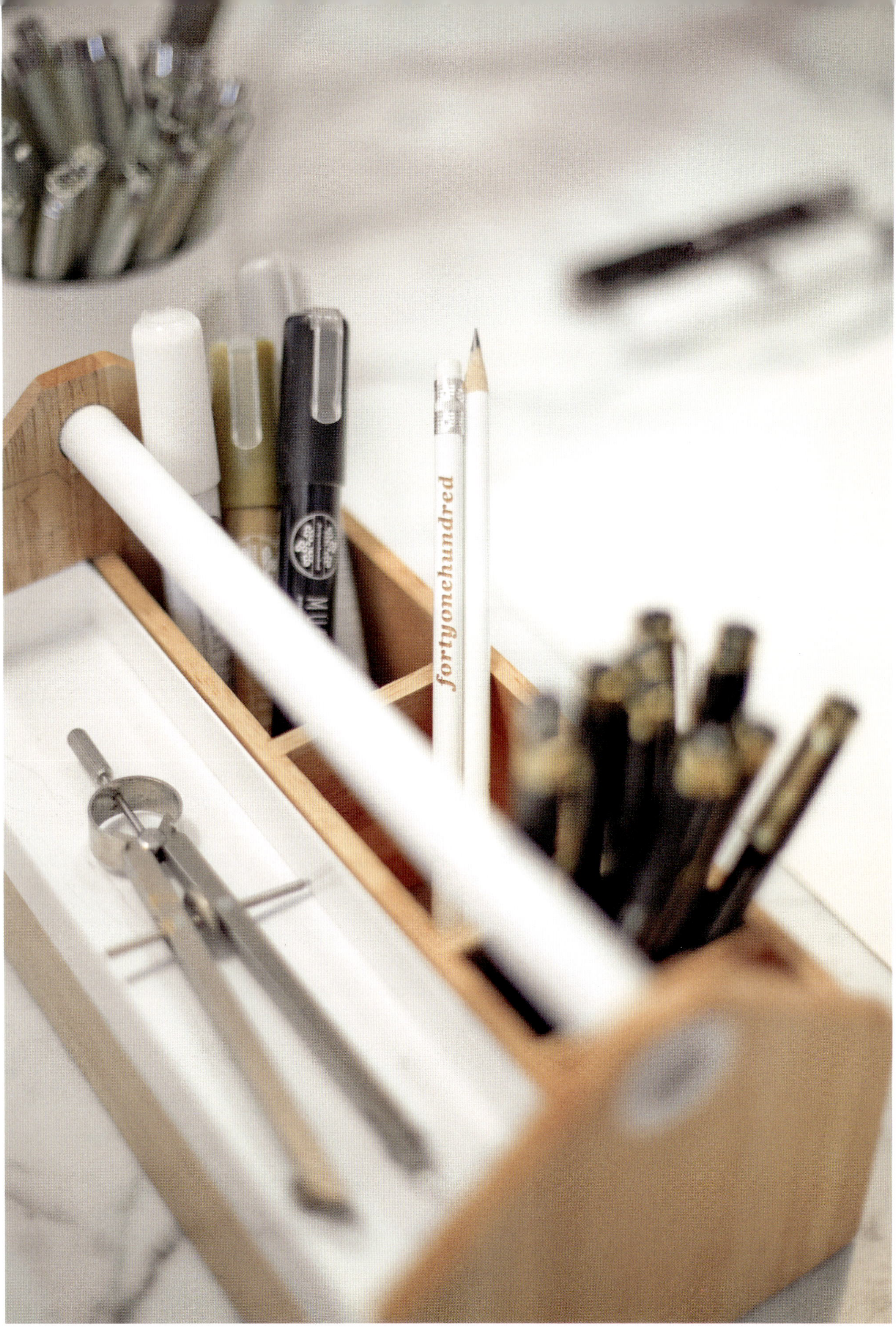
fortyonehundred

MATERIALS

All you really need is a pen or pencil and a piece of paper. However, as you progress in your art journey, you may want to seek out specialty and professional artist-grade tools to make the process more enjoyable and produce higher quality work, especially if you're considering selling your art.

The whole point of this book is to guide you toward finding and nurturing your own calming art practice. It's about experiencing the pure joy of drawing and the peace it provides, regardless of the materials used or how the artwork turns out. This section covers everything from paper and pencils to markers and paint and more.

Drawing Tools

The tool you use for drawing will be some kind of pen, pencil, or marker. The most popular option for this style of paper drawing is a fine liner pen, and then paint pens for canvas and wood.

FINE LINER PENS feature a small, precise nib that evenly distributes ink and flows beautifully on paper, allowing for detailed work and consistent lines. The archival ink used in these pens is permanent and resistant to fading, making them ideal for long-lasting artworks. My favorite brand is Sakura. Other popular brands include Micron, Faber-Castell, Staedtler, Uni Pin, and more.

PAINT PENS are a great option if you've chosen to draw on wood, canvas, walls, or anything other than paper. These are markers that contain opaque paint rather than ink. They are available in a range of tip sizes and colors, providing flexibility for creating both broad strokes and intricate details. They can also be used for murals and outdoor artworks. The paint pens I use are my own brand called Mural Pens, which are premium acrylic paint pens that I designed to have the perfect flow on walls, wood, canvas, and more. Other examples of popular paint pens include Montana, Posca, Molotow, Kuretake, and more.

If you don't want to buy and use professional artist tools at this stage, you can use anything you already have. Any pen or pencil is perfectly fine for meditative drawing. The key is to focus on the process and enjoy the act of creating, rather than worrying about what you're creating with.

Surfaces

Choosing a surface for your drawing is the next step and there are several options to consider. Each comes with its own characteristics and benefits. Examples include paper, illustration board, canvas, and wooden panels.

PAPER is of course the most common surface for drawing, available in various weights and textures, from smooth

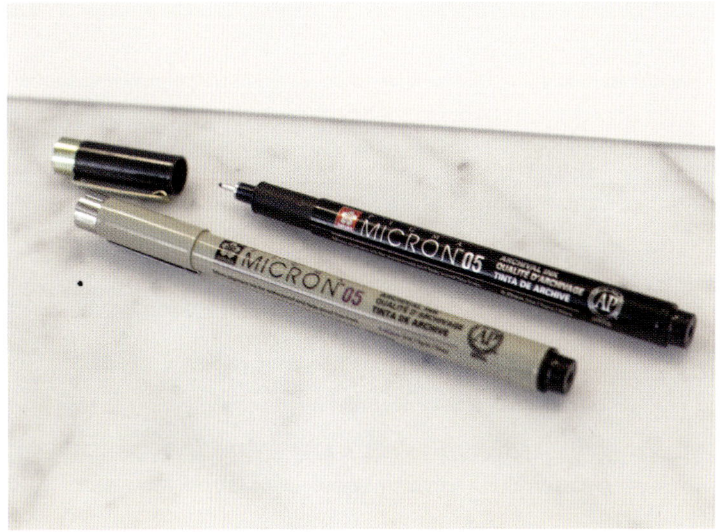

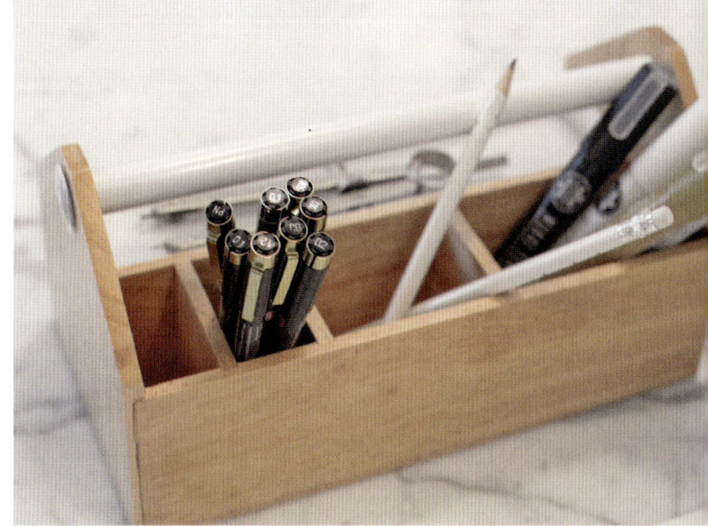

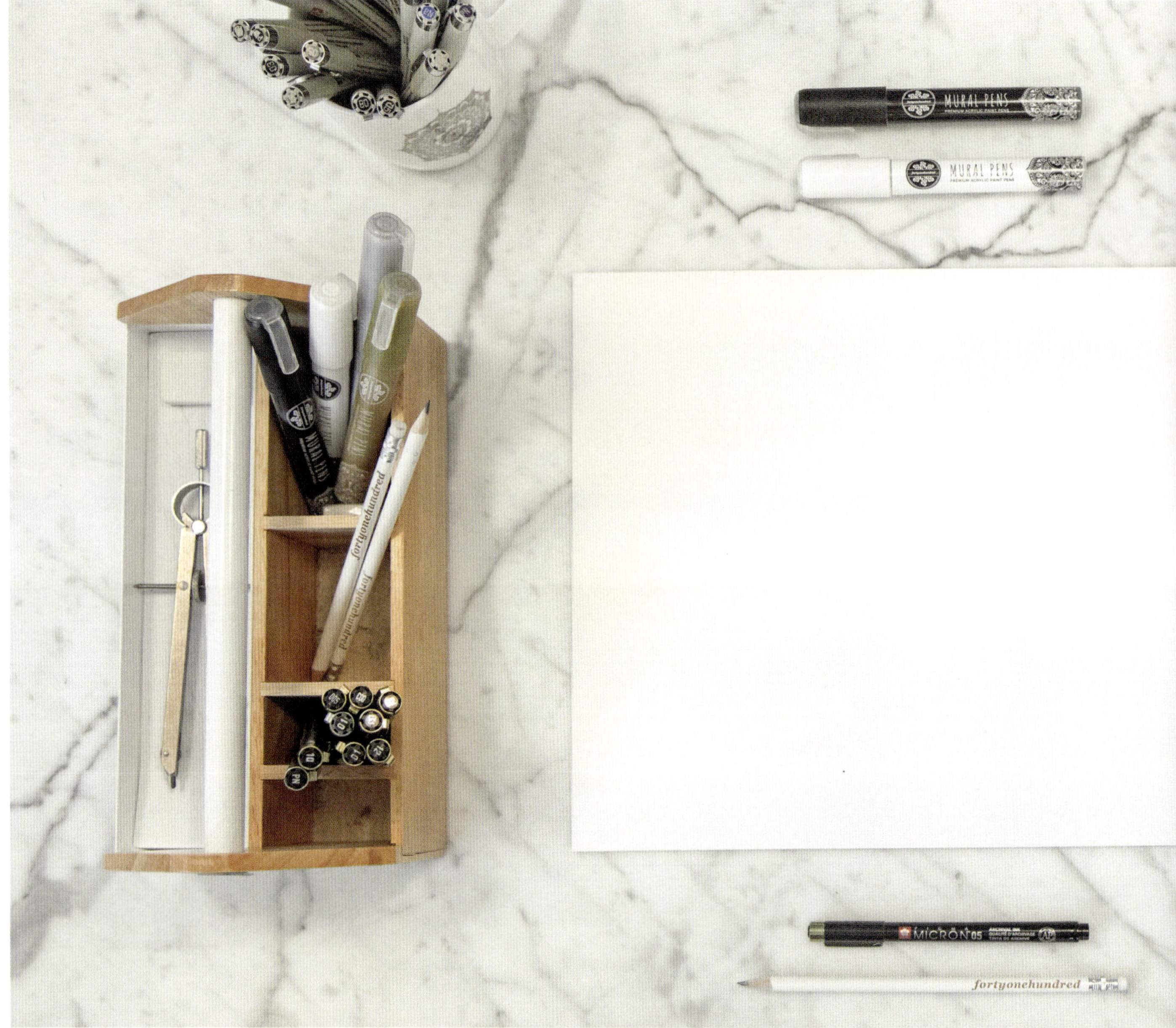

to rough. Smooth paper is great for detailed work, while rough paper adds depth to your artwork. Its main advantages are availability and ease of use, though it can tear easily and may not support a heavier medium like paint. I find paper ideal for daily practice but less suitable for artworks intended for display or sale, as I tend to be heavy-handed and end up damaging the paper.

ILLUSTRATION BOARD is a sturdier alternative to paper. It consists of a thick, rigid backing with a paper drawing surface on top. This board can handle heavier mediums like ink and paint as well as normal pens without warping. The main advantage of illustration board is its durability and resistance to impact, making it ideal for detailed and intricate work. However, it is more expensive than regular paper and can be less flexible in terms of portability (normal paper can be rolled into a tube, for example).

CANVAS is an industry standard choice for artists who use paint and other media that require a more robust surface. It can be "stretched" (bound over a wooden frame) or "unstretched" (in a roll or piece of fabric). The main

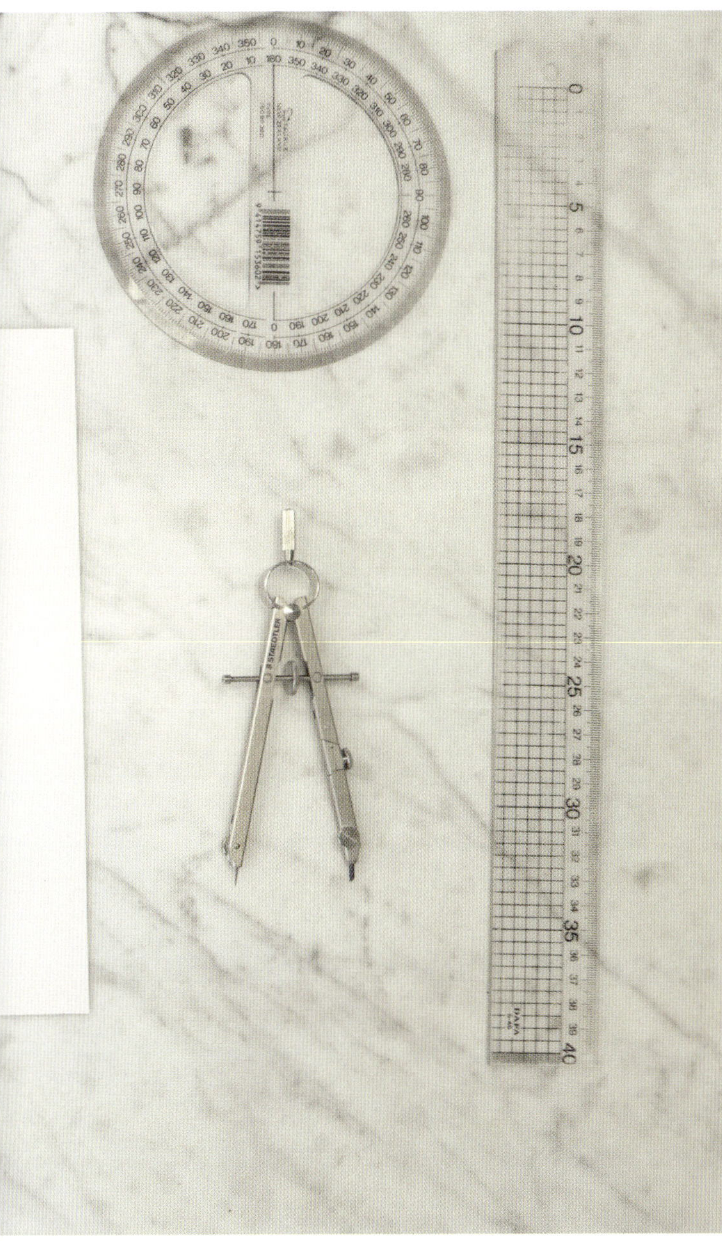

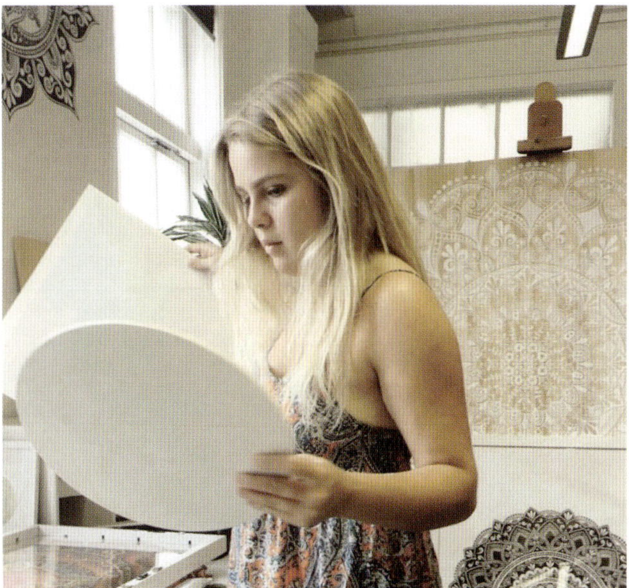

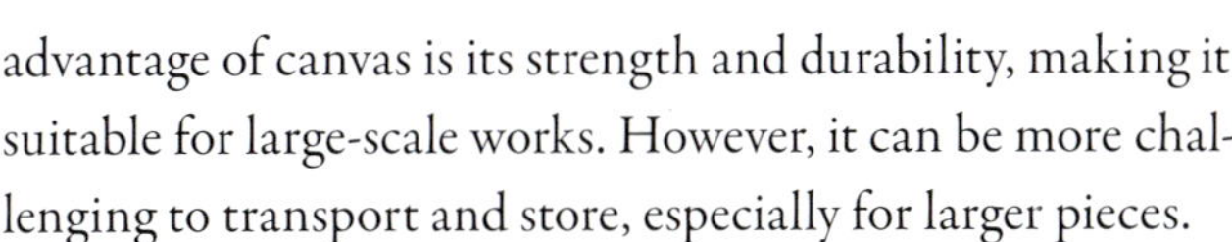

advantage of canvas is its strength and durability, making it suitable for large-scale works. However, it can be more challenging to transport and store, especially for larger pieces.

WOODEN PANELS offer a solid and sturdy surface that is excellent for heavy applications of paint and other mediums. It can be sanded and primed to provide a smooth drawing surface or left with its natural texture. The main advantage of wood panels is their durability and ability to withstand heavy media without warping. You can put a lot of pressure on the panel and it stays put, making it the best option for very detailed work that takes a long time. However, they are heavier and often larger than other art surfaces and can be more challenging to transport, display, and store. Another great reason to choose wood is if you find a panel with natural grain, you could leave some of it visible to add further character to your artwork.

DRAWING STRAIGHT ONTO A WALL offers a large, open surface ideal for creating murals and large-scale artworks. This process can be both exciting and liberating, encouraging expansive, expressive creations that engage your whole body. Wall paintings offer a unique opportunity for community engagement and collaboration, providing a space where creative ideas can truly expand. However, working on walls can be physically demanding and often requires special preparation or permission, particularly in public spaces. While it may not be practical for a daily art practice, it's a great experience if the opportunity arises.

OTHER OPTIONS for drawing surfaces include flat river stones, a fence, a front door, a piece of fabric, you name it. I recommend simply starting with paper you already have.

Choosing the right surface for your drawing depends on your medium, style, and the scale of your work. My favorite choice is illustration board for smaller drawings when I use a fine liner, and a wooden panel for larger artworks when I use a paint pen.

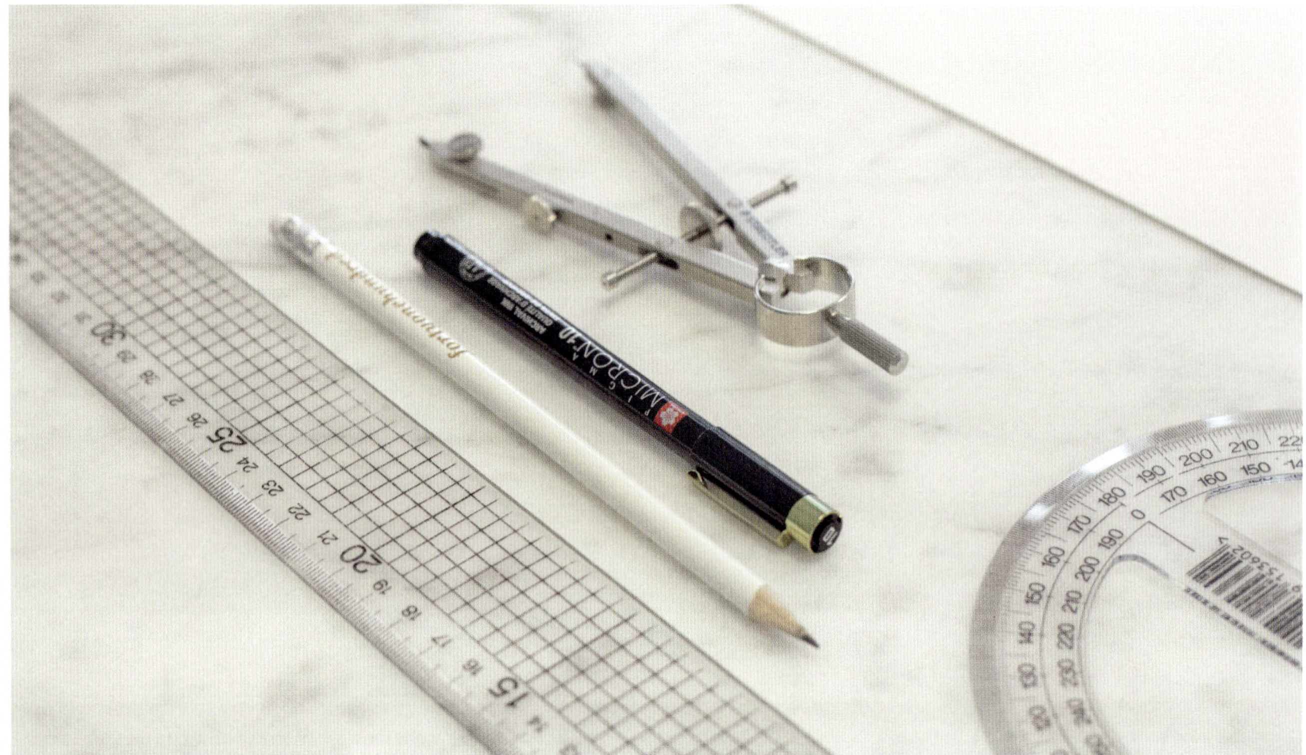

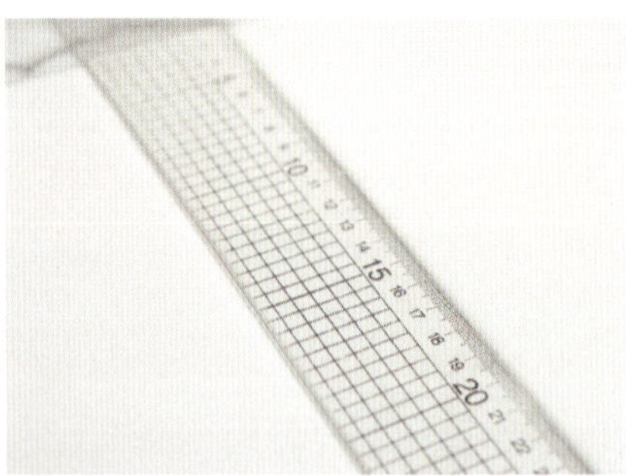

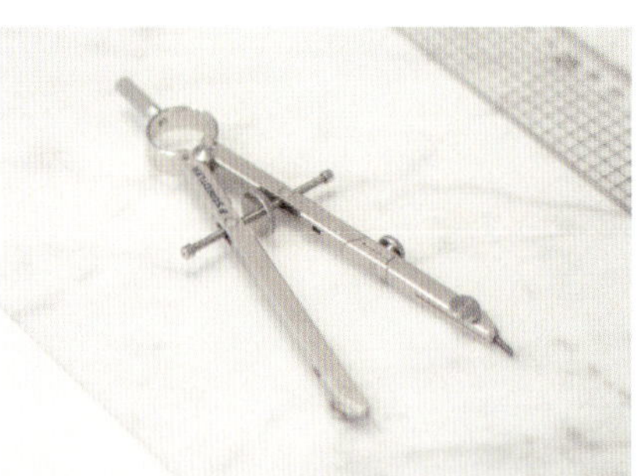

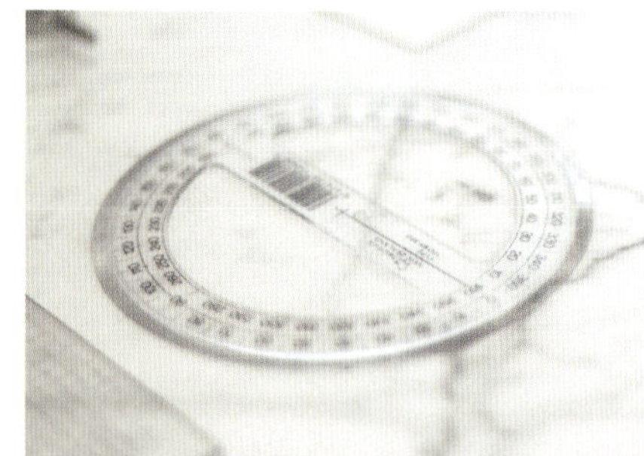

Measuring Tools

Measuring tools are vital for achieving precision and symmetry, especially in mandala drawing. If you're only interested in free-flowing designs, then all you need is a pen and some paper. Essential measuring tools for mandala drawing include rulers, drawing compasses, and protractors, each contributing to accurate and detailed designs.

CLEAR RULERS are most helpful for drawing straight lines and to ensure even spacing. Your ruler will be used to divide the surface into equal sections, create the foundational mandala grid, measure areas for evenness, and establish guidelines that will help maintain symmetry and accuracy throughout your mandala.

DRAWING COMPASSES are the most important tool for creating perfect circles and arcs in your mandala designs and guidelines. By adjusting the compass, you can create circles of various sizes, which form the basic structure of your mandala. The compass helps you maintain consistent proportions and symmetry, which are key elements in mandala art. You can buy a simple plastic compass for a few dollars, right up to a high-quality stainless steel artist-grade tool for around a hundred dollars. If you're just starting out, choose the former, but I have to say that investing in a high-quality compass really contributes to a lovely drawing experience, plus you can keep it for life.

PROTRACTORS are helpful for measuring and drawing specific angles as well as marking the measurements or segments around the circle in the mandala grid. This ensures that each section of your mandala is evenly spaced, adding another layer of precision to your work, especially if your design involves intricate geometric patterns.

Using these measuring tools ensures that your mandalas are balanced and harmonious, which truly makes all the difference. They help you achieve the precise, radial symmetry that makes mandalas visually appealing. You may wonder whether you truly need measuring tools, so I recommend trying with and without to see the difference.

Miscellaneous Supplies

Accessories to support drawing include pencils, erasers, and pencil sharpeners. I recommend using what you already own. But if you're buying from scratch, here is some information to help you choose your supplies.

PENCILS are the perfect tool for sketching out designs and planning your drawings. They come in various hardness levels, ranging from black (B) to hard (H). The softer black pencils (B) create darker lines and are great for shading, while harder pencils (H) produce lighter lines suitable for fine details. I recommend using H pencils because they are easier to erase.

ERASERS are for correcting mistakes and refining your work. A kneaded eraser allows you to mold the eraser into shapes for precise erasing, while a vinyl (standard) eraser is effective for removing large areas of graphite. My favorite eraser is called a Factis 36R, which is very small, soft, and inexpensive. It's made of synthetic rubber and erases well without tearing the drawing surface.

PENCIL SHARPENERS are essential for detailed work, as you need your pencil to be as thin and accurate as possible. Handheld sharpeners are portable and convenient, while electric sharpeners offer consistent sharpening and are ideal for frequent use. Sharpen more often than you think you need to. Faber-Castell creates high-quality, long-lasting sharpeners.

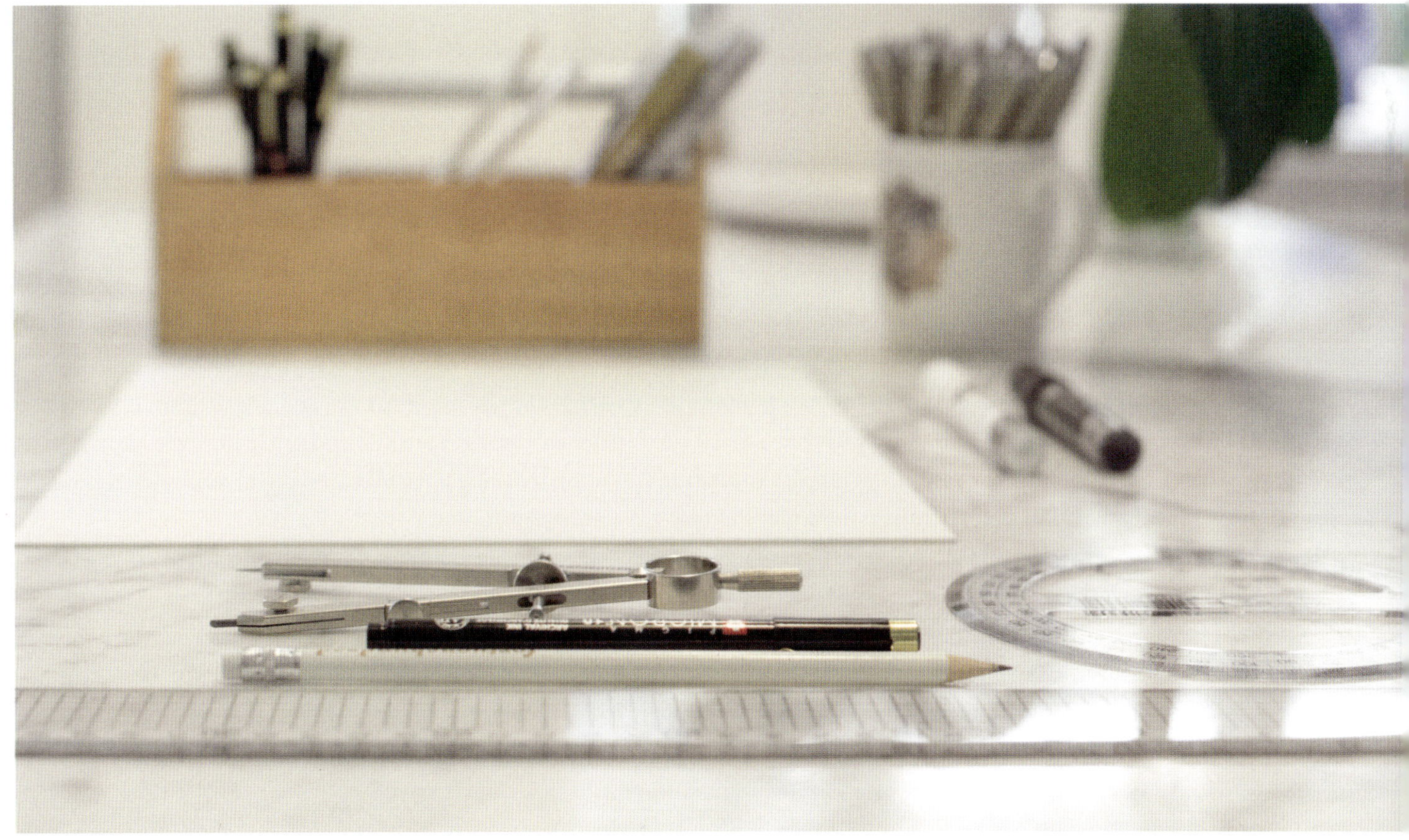

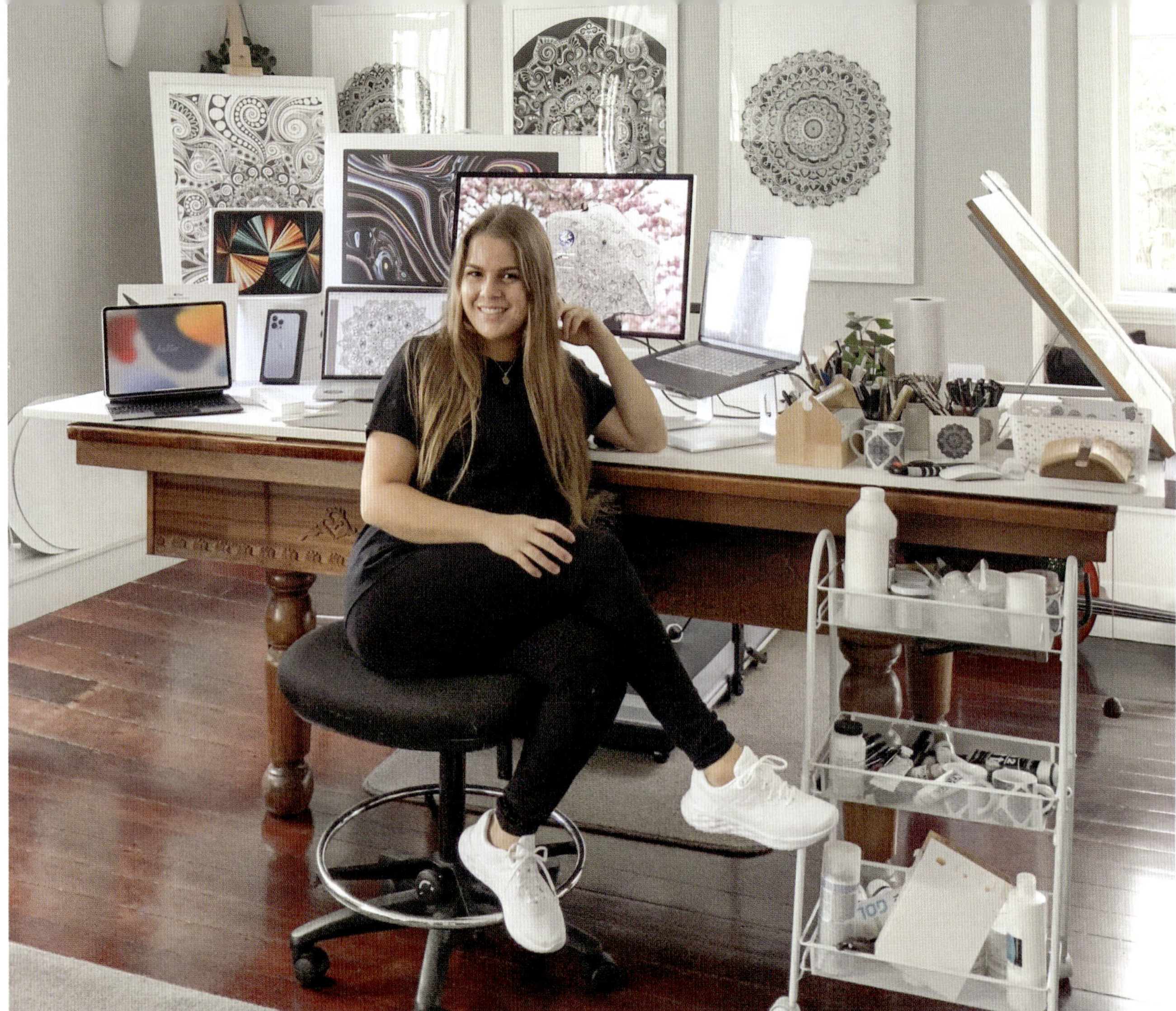

Helpful Digital Tools

For digitizing your work, photographing your work-in-progress steps, and experimenting with different options before committing ink to paper, digital tools can be incredibly useful. Here are some of my recommendations.

A CAMERA—whether a DSLR, mirrorless, point-and-shoot, or smartphone—can capture high-quality images of your work so you can document the art process, share your work with your audience online, or prepare your art to make prints. Smartphones, particularly the latest iPhones, offer a truly excellent camera quality. I used to only use a DSLR but now I mostly only use the iPhone as they have become so good.

A TABLET WITH A STYLUS AND DRAWING APP allows you to sketch ideas, plan compositions, and test ideas digitally before applying them to your physical artwork (more on this in chapter 6; see "Digital Pre-Visualization Techniques"). I recommend the iPad Pro with the Apple Pencil Pro, using the Procreate app for its versatility and wide range of tools.

A COMPUTER AND EDITING SOFTWARE allows you to transform a simple drawing into many possibilities. You can adjust the exposure, remove mistakes or smudges, change the size of the canvas, and prepare your images for print or sharing. I recommend using an Apple MacBook Pro with Adobe Photoshop. Powerful tools with endless editing capabilities.

Using tech alongside your hand-drawn works opens up a world of creative potential. I've always loved Apple products and couldn't recommend them more. All the products sync together so you spend less time thinking about your tech and trying to make it work, and more time creating and being in the flow state of mind.

FINDING INSPIRATION

Drawing inspiration can come from many sources—nature, art, architecture, and your personal experiences and surroundings. This section provides tips on how to seek out these sources to fuel your creative practice. Identify what resonates with you and use it to inspire your drawings.

Photography

The world around us is rich with patterns and details waiting to be discovered. One of my favorite methods for finding inspiration is through photography, to capture and appreciate the intricate designs that often go unnoticed in everyday life. Some of my inspirations include:

- Shells from a beach adventure in Whangamatā, NZ
- Romanesco cauliflower that I bought at the vegetable market
- The patterns on teacups bought at auction
- A chandelier and its shadows in my parents' home
- Ornate details in old architecture from travels in Europe
- A dandelion in my grandmother's garden
- A selection of stones collected on a walk
- The unfolding of a fern, hāpu'u, in Hawaii
- A mosaic tiled bathroom in my best friend's family home
- Fractal patterns in the sand in Tofino, Canada

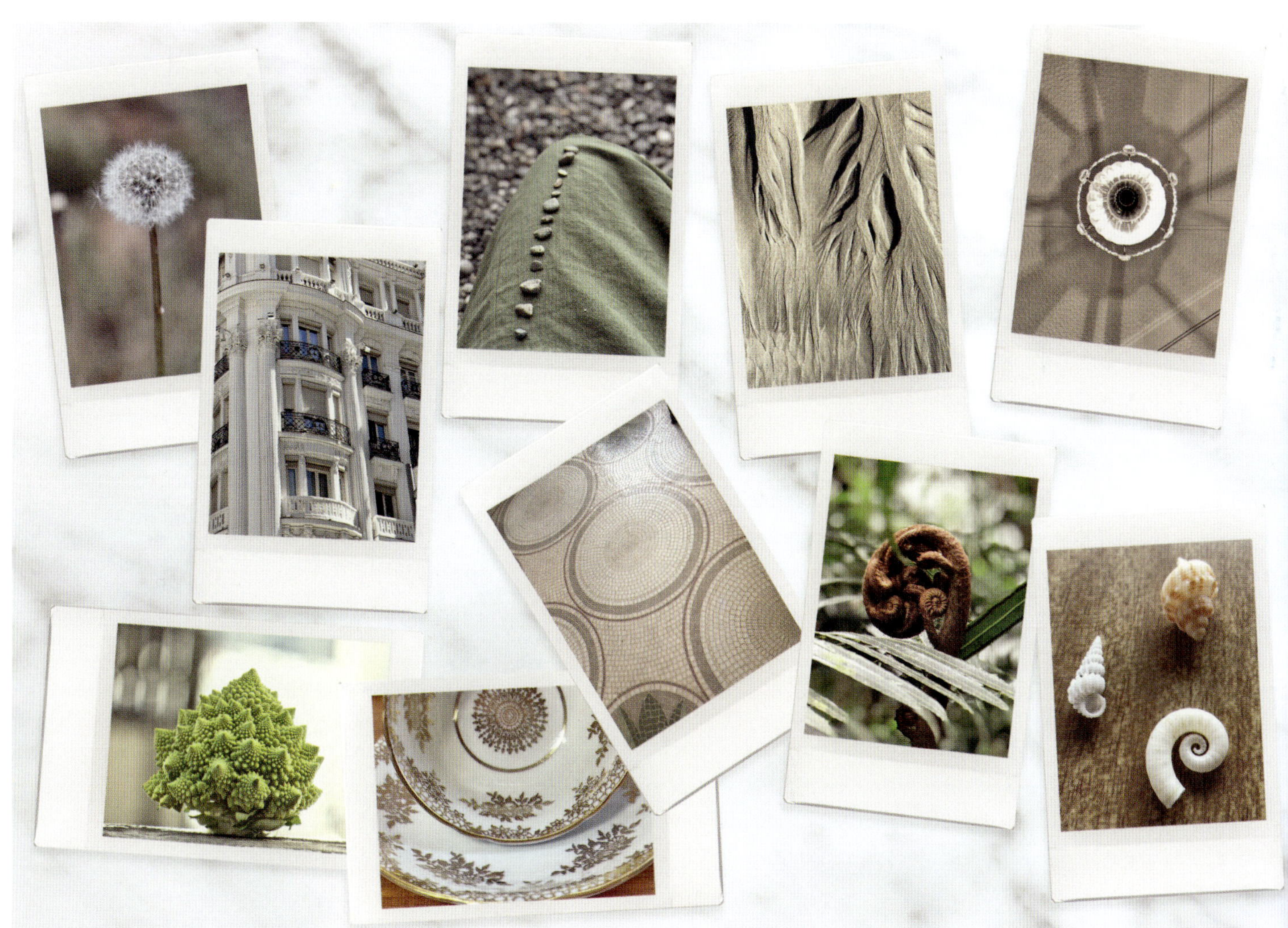

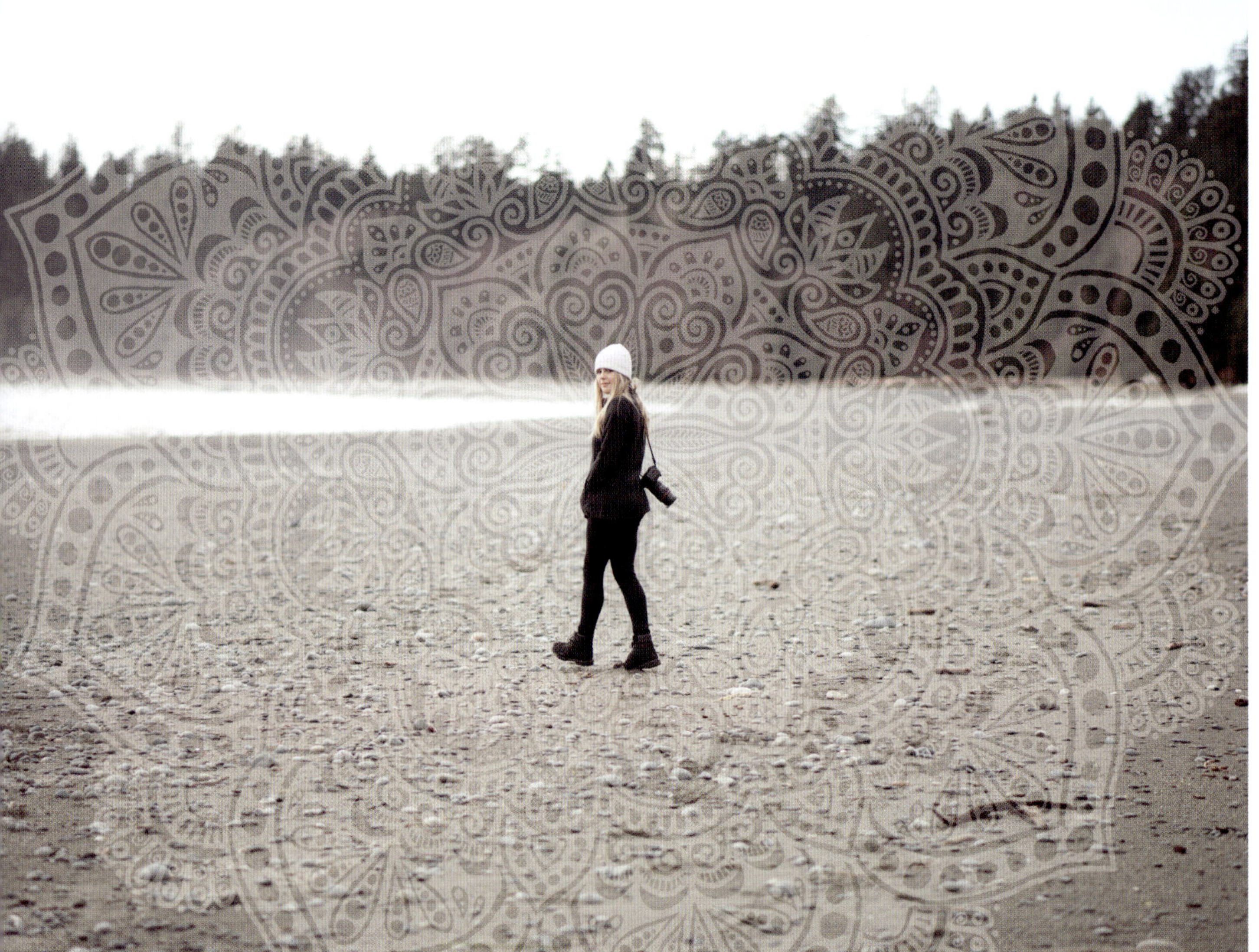

Paul Levy Photo

These normal parts of everyday life offer new perspectives and ideas for art, and they're also a beautiful way of documenting your life. Each observation helps spark creativity and inspire new drawings.

Starting my creative journey as a photographer originally, I developed a keen eye for noticing and interpreting these subtle nuances in the world around me. This attentive observation has been invaluable in my artistic journey. Our willingness to study through a lens of curiosity is a tool that we all possess. So, go out and immerse yourself in your surroundings. Pay attention to what captures your interest, whether through photography or sketching in a notebook. Documenting these observations helps fuel your creativity and provides a wealth of inspiration for your drawings.

INSIGHT

Many years spent with a brilliant photographer helped shape my approach to "conscious seeing." We would take our cameras on nature walks, hunting for perfect light, interesting compositions, and tiny details. His mother, also an extraordinary artist, seemed to master every style and medium she tried. When we went on holiday, she'd bring along pocket-size watercolors to quietly sketch whatever caught her eye, from beach scenes to fleeting moments. Her way of capturing the world around her continues to be a source of inspiration for me.

Other Artists

Exploring the work of others is an essential part of the creative process, offering both new insights and a powerful motivation to keep creating. Study what has come before you. Two artists whose work I admire are Yayoi Kusama and Ernst Haeckel.

YAYOI KUSAMA (b. 1929) is a Japanese artist renowned for her use of circles, dots, and infinite patterns. Her mirrored "infinity" rooms create the illusion of endless space, immersing viewers in a realm where simplicity evolves into complexity and they become part of the artwork themselves. Kusama's work explores the concept of the infinite, transforming ordinary elements into profound, immersive experiences that invite deep reflection. Her art often explores themes of repetition and scale, reflecting her own experiences with mental health and personal obsessions.

Kusama's exploration of infinity deeply resonates with my fascination in how fractals can allow us to visualize the infinite through their endless expansion and contraction at every scale. Her focus on patterns and repetition mirrors my desire to find aesthetic beauty, as well as depth and meaning, through relatively simple, creative expression.

BELOW: Pumpkin art, Yayoi Kusama

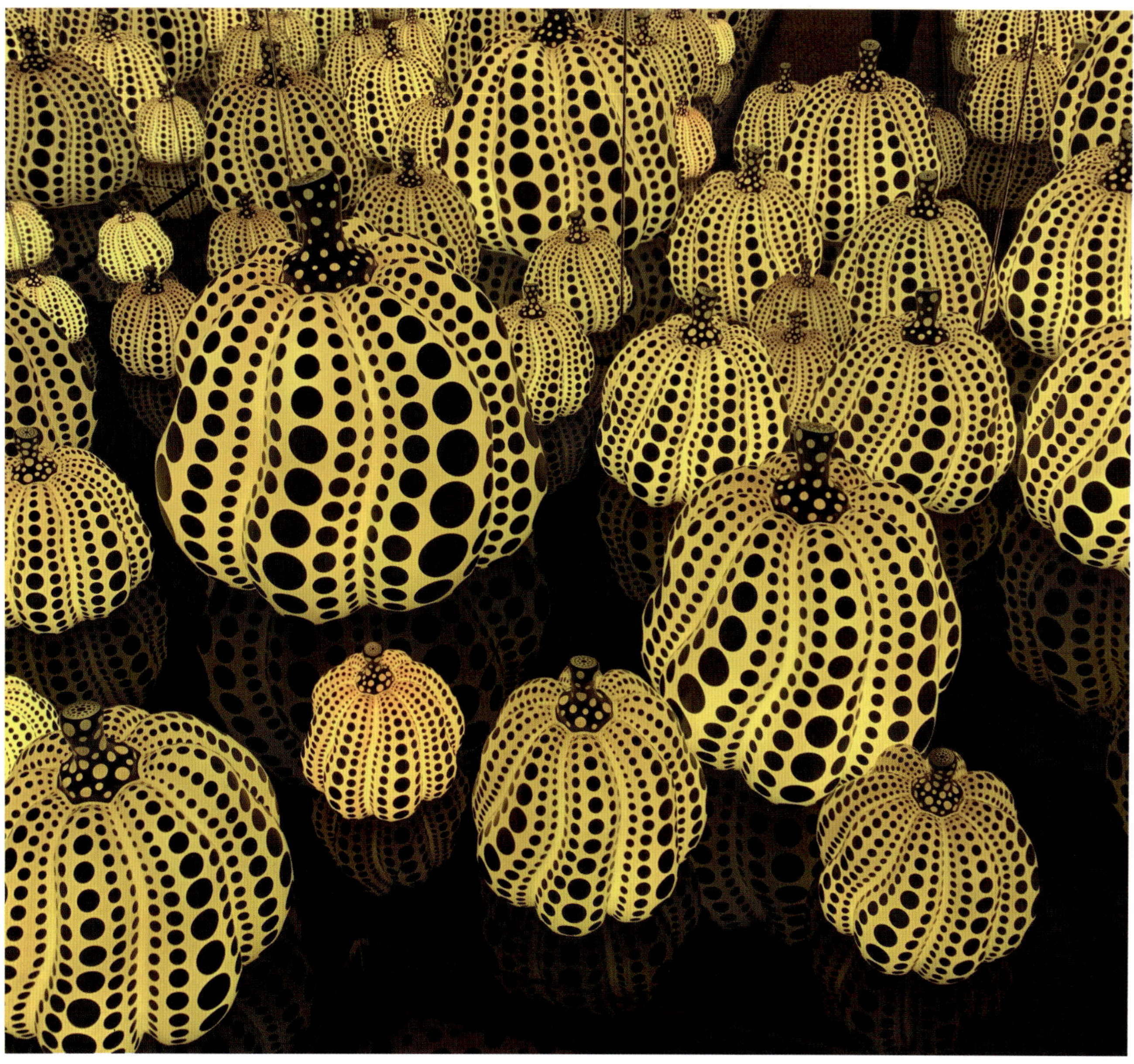

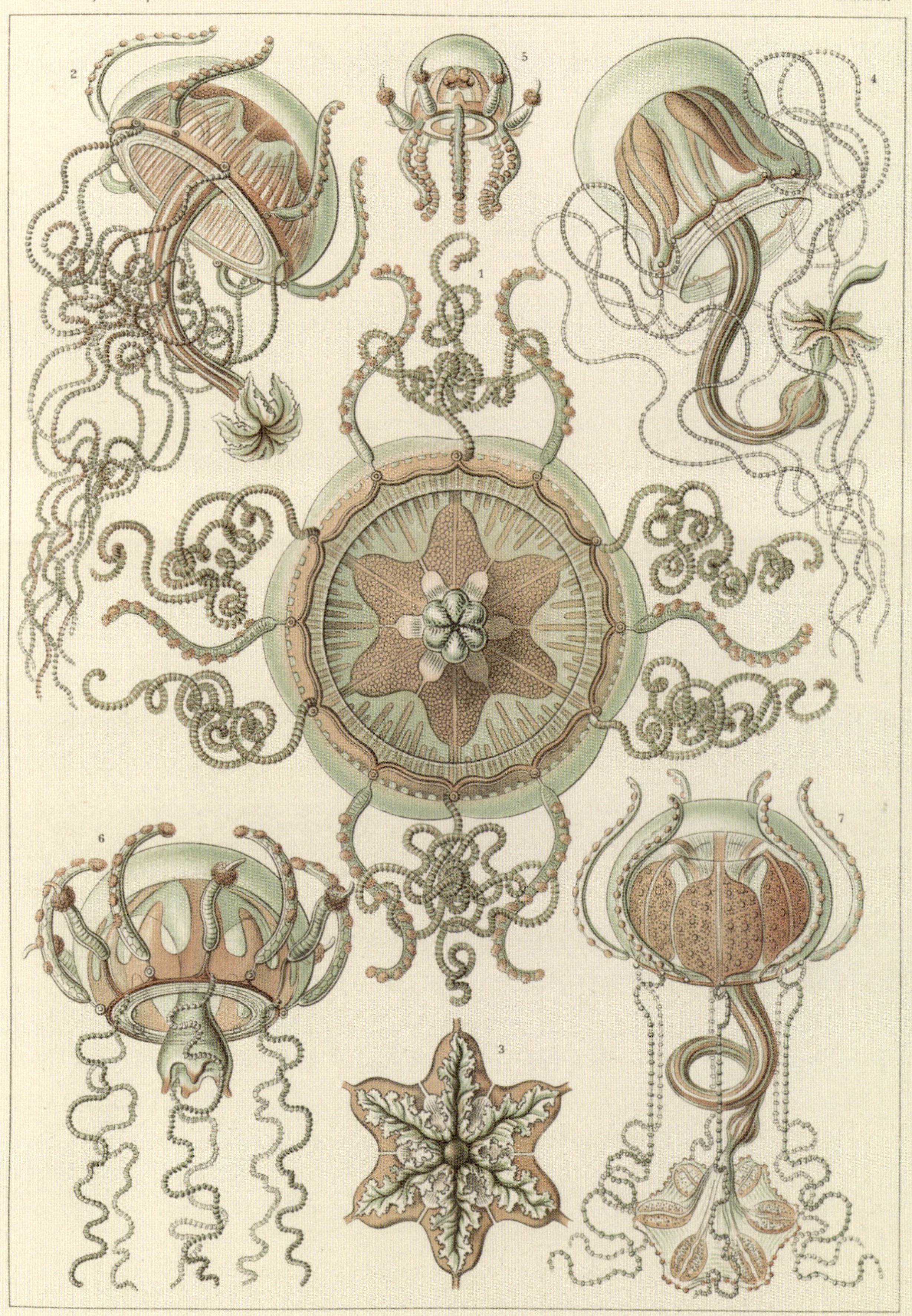

Trachomedusae. — Kolbenquallen.

ERNST HAECKEL (1834–1919) was a German biologist, naturalist, and artist known for his detailed and scientifically precise illustrations of marine life and other organisms. His work combined scientific research with artistic interpretation, contributing significantly to the fields of marine biology and evolutionary theory. He coined several biological terms and was an advocate of Charles Darwin's theory of evolution. Haeckel's intricate drawings showed the complex beauty and symmetry found in nature.

I find inspiration in Haeckel's work because of his meticulous observation and artistic interpretation of the natural world. His ability to capture the delicate intricacies of nature's design encourages me to appreciate and replicate similar patterns in my own artwork.

Drawing inspiration from artists broadens your artistic perspective and stimulates new ideas. Studying different artists can deepen your appreciation for art and encourage innovation within your own skills and projects.

Galleries and Travel

Traveling offers an incredible opportunity to broaden your horizons, whether you're exploring your local town, venturing across your country, or journeying overseas. Each destination opens your eyes to new perspectives and inspirations.

One of my favorite parts of traveling is photographing mandalas in various forms around the world. From intricate coins and decorated manhole covers to stained glass windows and temple artworks, mandalas appear in every country and culture. This recurring motif highlights our universal appreciation for circular, intricate patterns found in nature. Witnessing how these designs are woven into different cultures globally is truly inspiring and enriches our creative vision.

INSIGHT

Some of my favorite galleries include the National Gallery in London, the Prado in Madrid, the MMCA in Seoul, The Met and Guggenheim in New York, and the Louvre in Paris. I feel fortunate to have explored these institutions during both art commission trips and personal adventures with family and friends. Including galleries as a central element of travel creates deeply enriching and memorable experiences.

Dive into the world of art and inspiration by immersing yourself in it. Go to art galleries and museums, read about art, and watch documentaries to gain deeper insights into different movements and artists. Follow the threads of pieces that captivate you and let your curiosity lead you on an inspiring journey. There's a wealth of artistic exploration available and endless opportunities to enrich your understanding and appreciation of art, if you seek it out.

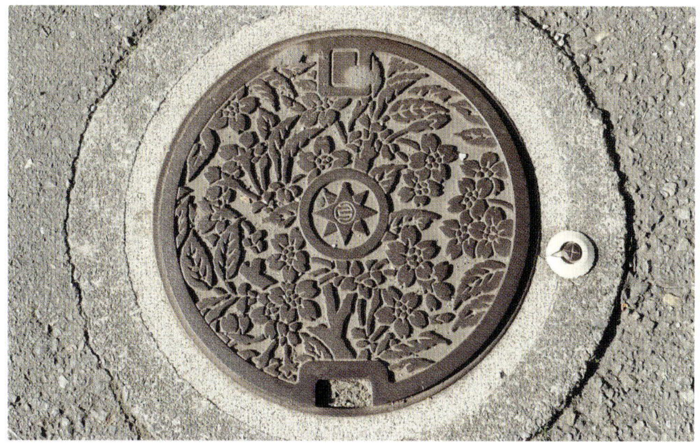

MANHOLE COVER IN JAPAN

LEFT: Scientific illustration of flora and fauna, Ernst Haeckel

SKETCHING IDEAS

Keeping a diary or notebook dedicated to sketching out your ideas is an invaluable practice for translating your observations and inspirations into tangible forms. Whether you're jotting down quick pencil sketches or more detailed pen drawings, this private space can become a home for your creative thoughts and experiments. Embrace the freedom to make these sketches as rough or detailed as you like; they don't need to be perfect and they don't need to be shown to anyone.

Capture the essence of your ideas through drawing, while having the freedom and permission to explore different approaches (and make mistakes). Over time, your notebook will evolve into a personal library of patterns and motifs that you can reference and build upon. This process not only helps in refining your artistic vision but also provides a rich resource for future projects. By continuously documenting and sketching your inspirations, you create a dynamic and evolving dictionary of your own artistic language.

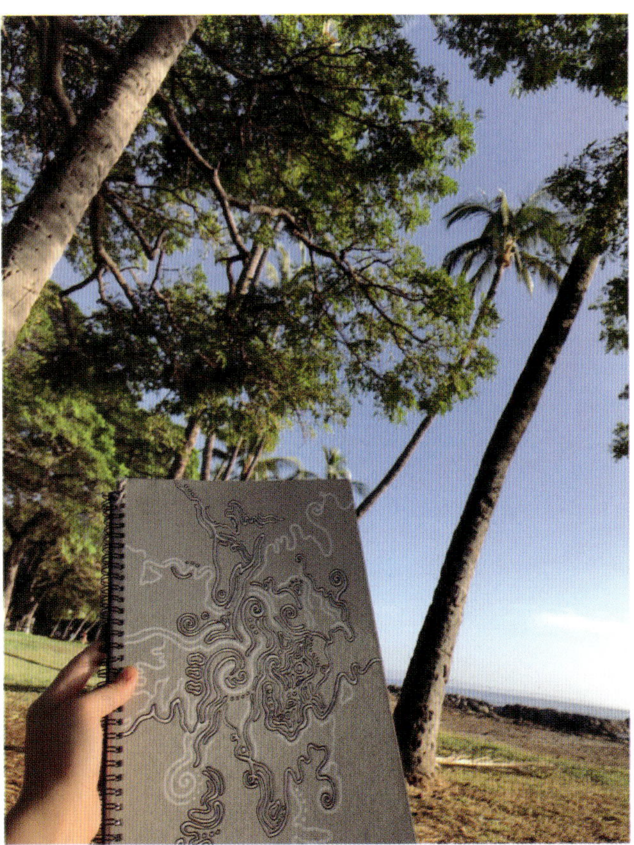

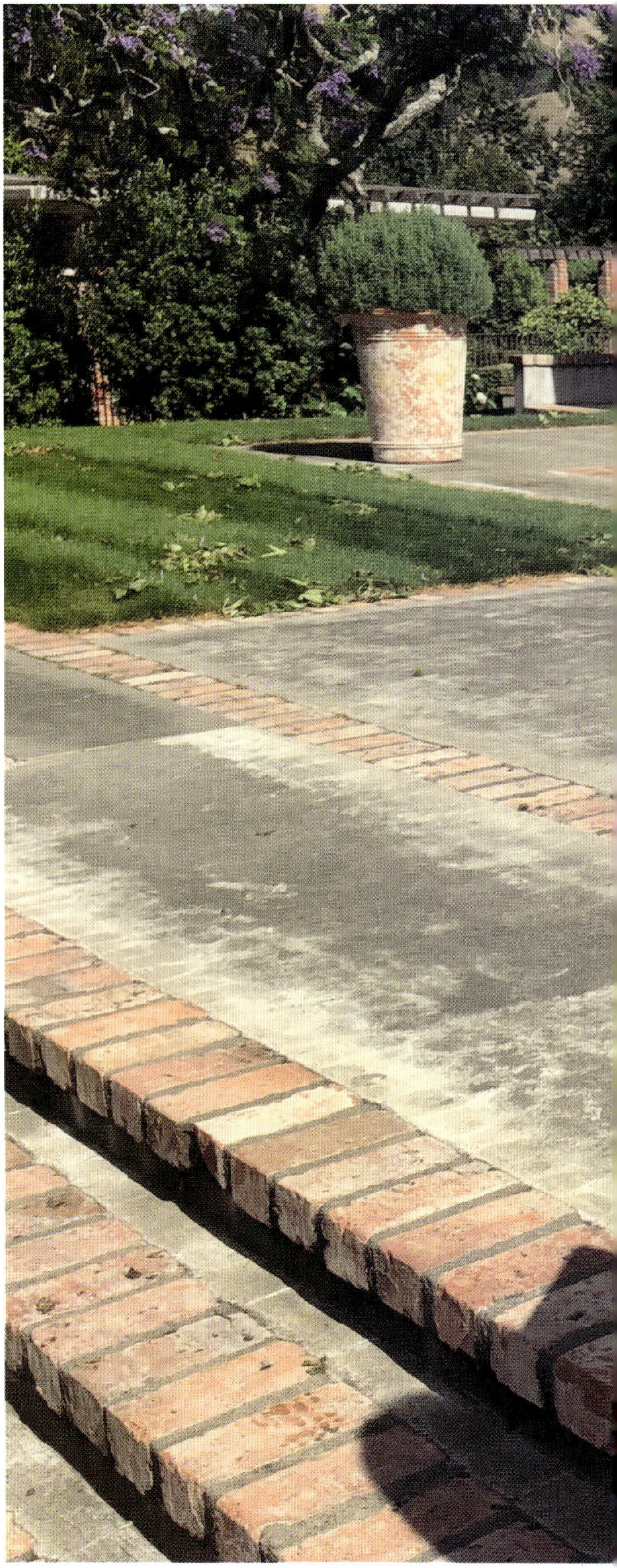

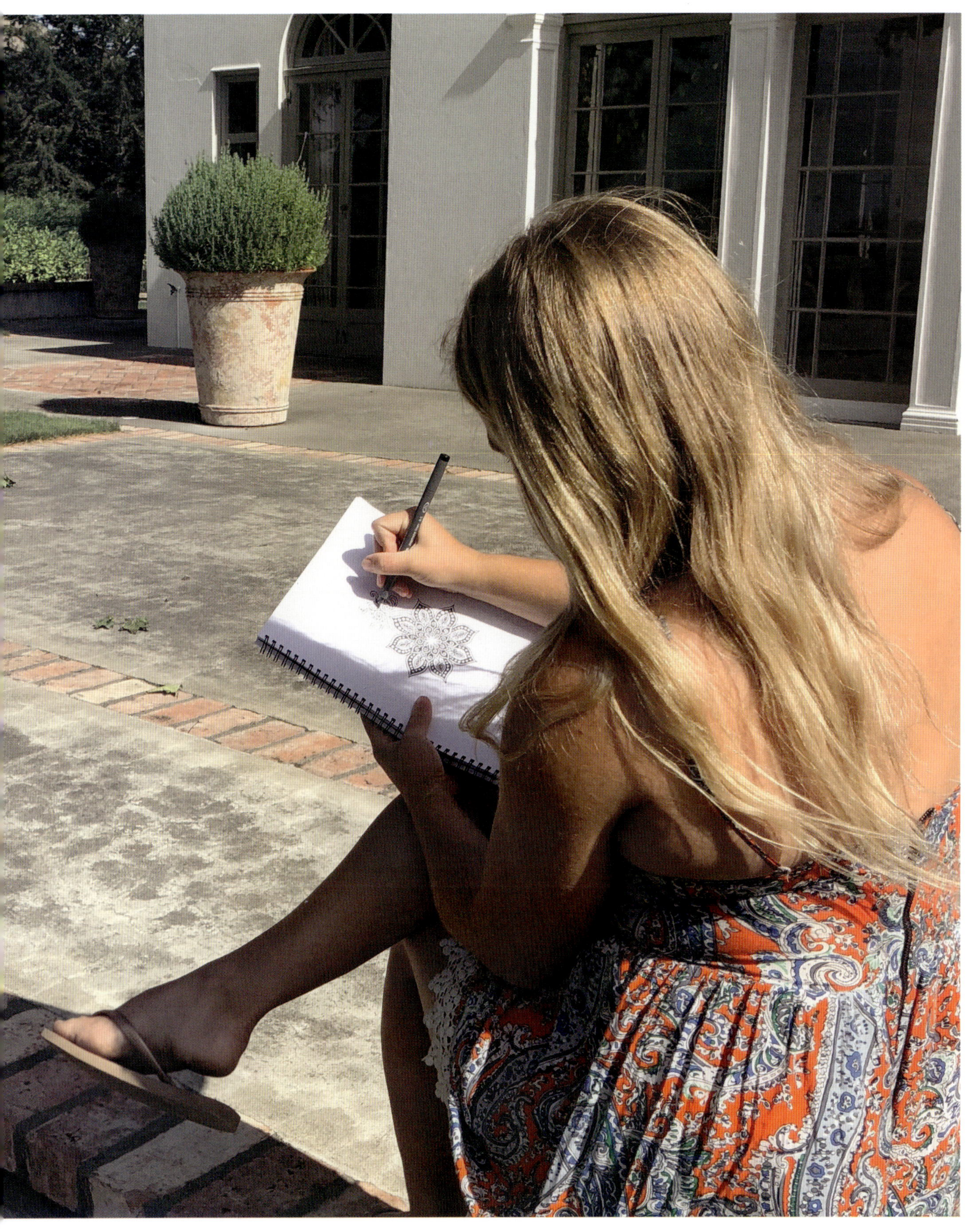

4

BASIC PATTERNS + MOTIFS

IN THIS CHAPTER, WE WILL EXPLORE the art of drawing basic patterns and motifs. The key is selecting designs that are intricate enough to captivate your attention, yet not so complex that they lead to frustration. I'll guide you through the process of choosing and creating patterns that encourage concentration and mindfulness. Additionally, I'll share insights on setting themes and artwork rules to streamline your creative process, making it easier to engage in a fulfilling and meditative drawing practice.

DESIGNS THAT ENCOURAGE THE FLOW STATE

INSIGHT

I find it takes ten to fifteen minutes to get fully absorbed in drawing, similar to what I experience when cooking or playing the cello. Those first moments feel restless and I have to really convince myself to stay focused, before eventually the flow state takes over and a wave of ease and enjoyment arises. Then all sense of time is lost, and I can draw for hours without a break in a very meditative state.

Considering that a state of focused creativity requires you to be equally challenged and engaged (see page 35), the designs you choose to draw should strike just the right balance between being difficult and enjoyable. Patterns and motifs that are too simple might not capture your full attention, while those that are overly complex can become overwhelming. The goal is to select designs intricate enough to hold your focus and slightly push your skills, but not so difficult that they lead to stress (or wanting to give up).

Drawing repetitive geometric shapes alongside fluid, organic patterns can be particularly effective in cultivating sustained attention. These designs encourage focus and help you become fully absorbed in your artistic practice.

It's also important to recognize that reaching a deeply absorbed creative mindset often takes time. Transitioning from daily distractions to this level of focus requires a few moments. To make this process smoother, eliminating distractions and interruptions can significantly enhance your ability to concentrate. By creating a distraction-free environment, you allow your mind to settle into the rhythm of your drawing and enjoy a more fulfilling and seamless creative journey.

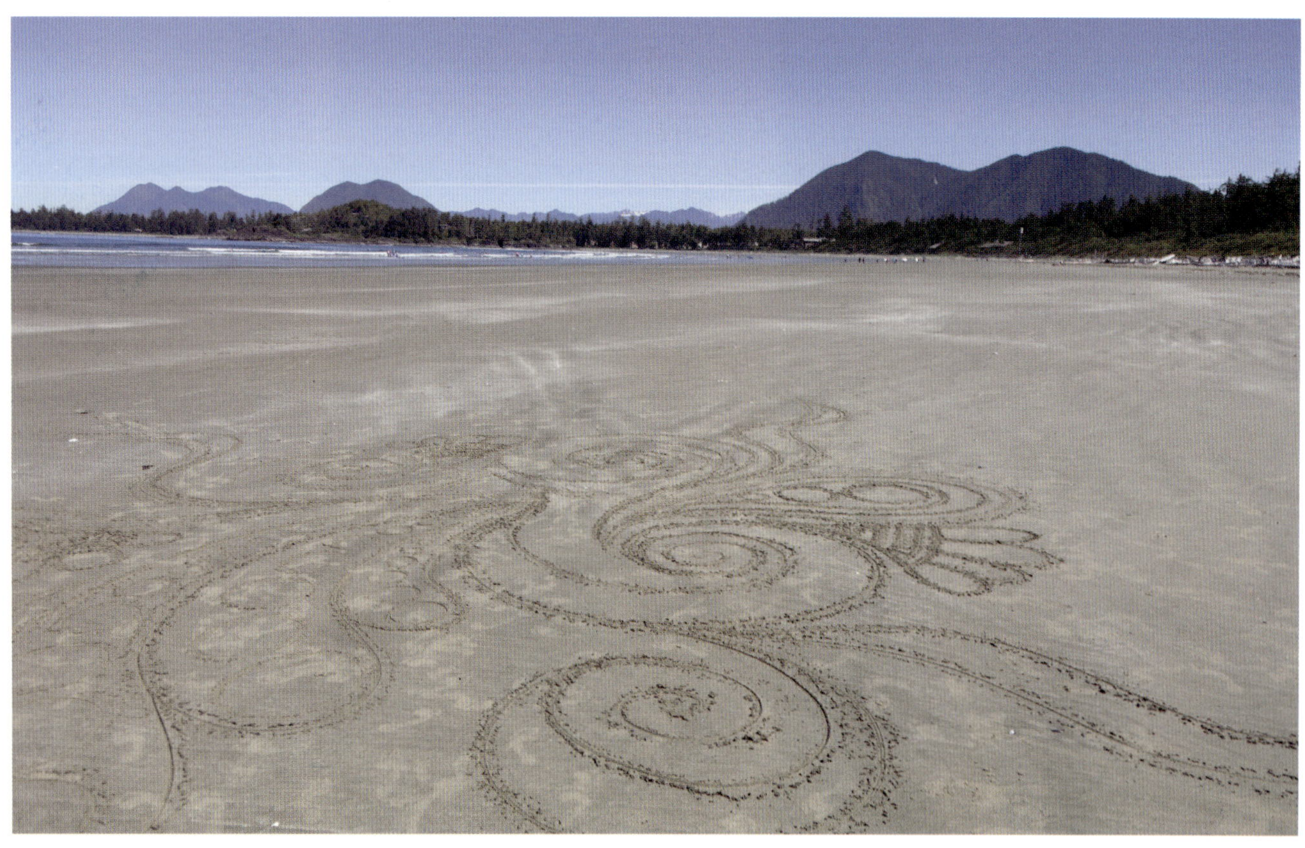

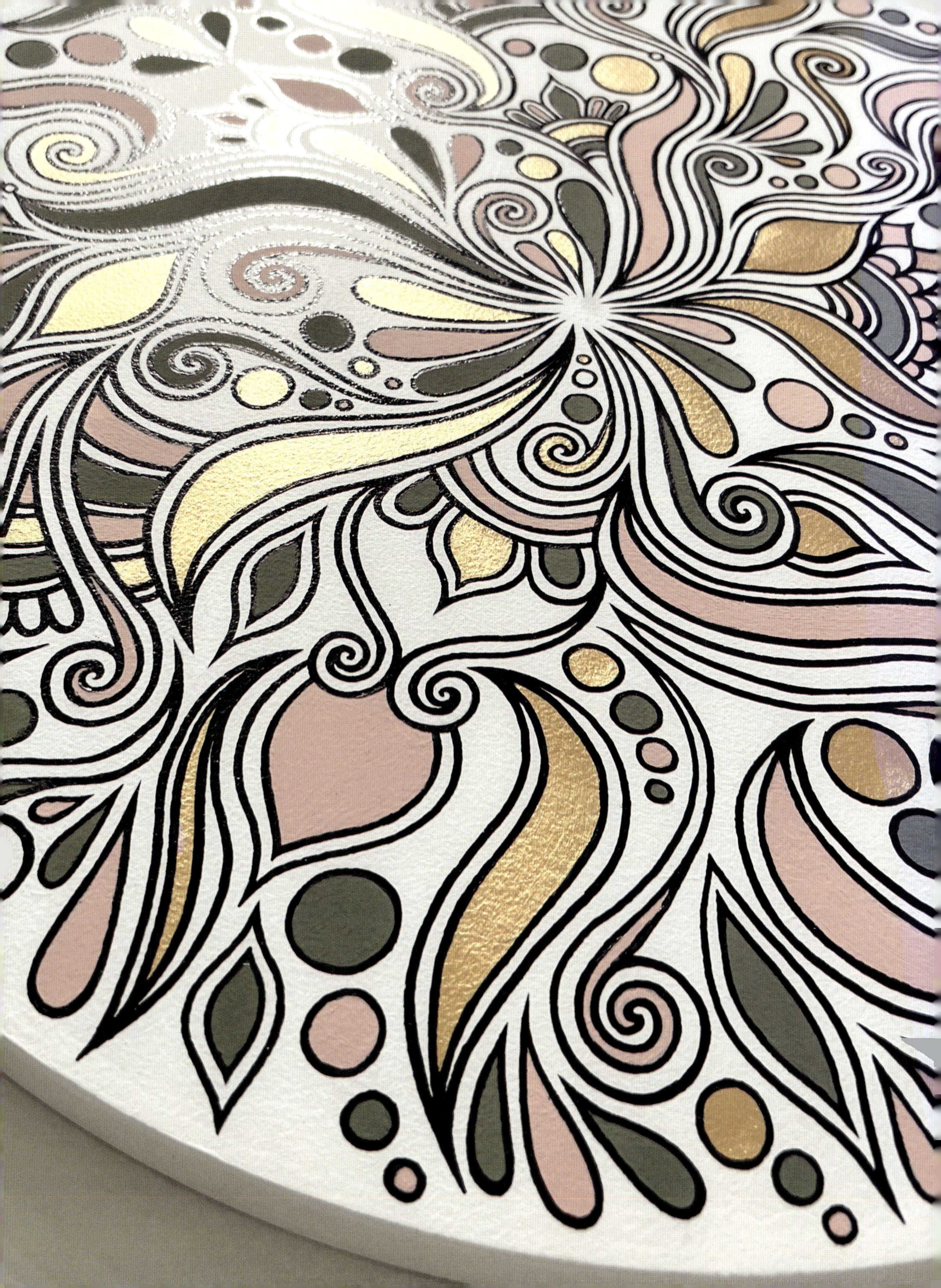

SETTING THEMES AND ARTWORK "RULES"

Establishing themes and guidelines for your artwork can bring clarity and enhance cohesion by introducing simplicity and control. These boundaries help focus your design process, turning chaos into a more structured, impactful composition. Clear rules or themes allow for a focused approach, ensuring that each decision serves the overall concept and contributes to a unified, striking visual effect. This simplifies the process of entering the flow state, as it reduces the number of decisions and interruptions, allowing for a more seamless and mindful creative experience.

For example, you might decide to use a "rule" of selecting only four shapes or patterns to use in your artwork, varying their scales and complexities throughout. Choosing to work with a limited number of patterns like this can encourage you to delve deeper into variations and detail level of those elements too.

Another option is to set a "theme," such as creating an artwork that is entirely based off the patterns and shapes found in the architecture of a particular museum, or the theme of "spring," or basing an artwork on the patterns in cut-crystal vases found in an antique shop. There are endless options, and these self-imposed rules provide a framework that fosters your creativity through setting defined boundaries.

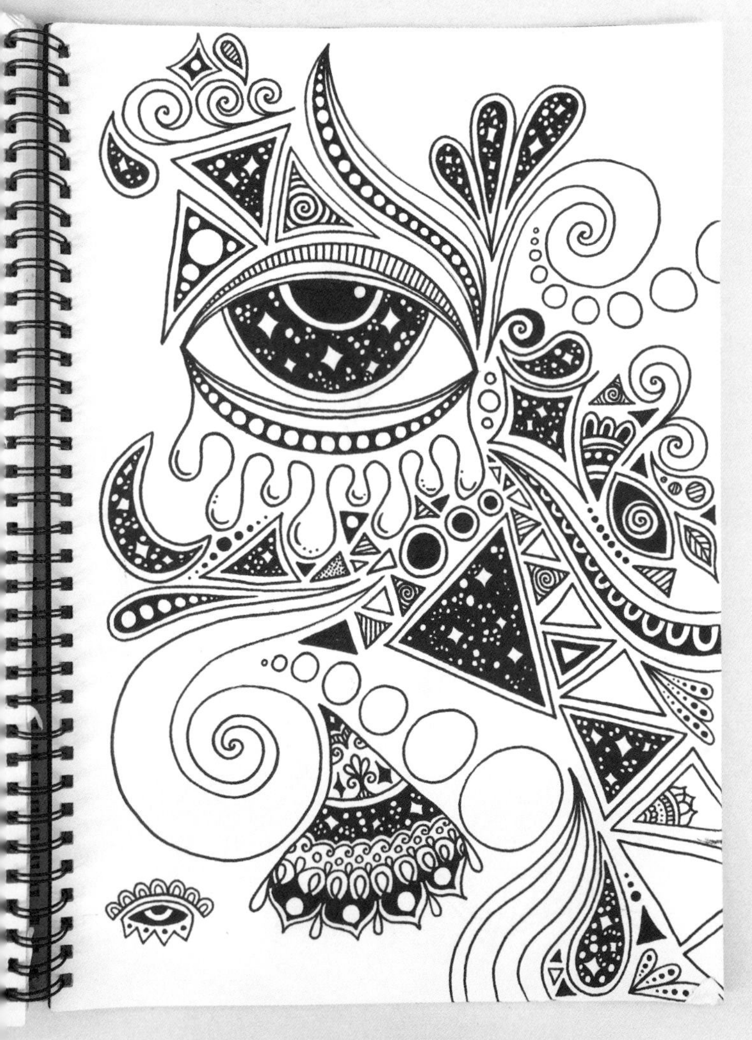

INSIGHT

At times, I've been asked if I ever get bored of this style of drawing, but I truly don't. As we continue to draw, our skills evolve, and new ideas emerge, leading us on a path of continual creative expansion. Establishing "rules" and themes doesn't limit creativity; rather, it pushes us to explore and discover fresh approaches within those constraints. These boundaries encourage us to innovate and find new ways of thinking, making the creative process an ever-evolving journey. There are infinite possibilities within our minds, and this style of drawing offers a deliciously rich way to tap into that endless potential.

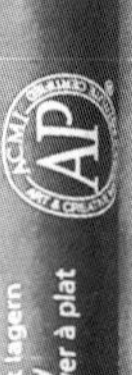

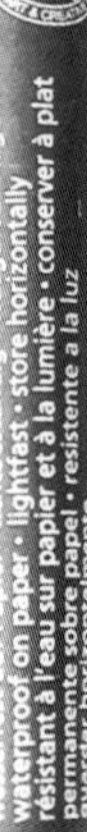

BUILDING PATTERNS FROM SIMPLE SHAPES

By drawing simple shapes over and over again, we can observe how they gradually build into mesmerizing, complex patterns. Focus on the process here—relax into the repetition and see how the drawings evolve. Whether it's a simple dot, circle, or line, repetition allows these basic marks to develop into striking designs. In this way, foundational drawing prepares us for the next steps, where we'll explore drawing more intricate artworks. This might be the extent of your meditative art practice, and it's a perfectly fine way to enjoy drawing—a rhythmic and grounding journey of creating beauty through simplicity.

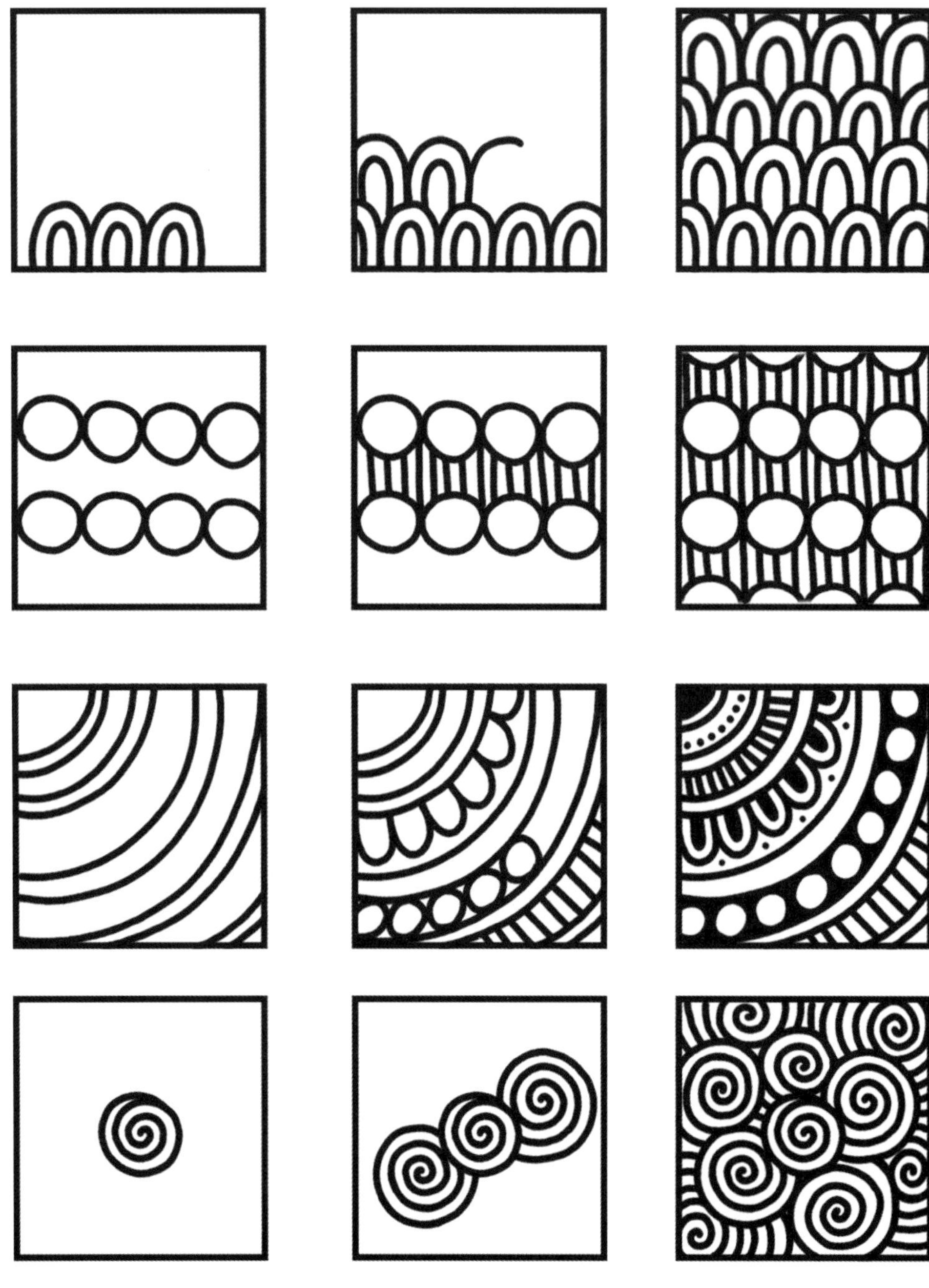

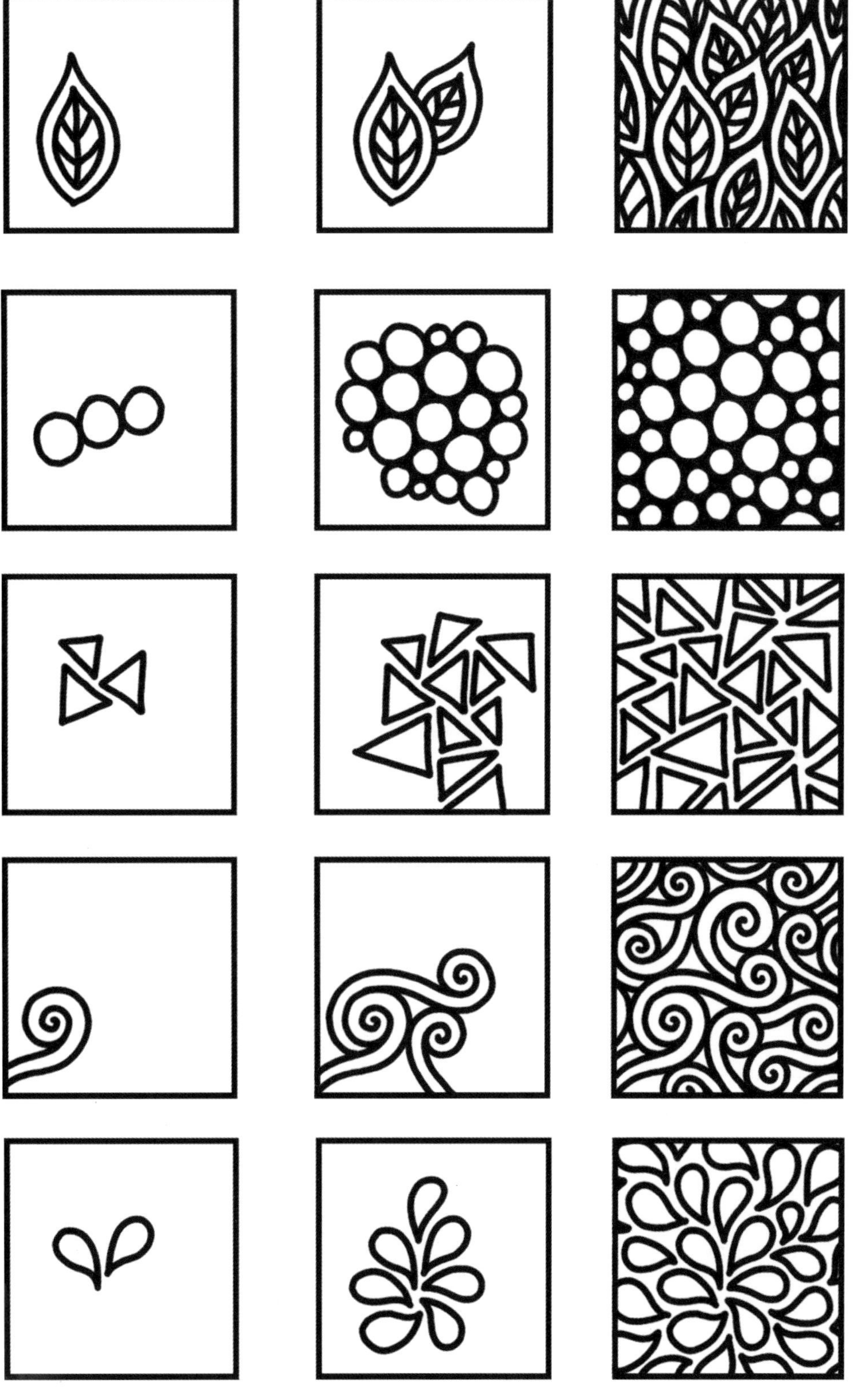

MOTIF PRACTICE

As we begin to explore more intricate shapes and designs, we can experiment with more detailed drawings and literal forms, expanding our creative possibilities. Over time, we naturally gravitate towards certain patterns, helping us define our unique style. With consistent practice, we also start building a library of ideas and designs, creating a personal bank of inspiration to draw from. This framework supports a meditative approach, providing clear direction and removing hesitation each time you pick up the pen.

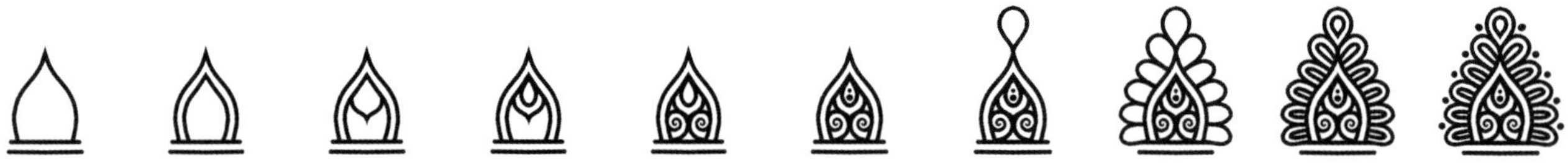

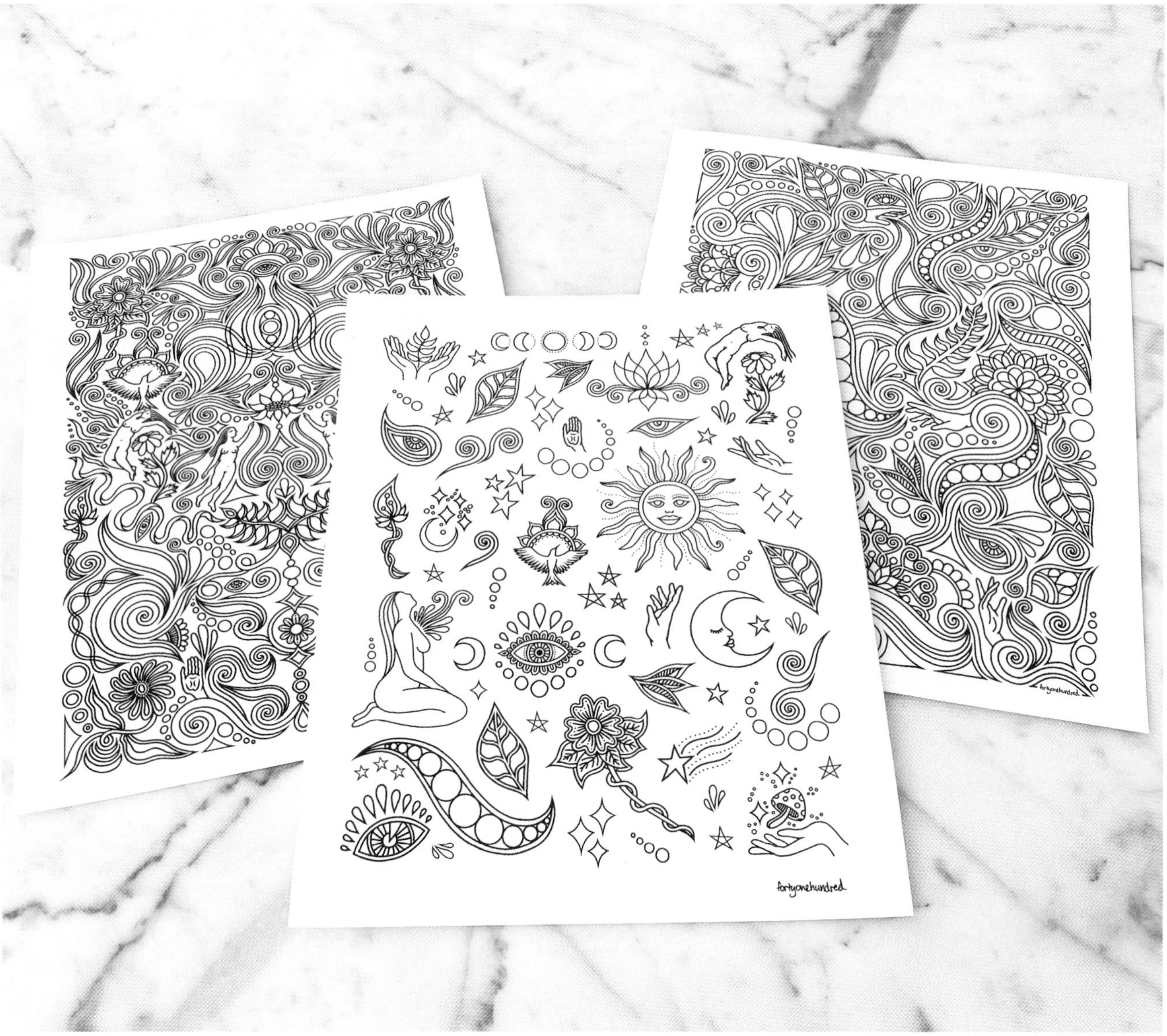

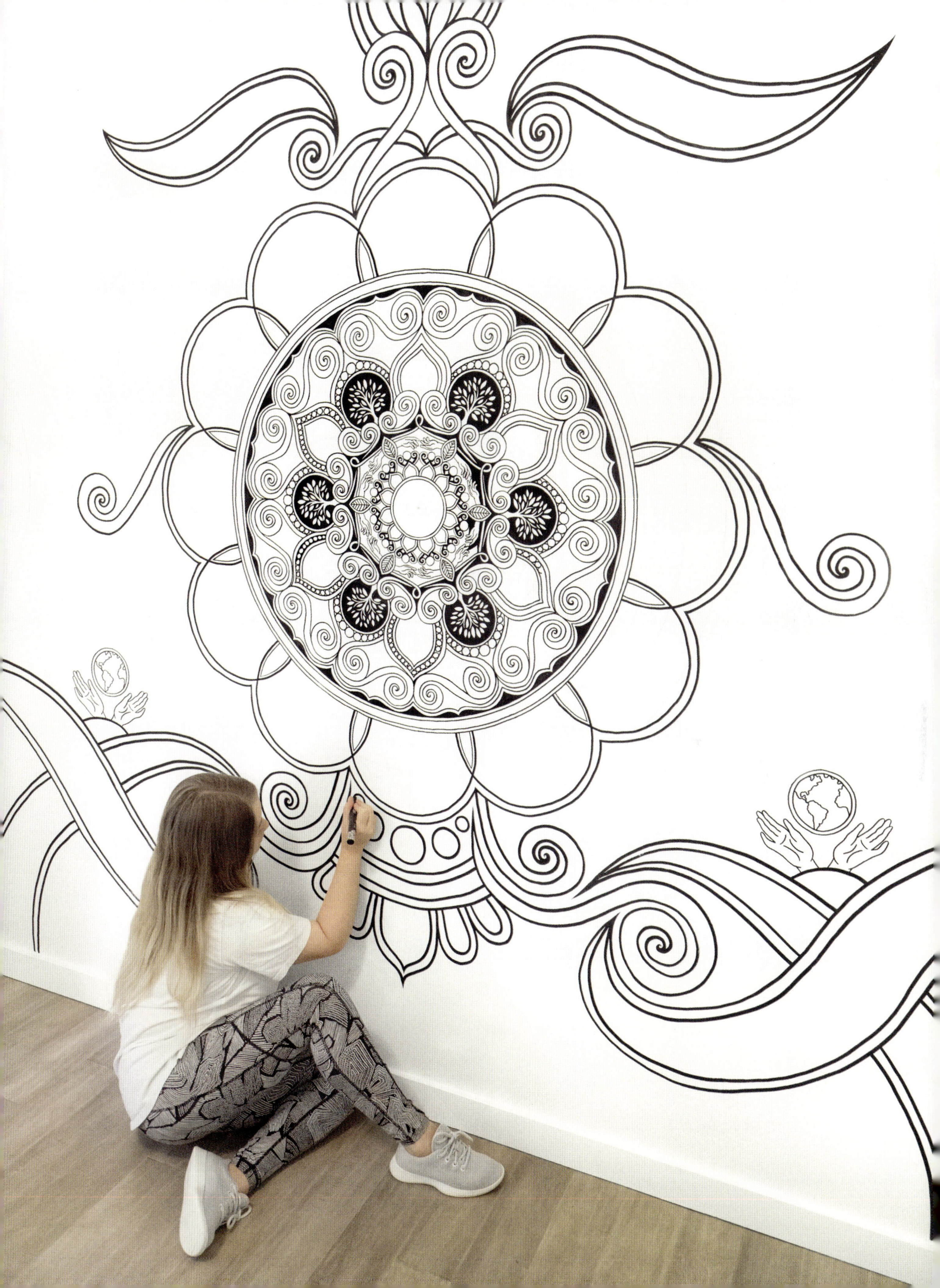

Here is a selection of my designs and motifs that you might incorporate into your own artwork. You can trace these designs onto paper or use your iPad/tablet to create a semi-transparent layer to draw over. From there, try replicating them freehand or use elements from these designs (and other inspirations) to create your own. Starting with simple shapes and gradually building them into more intricate designs is a natural way to develop your patterns.

INSIGHT

While we should always strive to create our own unique art, it's perfectly acceptable to begin by copying. Imitation can help us develop our skills and find our own artistic voice, and eventually lead us to create our own signature style. As you continue to draw, you'll find that over time you won't need to reference other inspirations as much, as your own style will evolve and reveal itself. During this process, it's important to respect intellectual property and give credit to original artists and creators when using their work as a reference.

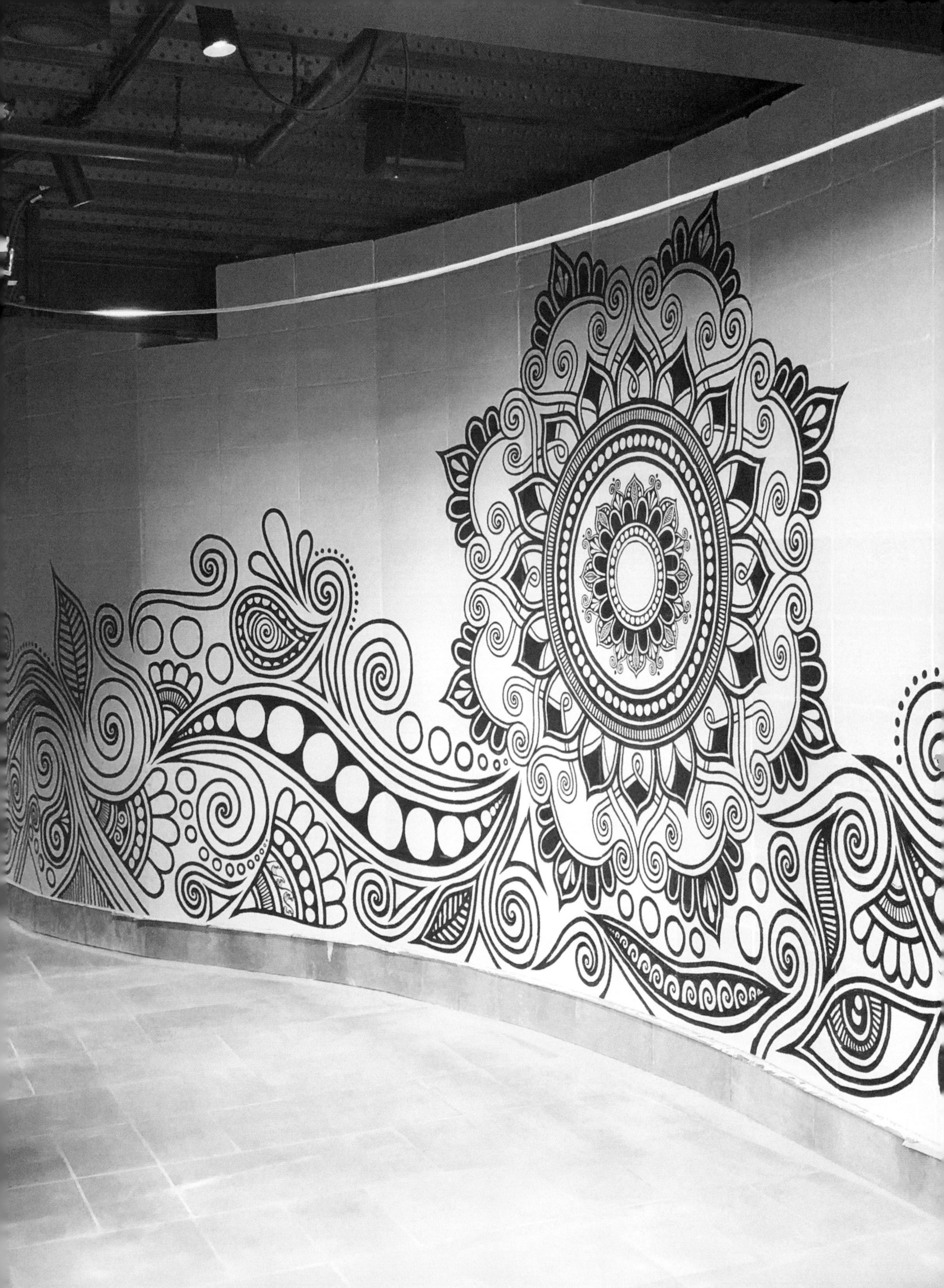

5

FREE-FLOWING DESIGNS

IN THIS CHAPTER, WE DELVE INTO the art of free-flowing designs, where creativity takes the lead in shaping your patterns into a unified artwork. You'll learn to seamlessly integrate various motifs, creating a dynamic composition that embodies fluidity and connection. We'll explore techniques for selecting layouts, making your designs flow naturally, and adjusting patterns to enhance movement and continuity. By embracing repetition and letting your creativity guide each element, you'll transform individual patterns into a harmonious piece of art.

STEP-BY-STEP PROCESS

Free-flowing designs can be spontaneous expressions of creativity where patterns come to life. We can find a way to thoughtfully assemble these patterns into a cohesive artwork.

Whether your design sprawls across the page or is contained within a defined shape, letting the elements flow smoothly from one to another creates a dynamic sense of movement and connection.

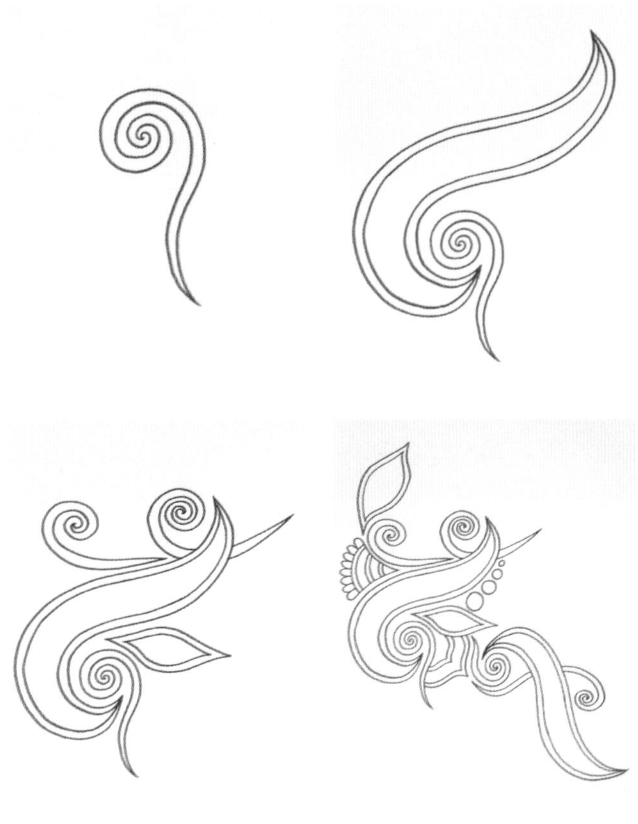

1. Review Your Patterns

Start by revisiting the patterns and motifs you have developed from previous inspirations. Look at how they relate to one another and consider how they can interact in a larger composition. You might choose one, or a few, or many to work with.

2. Select a Layout

Decide whether your design will span across the whole page or be contained within a space. This choice will influence how you arrange your patterns. (For example, will you work within a set space, or have the designs moving off the page?)

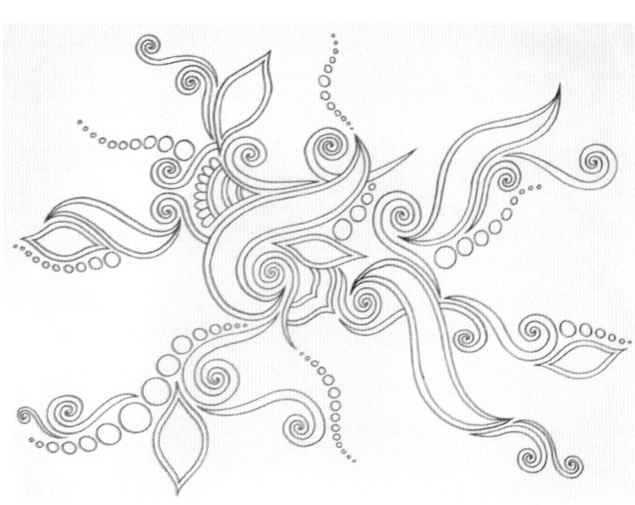

3. Make the First Mark

Draw your first icon, pattern, or motif in a space on the page.

4. Draw the Next Designs

As you draw the next shape, and the many after, focus on how they complement or transition to the next, aiming for a sense of movement and continuity.

5. Create Flow and Movement

Adjust the spacing, orientation, and scale of your patterns. Look for ways to make the patterns connect seamlessly, so that your eye is naturally guided through the design.

Embrace the freedom of flowing designs, where each pattern contributes to a larger, interconnected whole, and let your creativity guide the transformation of individual elements into a captivating and unified composition.

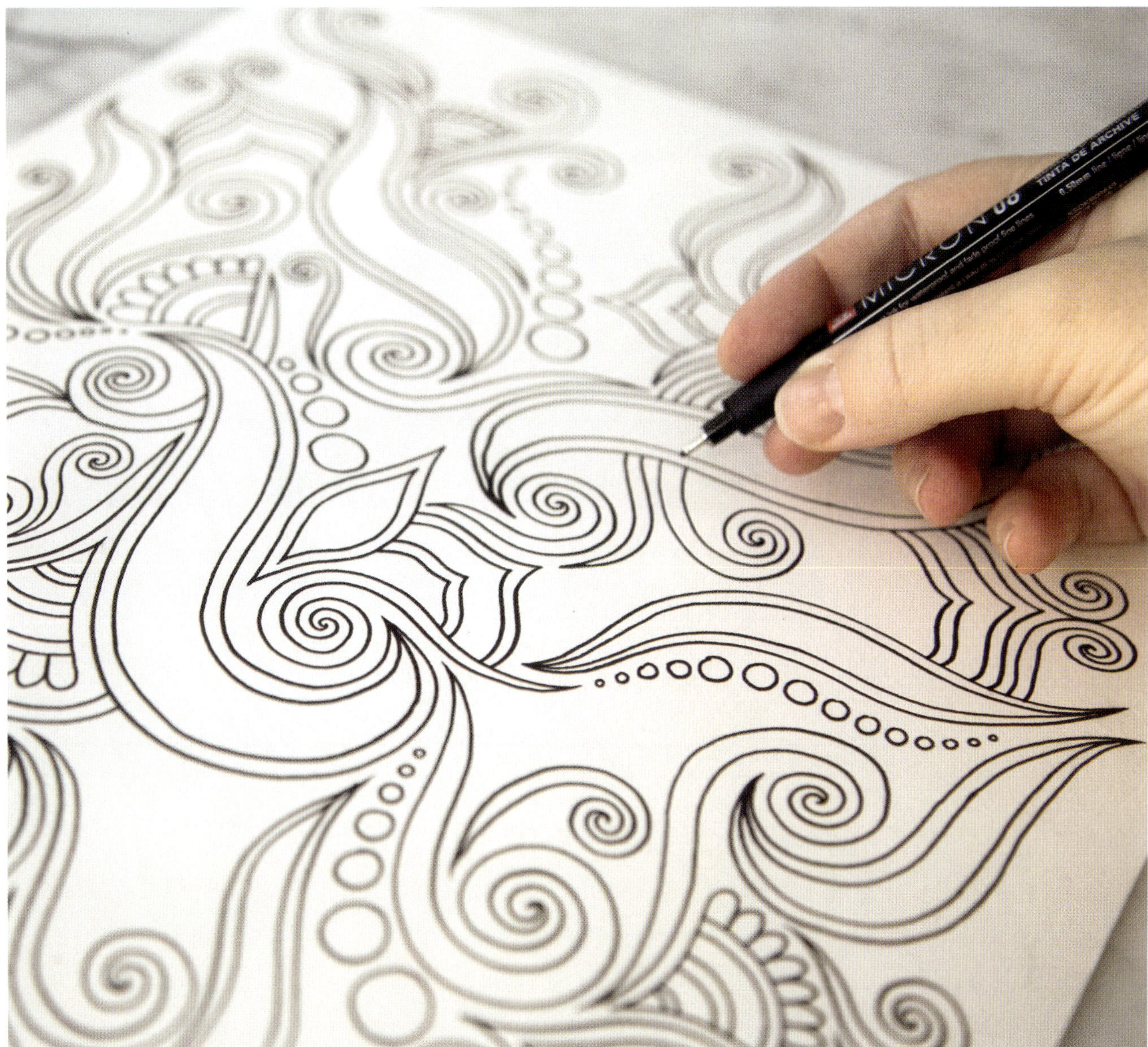

INSIGHT

In my free-flowing drawings, my favorite pattern to use is spirals, inspired by the many examples found in nature. These can be seen in nautilus shells, weather patterns, galaxies, the unfurling of ferns, sunflower seed arrangements, pine cones, and more.

Where one spiral ends, it creates curves and spaces for another drawing to stem from. This process contributes to the meditative quality of the artwork, as each drawing leads to the next without requiring much thought, allowing a continuous and relaxing creative flow. For example, where the spiral moves into its circular head, a triangle of negative space is formed, offering the perfect opportunity to fit in a pattern or an icon of a similar or different shape, further enhancing the intricate and interconnected nature of the design.

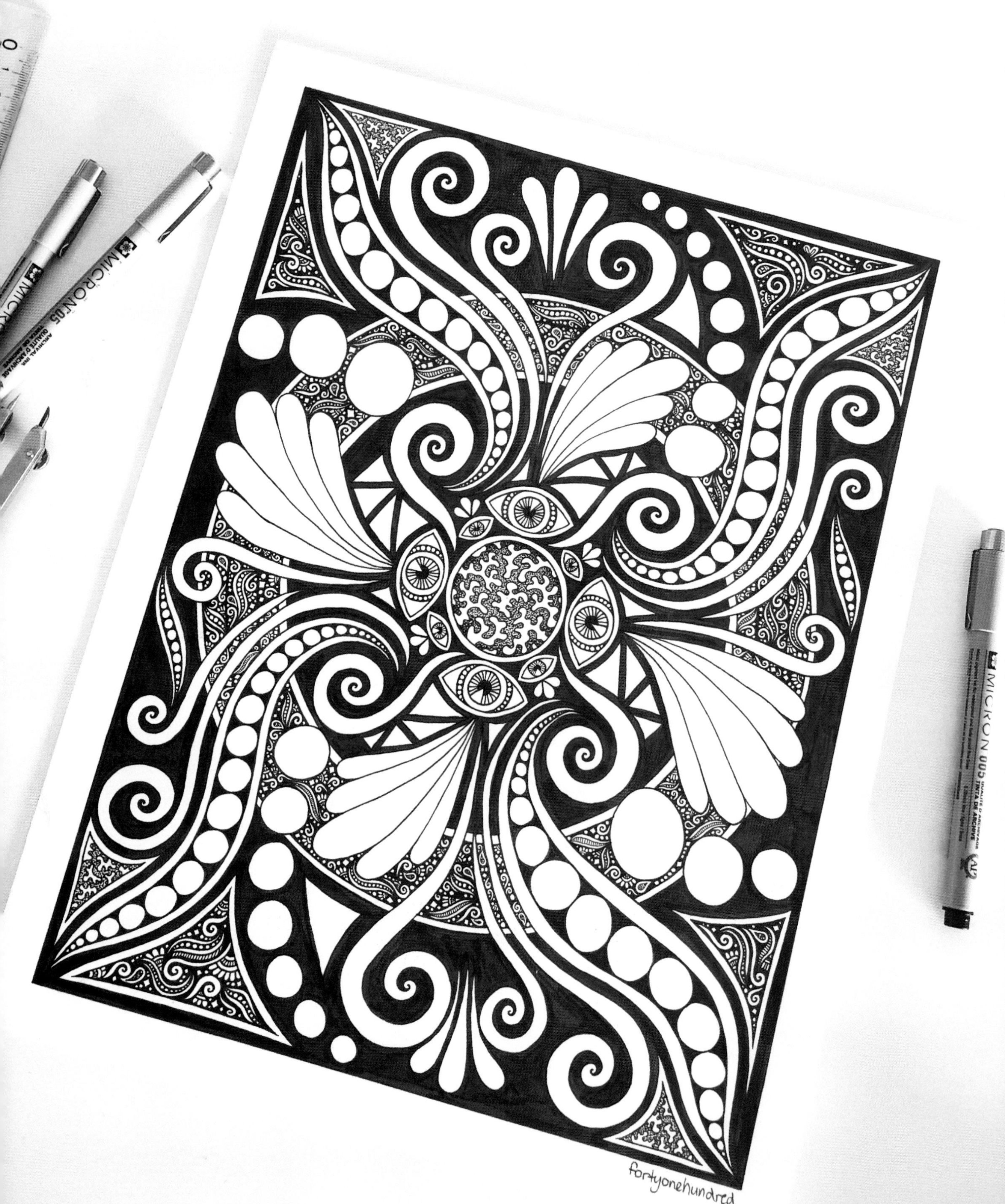
MICRON 05
MICRON 005
fortyonehundred

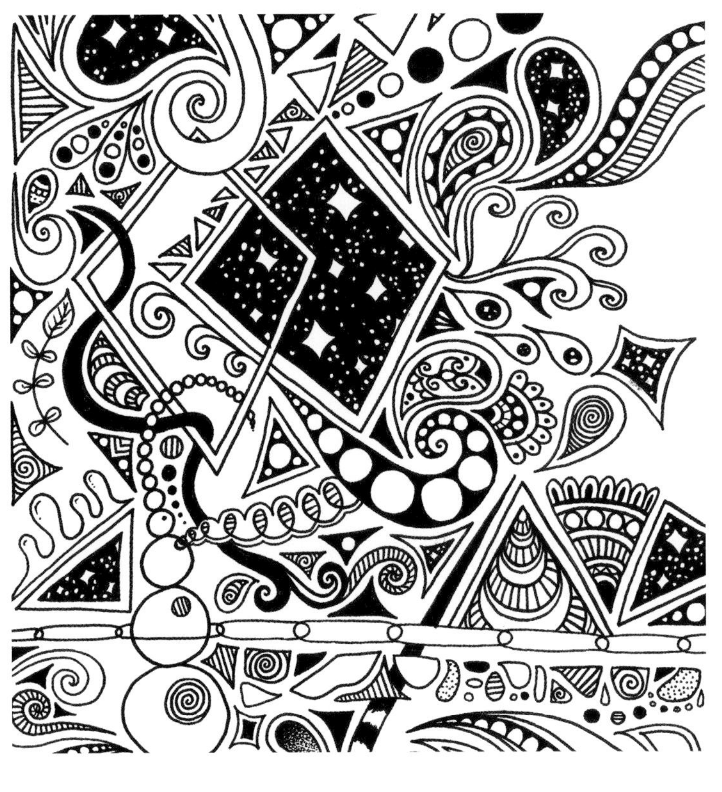

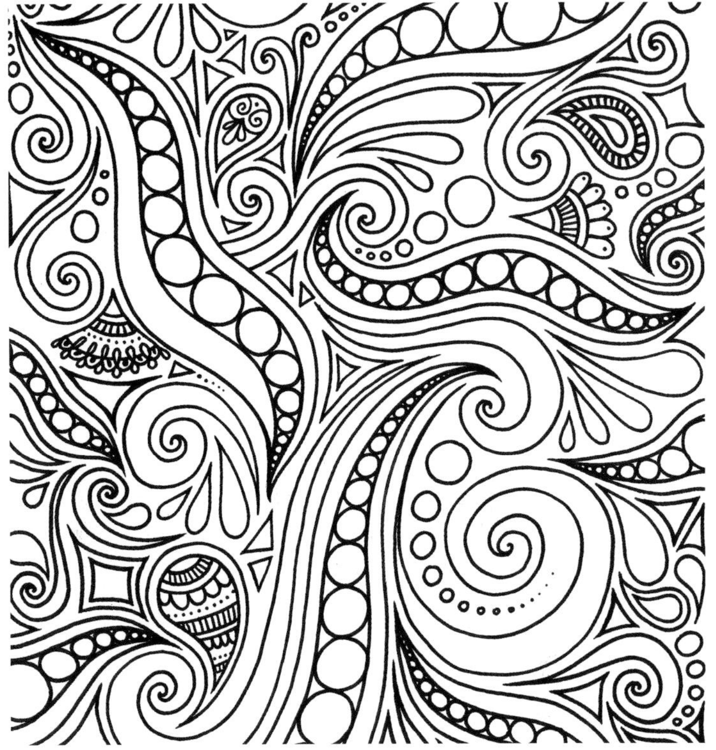

SCAN TO WATCH A VIDEO creating a free-flowing design based on fractals.

ABOVE AND LEFT:
Here are three free-flowing designs created using this process.

ENJOYING THE REPETITION

Repetition taps into our innate love for patterns, much like our enjoyment of rhythm in music or a toddler's fascination with hearing the same story repeatedly. In meditative drawing, this instinct is harnessed to cultivate calm and focus. This repetition reflects patterns found in the natural world, such as the rhythmic waves on a beach or the repeating leaves on a stem.

By engaging with repetition, both in concept and visual outcome, we immerse ourselves in a process that mirrors these natural inclinations, allowing us to experience the soothing effects of repetitive motifs and find deeper satisfaction in our creative practice. Each repetition brings you closer to a state of serenity and concentration, making the creative process both soothing and fulfilling.

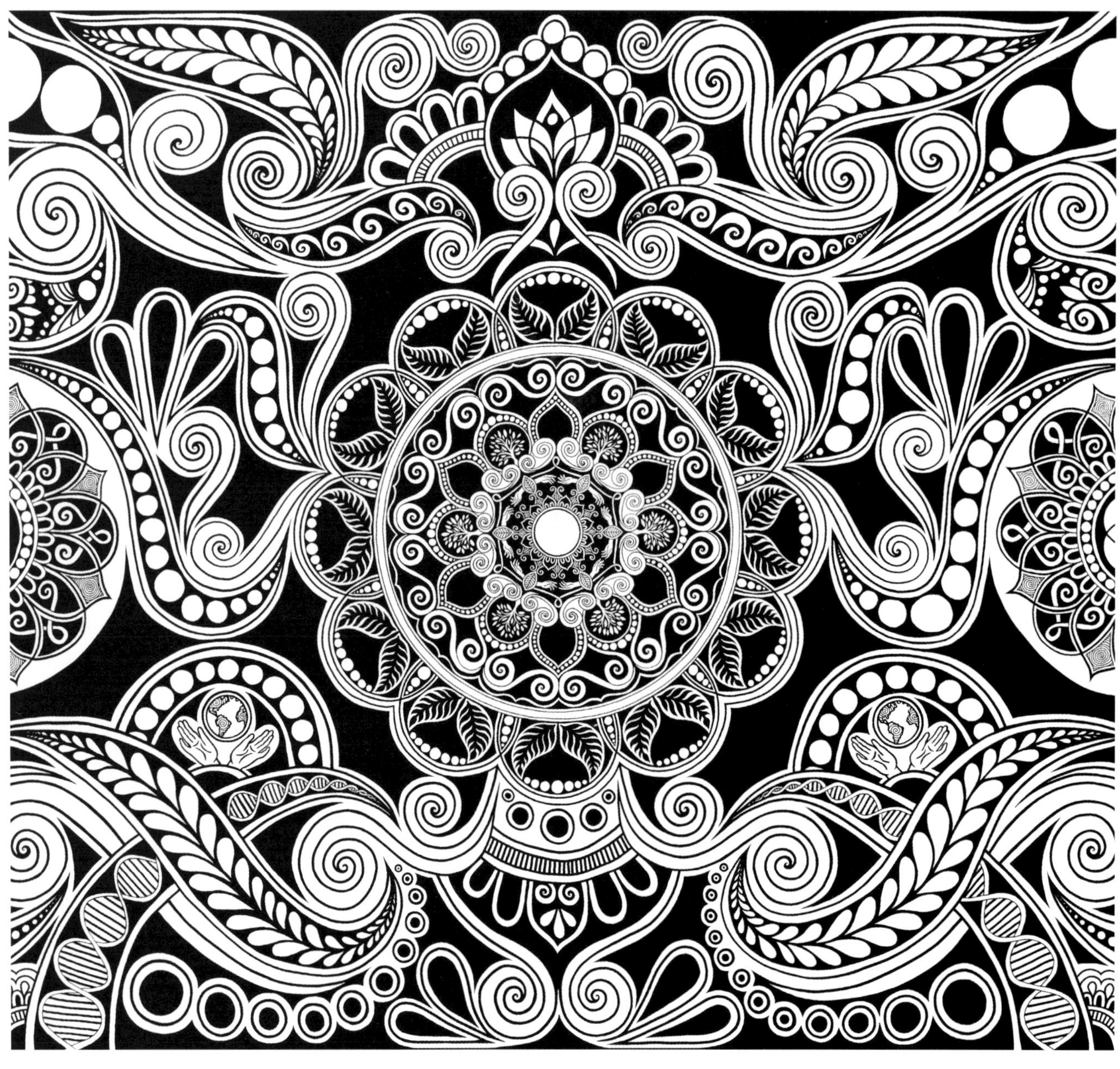

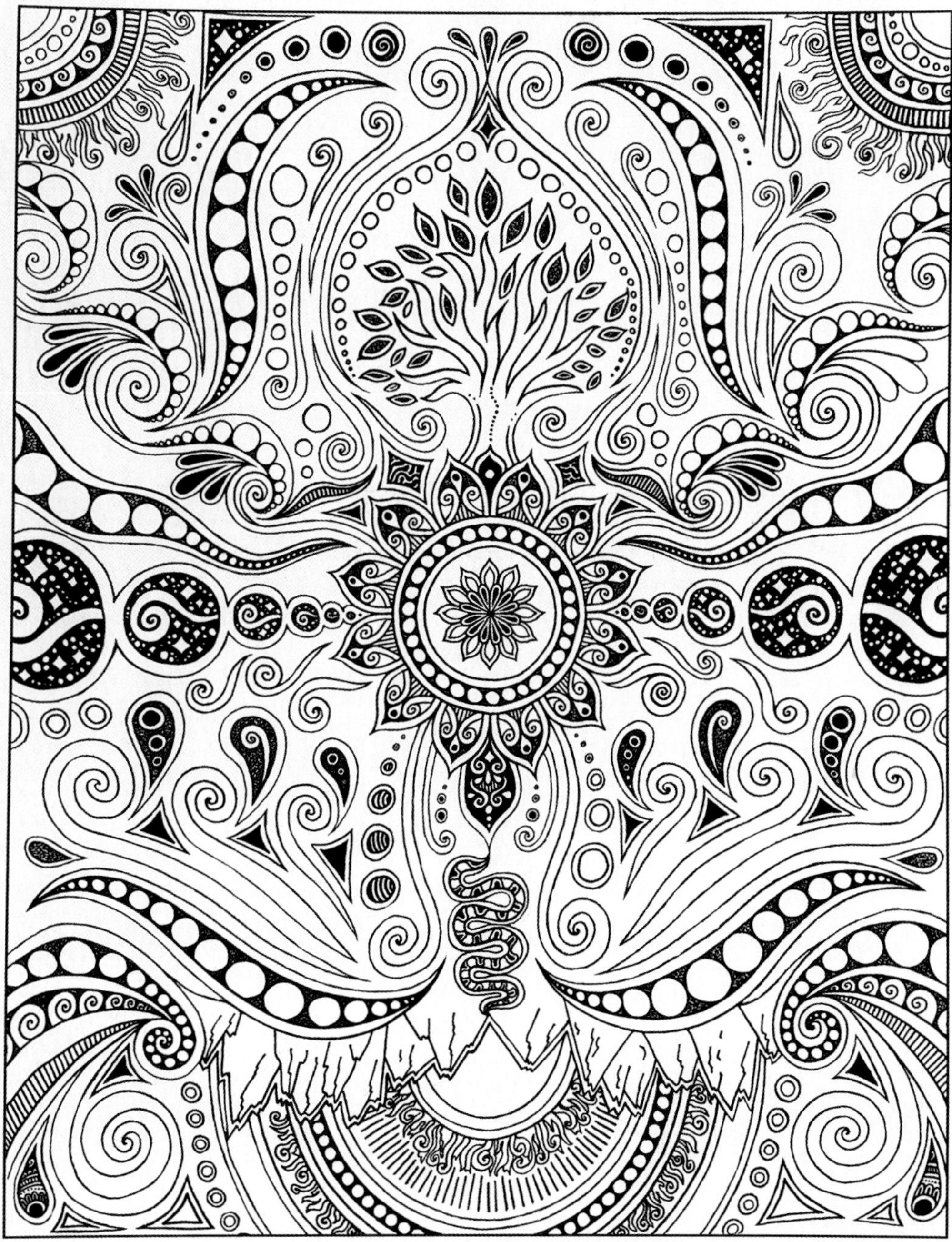

fortyonehundred

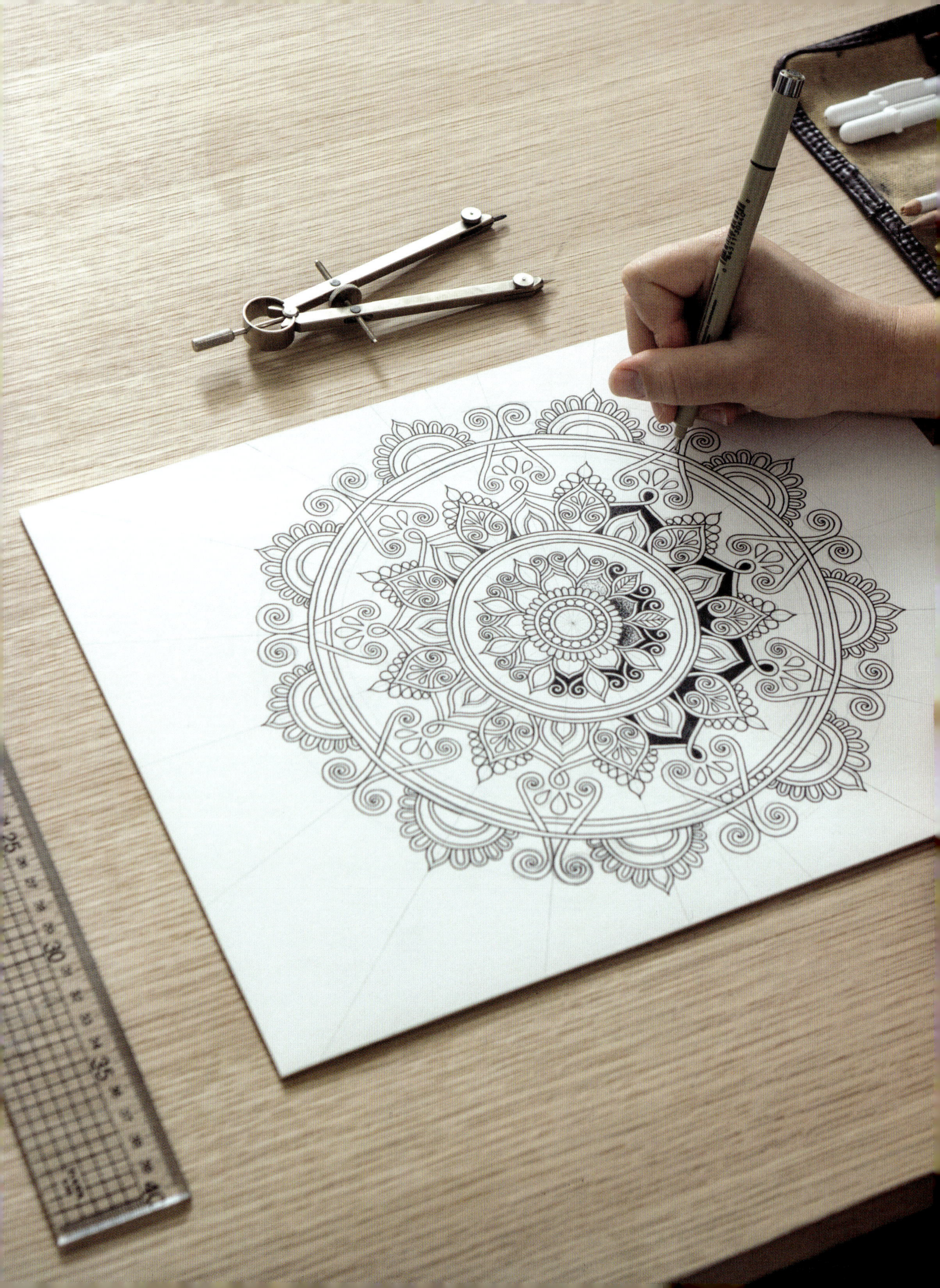

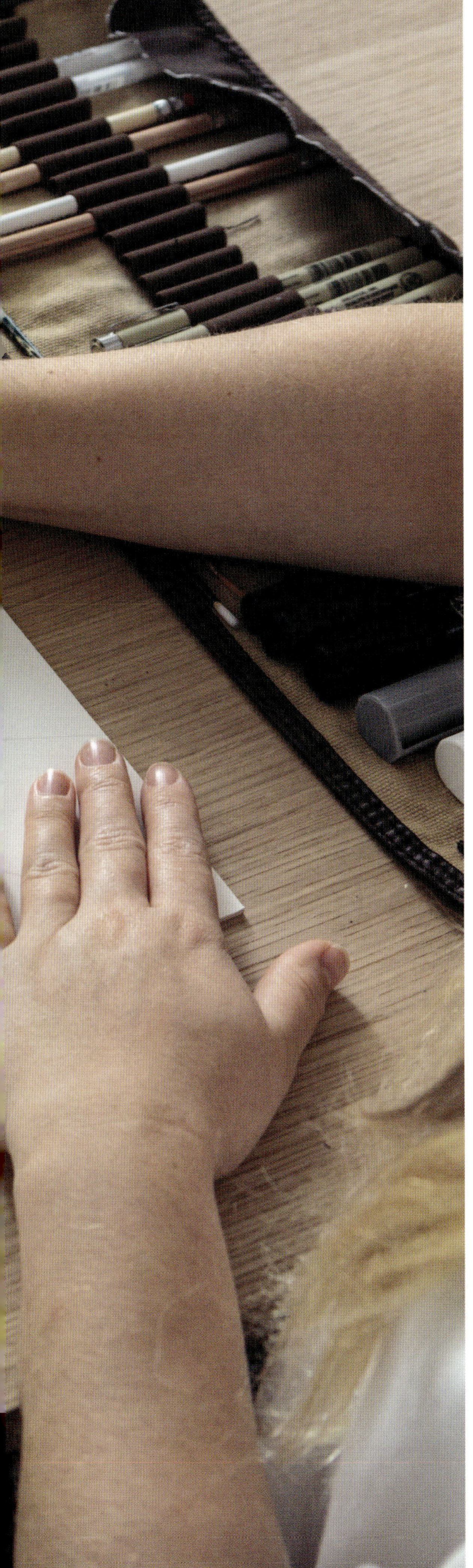

6

DRAWING MANDALAS

NOW THAT WE'VE DRAWN INSPIRATION from different spaces, and perhaps tried free-flowing patterns, we can structure these shapes through rules such as circularity, radial symmetry, scaling, and repetition to create a contemporary exploration of the mandala.

The intricate patterns, symbols, and motifs within a mandala hold different meanings for each artist or viewer, resonating uniquely with each of our personal beliefs, cultural backgrounds, interests, and experiences.

A mandala is an art form that transcends specific doctrines or ideologies, inviting everyone to find their own joy and meaning within its patterns. It serves as a universal canvas where diverse interpretations coexist, allowing each of us to access and appreciate the significance it holds, regardless of our way of thinking. Embracing mandalas in this inclusive manner emphasizes our shared human desire for connection and the various paths we take to find peace and understanding in our lives.

DRAWING THE GRID

Creating a grid is the foundational tool for achieving balance and symmetry in your mandala design. It helps ensure that your design is evenly distributed, creates a visually pleasing composition, and maintains precision and accuracy.

It's worth taking your time to create a well-executed grid, as it will set you up for success in your artwork. Our eyes are well trained to symmetry, and we notice very quickly when something is a bit "off." It's incredibly difficult to create a mandala without a grid, but you could give it a go with and without to see the difference.

To create the grid for drawing a mandala, we need to measure the center of the page, draw circles with a compass, and then divide the circles into sections with radial lines.

YOU WILL NEED

Ruler
Pencil
Compass
Protractor
Eraser
Pencil sharpener

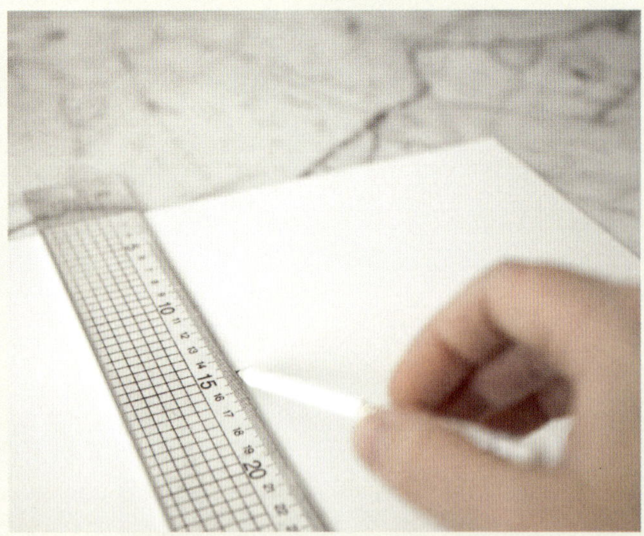

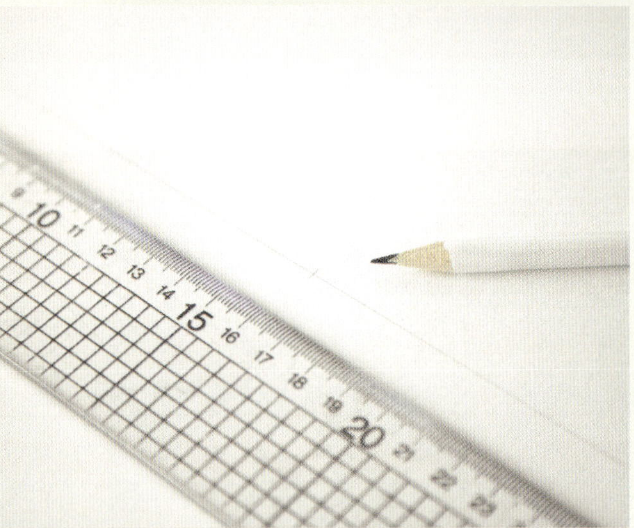

Measure the Center of the Page

STEP 1

Find the midpoint of each side of your page. Measure one side of your page's length using a ruler. Divide this length by two to find the midpoint. Mark this point lightly with your pencil. Repeat on all four sides of your page.

STEP 2

Where the midpoints intersect is the center. Use a ruler to draw two light, straight lines connecting the points.

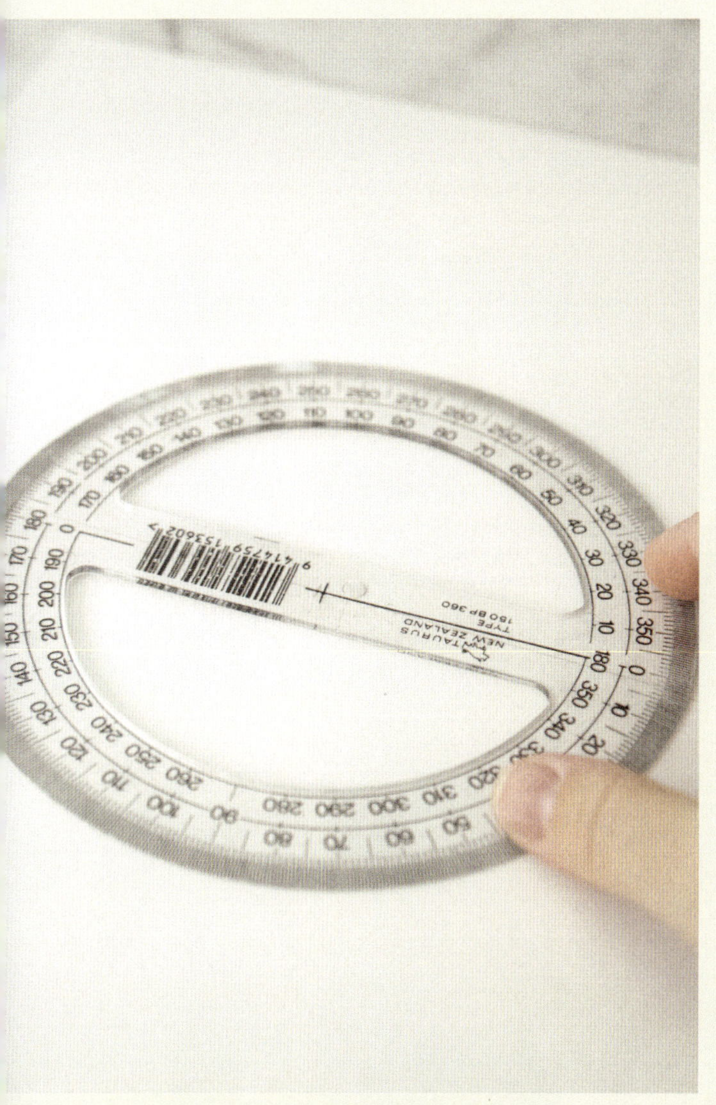

STEP 3

Make a slightly larger mark to clearly indicate the center of your page. This will be the starting point for your mandala design and where your compass will go in the next step.

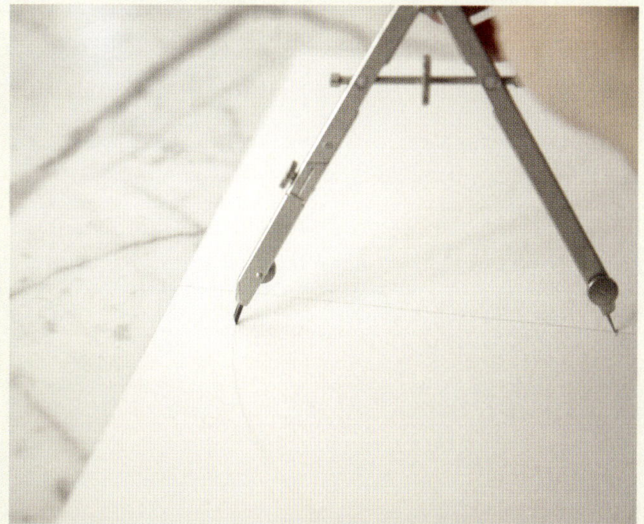

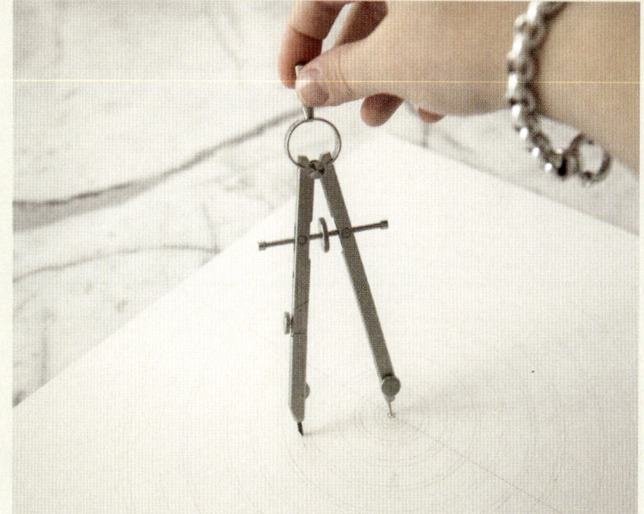

Draw Circles with a Compass

STEP 1

Place your compass point in the center of the paper.

STEP 2

Expand your compass and draw a small circle in the center.

STEP 3

Gradually increase the radius for each subsequent circle, drawing ten to twenty circles of increasing diameters.

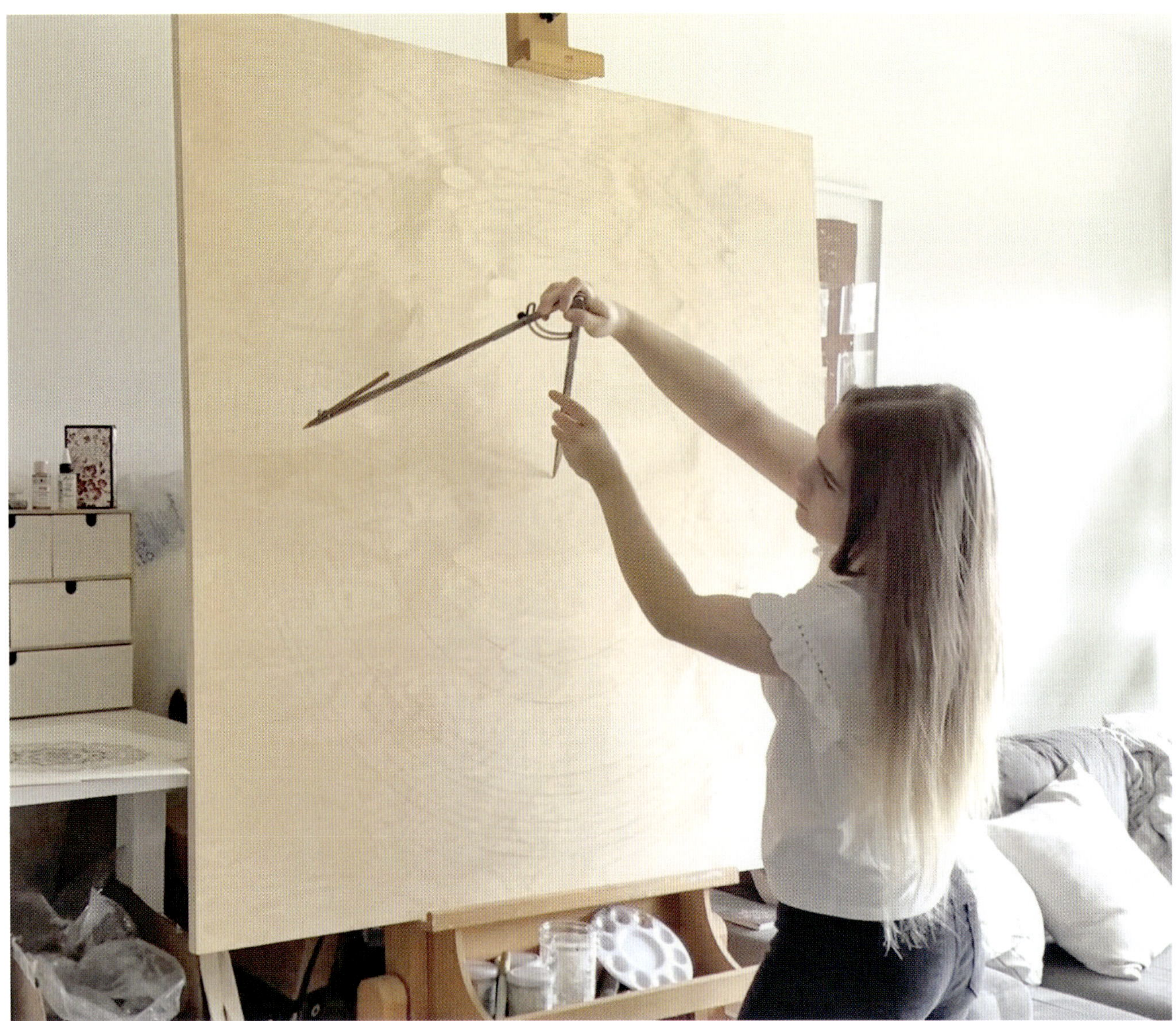

ABOVE:
Creating large circles on a wooden canvas using the *fortyonehundred XL compass*.

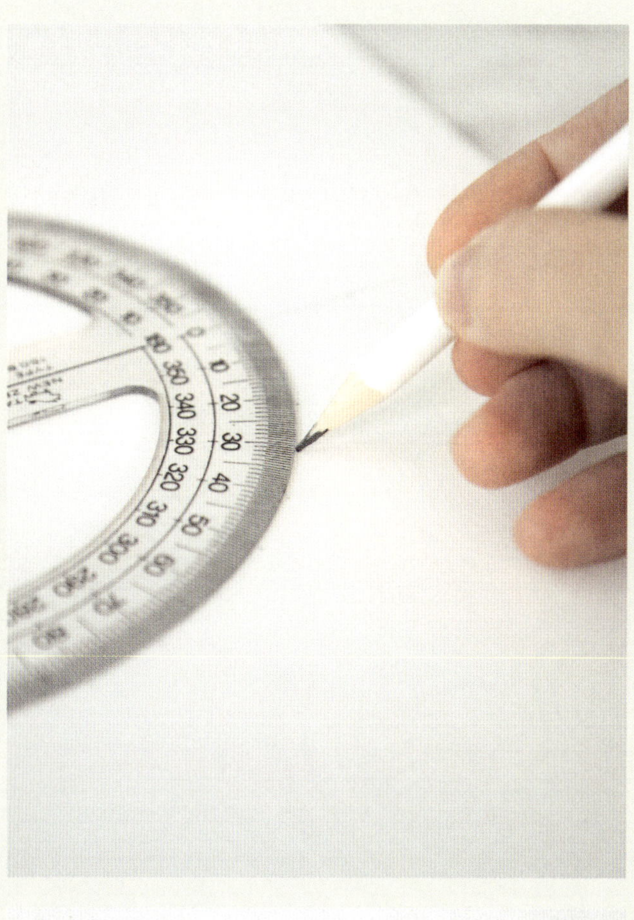

TIPS

Keep sharpening your pencil throughout this process; it makes a huge difference.

Use as light of a hand as possible, as all these lines will be erased at the end.

Divide the Circles into Sections with Radial Lines

STEP 1

Place the protractor so that its center aligns with the page midpoint. Using a pencil, mark a dot at each point of the protractor. Repeat around half of the page.

STEP 2

Take your pencil and place it in the hole in the middle of your page. Hold the ruler against your pencil, aligning its end with a protractor dot. Draw a line across the entire page, intersecting these points. Repeat this with the next dot, creating radial lines out from the center.

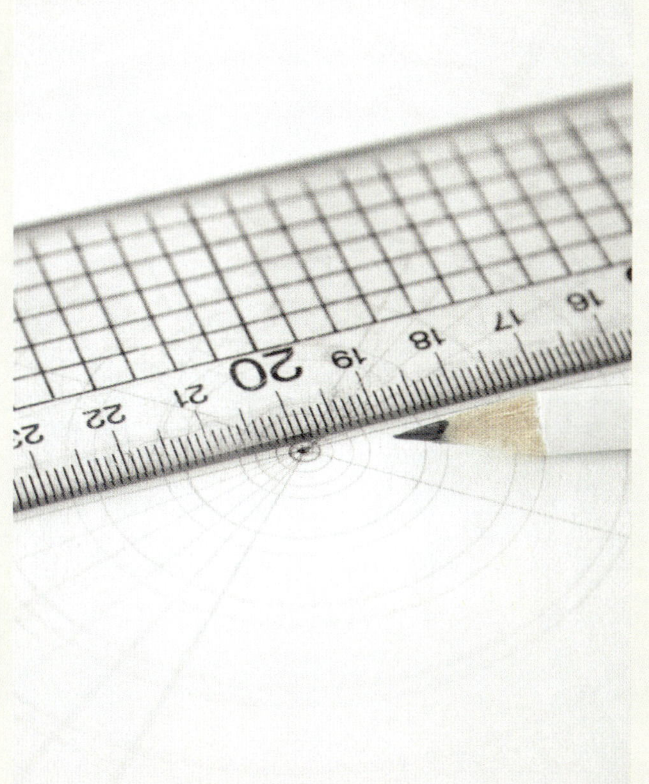

SCAN THIS QR CODE to watch a video of setting up a grid from scratch.

DOWNLOAD

Your grid-making skills will get better with practice. If you're eager to get going on the drawing without having to measure and create the grid, **scan this QR code** to download the fortyonehundred "Mandala Drawing Grid Template." You can print this out (or use as a layer on your iPad) to draw on top of or use the blank grid provided on page 119.

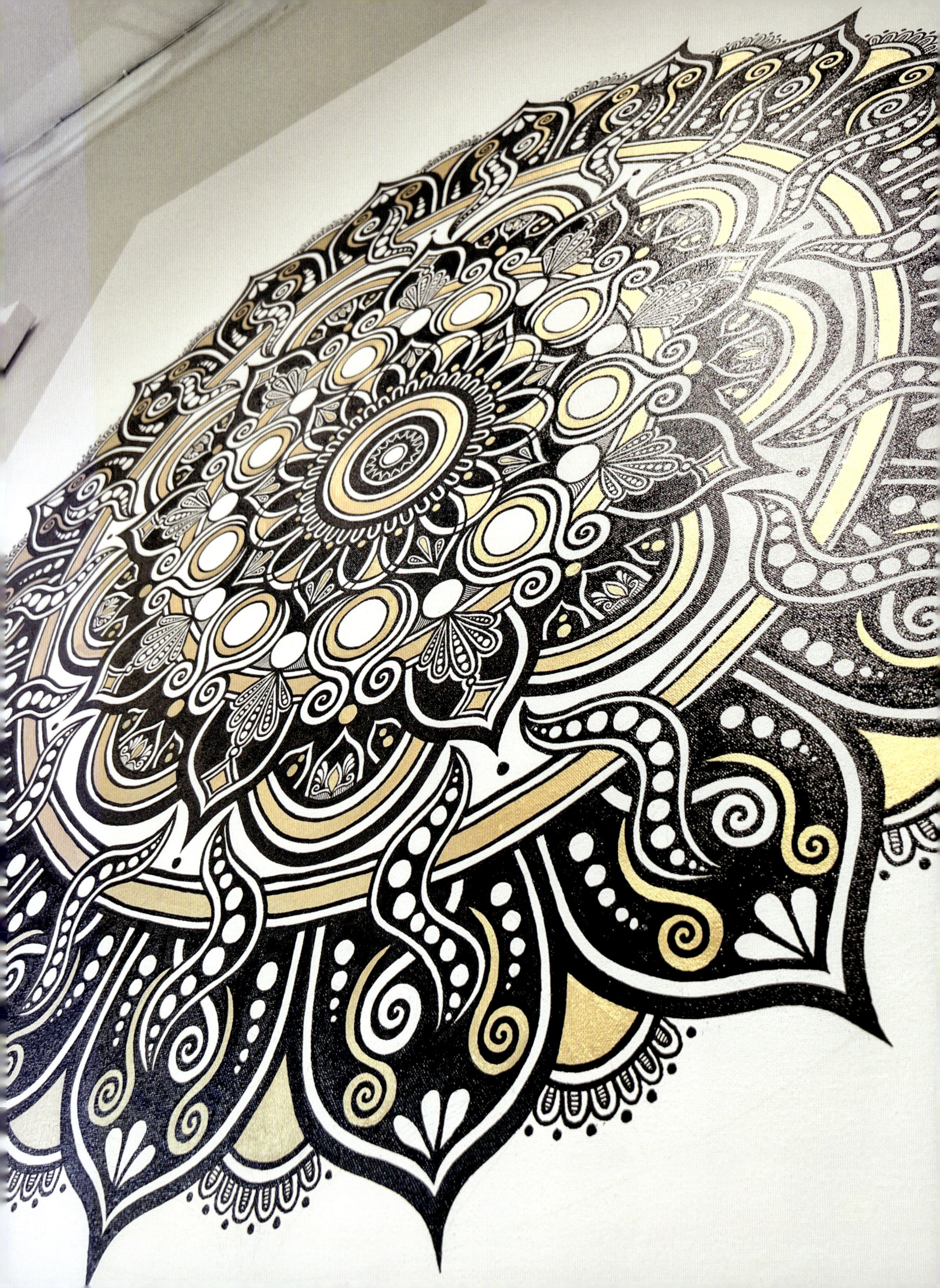

METHODS TO CONSIDER

When it comes to creating a mandala, you have two methods to choose from: the circular (or "layer-by-layer") method and the wedge (or "create-first-repeat-later") method. Both offer their own unique benefits and challenges, and the choice ultimately depends on your personality, mood, and creative inclination.

The Circular (or "Layer-by-Layer") Method

This method involves drawing one circle or ring of the pattern at a time, allowing the design to evolve organically as you move from one circle to the next. This method is highly meditative and creative throughout the entire process. With each design element flowing naturally into the next, the finished mandala may surprise you at the end.

PROS: One of the positives of this method is that it allows your intuition to take charge. With less thinking and more natural progression, the design evolves organically as you move from one circle to the next.

CONS: One downside is that you might end up with a completed design that lacks a certain aesthetic harmony than if you had planned the artwork in its entirety.

The Wedge (or "Create-First-Repeat-Later") Method

This approach begins with drawing an entire slice of the design from the middle to the outer edge, a sector of a circle. Once this initial section is complete and you've made tweaks to the design to your satisfaction, you can then repeat the pattern around the mandala's circumference until the whole artwork is complete. This method offers a burst of creativity at the start, followed by a more meditative process of repetition to complete the mandala.

PROS: The upside to this method is that you have the chance to make the artwork as beautiful as possible by tweaking the design before continuing around. Additionally, this method allows you to enter a flow state of mind for the longest duration of time, as once you've drawn the first part, you can simply zone in and spend many hours engaged in automatic drawing.

CONS: A downside is that this method has the potential to feel tedious because the creativity is all at the start.

Personally, I tend to use a mixture of both methods interchangeably. Sometimes I start with the wedge method to encourage my creativity and to get the ball rolling. Once I'm in the swing of things, I switch to the circular method to allow the design to flow organically. This way, I can enjoy the benefits of both approaches and create a beautiful, symmetrical design that's truly unique. I also like to draw simple line work patterns, and then expand upon the design bit by bit. For the sake of this book, I've written each step in order, so you can certainly do this, or flow back and forth between each step and method. Choose what works for you.

Pencil vs. Ink

When it comes to creating mandalas, there are several approaches to using pencil and ink. One option is to draw the entire design in pencil first, then go over it in ink. Alternatively, you can work section by section, starting with pencil, immediately going over it with ink, then moving on to the next space in pencil. The latter is my preference.

Some artists prefer to skip the pencil altogether and go straight to ink, although this is less common (and I don't recommend it!) as it leaves less room for refining the design or fixing mistakes. You can also use the pencil to mark guides—often I'll draw a dot in pencil referencing where the middle of an area is, so that my pen will follow the correct spacing. Ultimately, the choice between pencil and ink depends on personal preference and how confident you feel working in ink.

CIRCULAR METHOD

Now that our grid is set up, we can begin drawing our mandala. In this example, I've used the circular method, where we draw one layer—or ring—of design at a time, working outward from the center. We'll start by creating the base design (or outline), and then expand the artwork by eventually adding more features and elements.

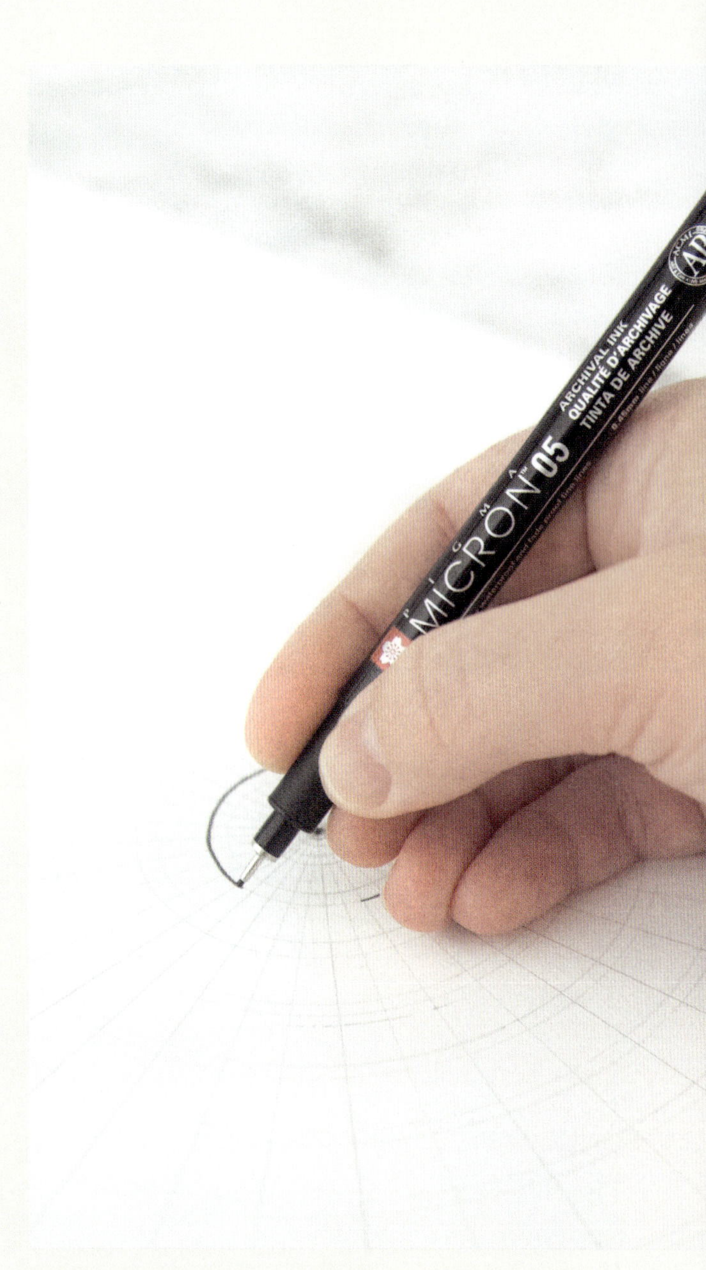

STEP 1
Let's start the design by using one of the circles that is already drawn from the compass and go over it in ink. This is an easy way to start the artwork.

STEP 2
Expanding off the circle, draw a simple semicircle (or petal shape) in one of the grid spaces. Repeat this shape all the way around the circle, creating a ring of design.

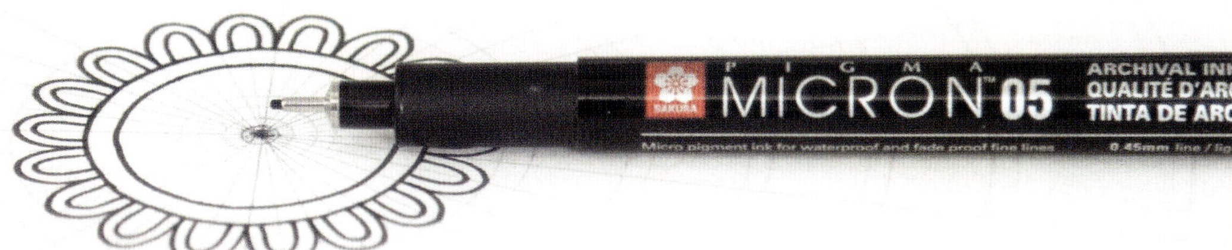

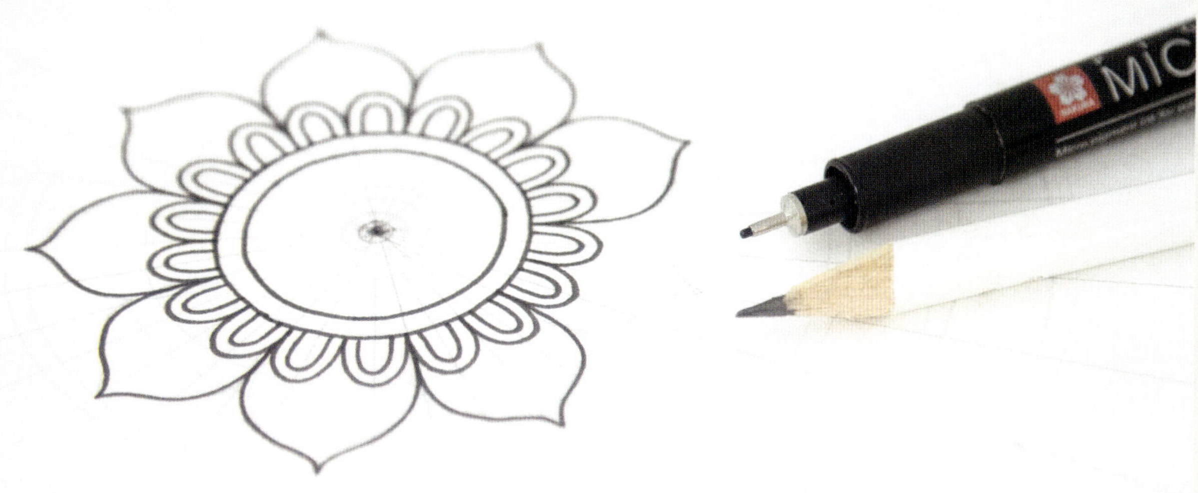

STEP 3

Create the next ring with a larger petal shape that intersects the original shape in the center. Repeat this all the way around. This is where your creativity comes into play as your designs start to evolve and fit into one another.

TIP

I recommend drawing two lines close together all throughout the mandala design. This second line is what I call the “Double Line Trick”—which defines the area and makes each element stand out.

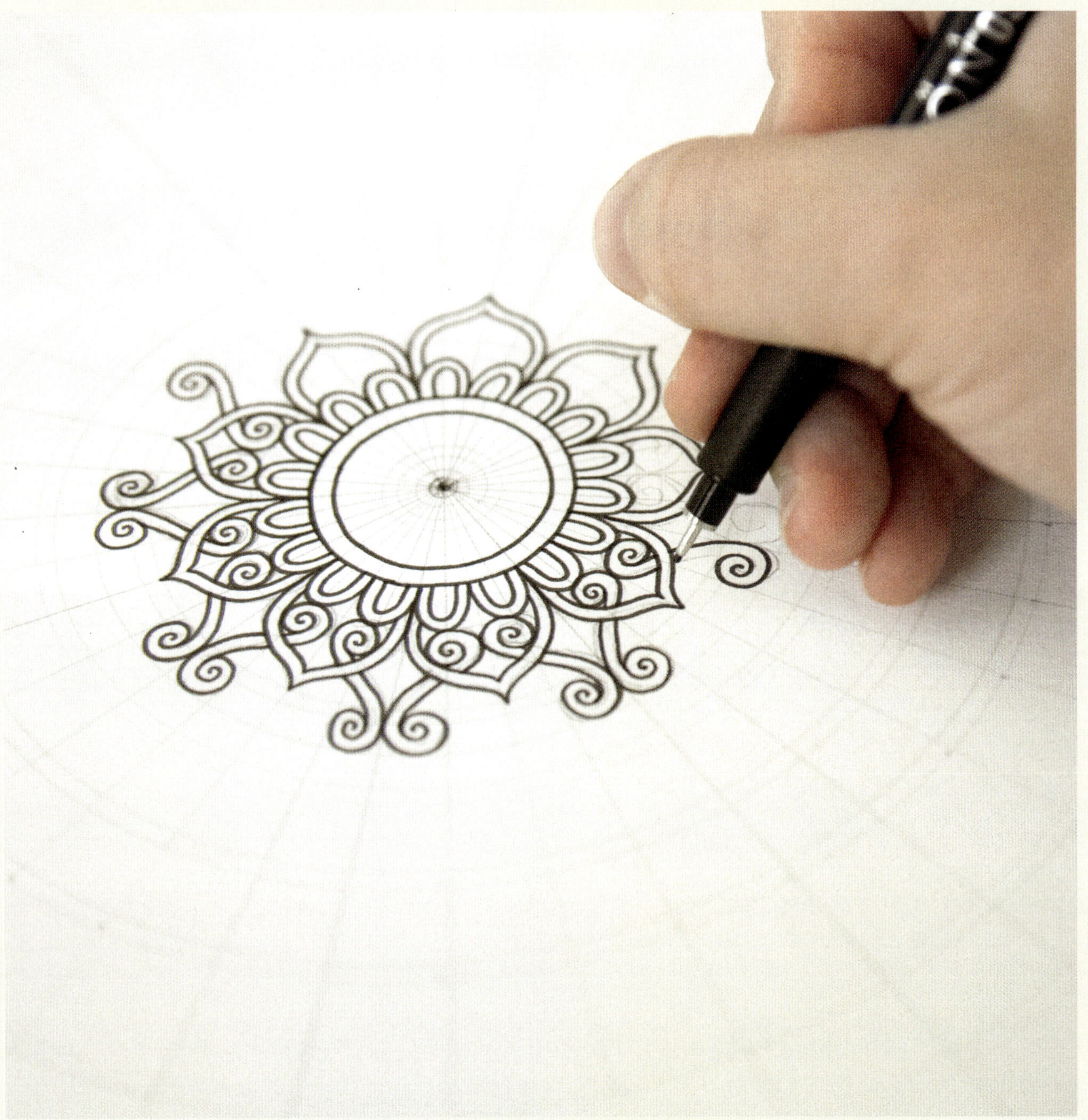

STEP 4

The design is already beginning to take shape. Try adding a third layer. This time you could curve your petal into a point, replicating a leaf shape, or add a spiral, or a circle, or a shape from your prepared designs.

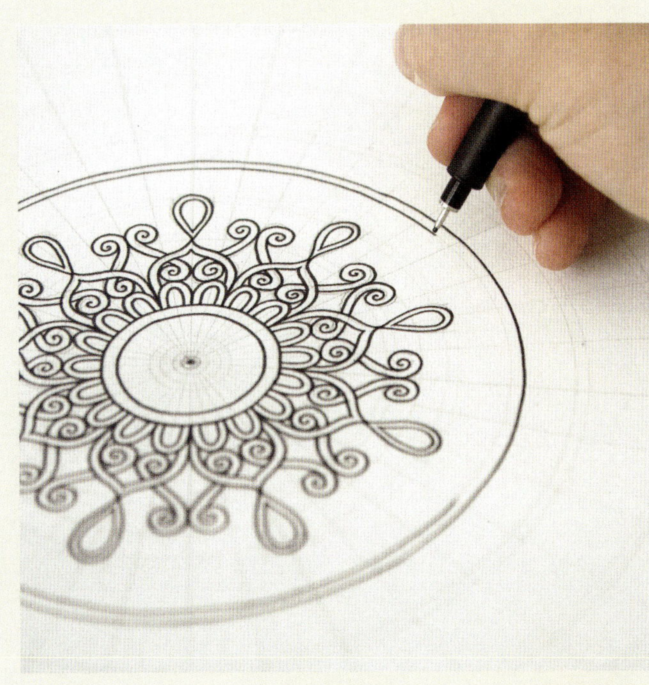

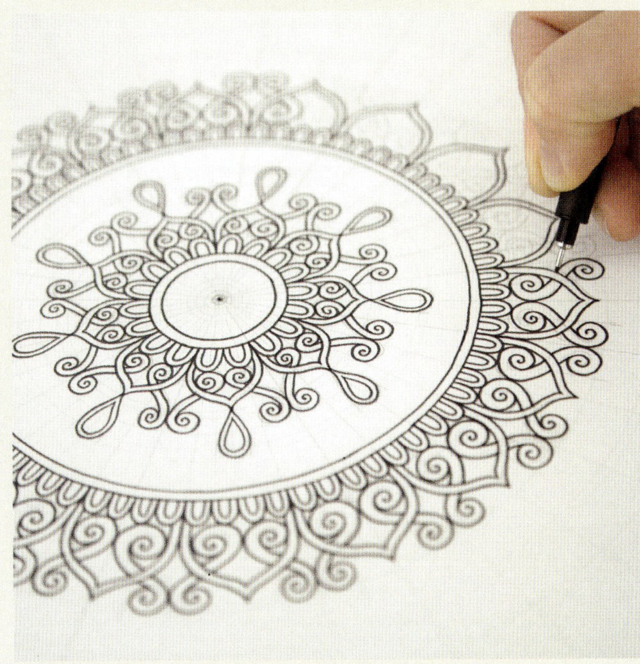
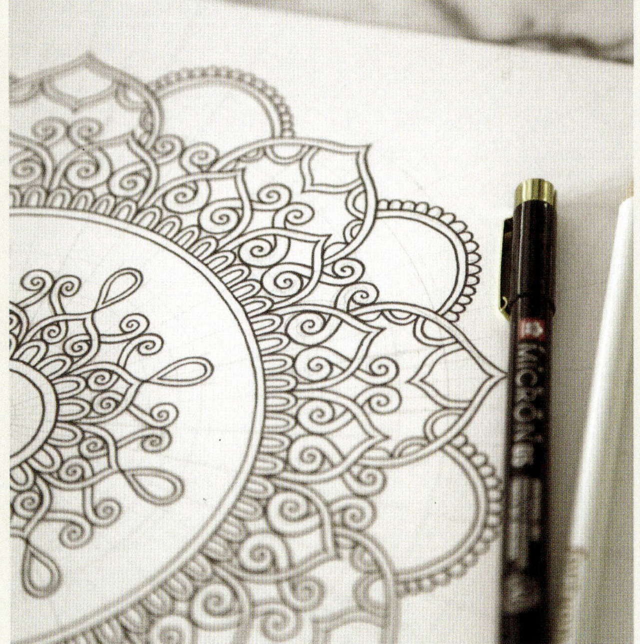

STEP 5

Repeat and add rings of patterns at larger and larger scales. Notice the fractal element of the design evolving. The same patterns exist at different scales, giving a sense of infinity in both directions.

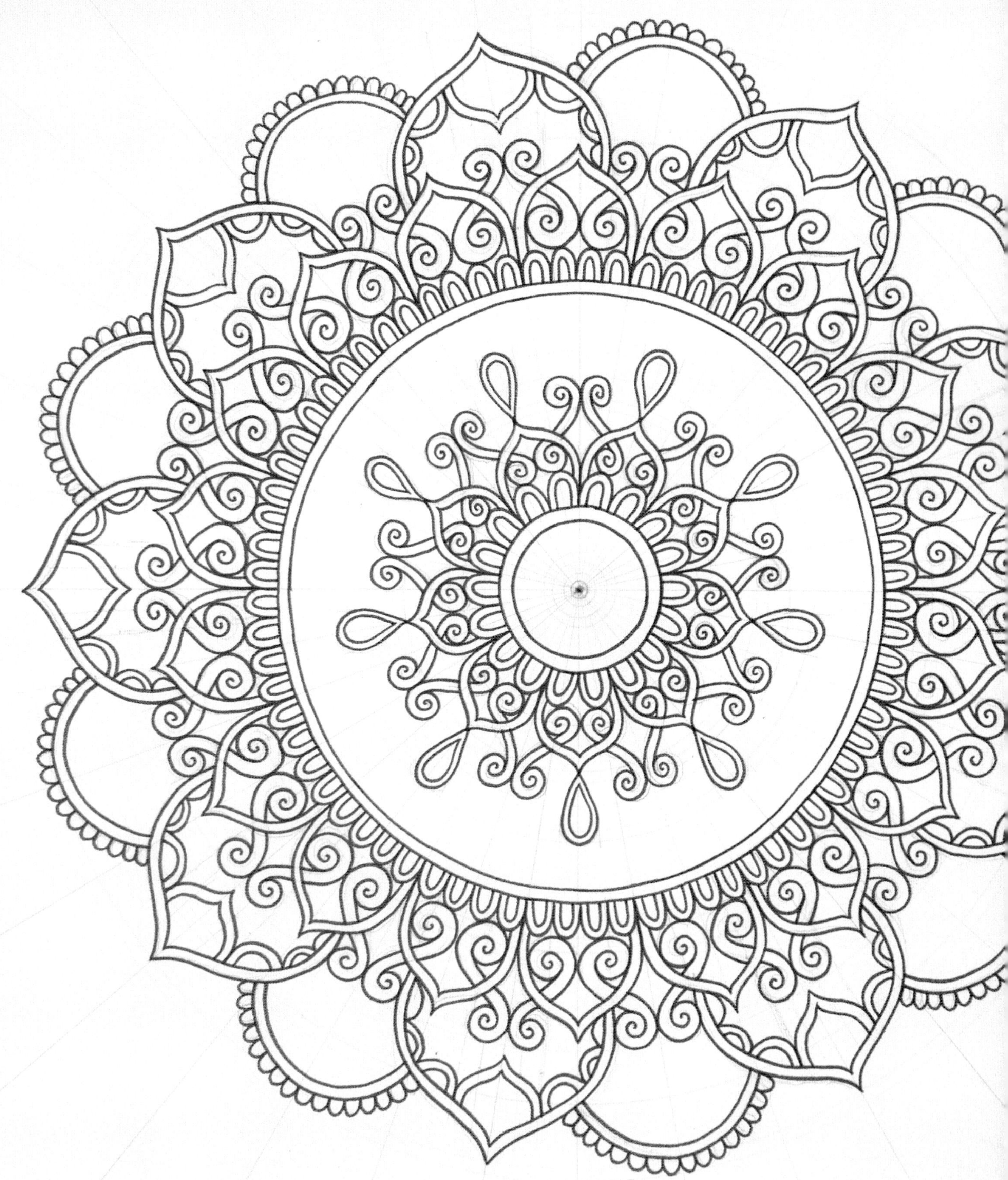

TIPS

- Use an extra piece of small paper under your drawing hand to keep the paper clean.
- Allow your intuition to guide you as you create your mandala. There are no strict rules to follow, so feel free to experiment and let your imagination run wild. Take your time with each section of the mandala, allowing the design to evolve naturally as you move from one circle to the next.
- Take breaks when needed, and don't be afraid to make changes as you go. There's no right or wrong way to create a mandala, so have fun with the process and enjoy the journey of self-expression.

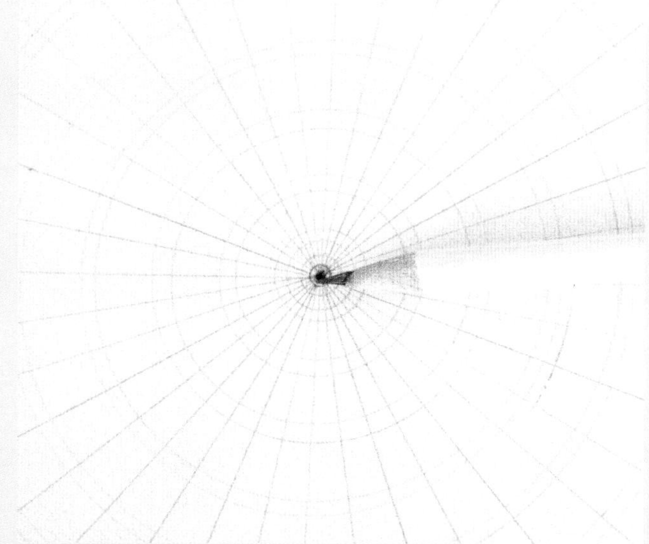

SCAN THIS QR CODE to watch a video showing a mandala being drawn from start to finish in the linework stage.

INSIGHT

Often I find that when I'm partway through an artwork, I feel it isn't looking as refined as I'd hoped. Trusting the process is crucial as it (almost always) develops into something of beauty in the end. It's a lovely metaphor—the artwork as a whole looks stunning and perfect, even if there are many imperfections. These inconsistencies are actually what give the artwork character (if it were flawless, it would look computer-generated and lose the organic appeal that makes it interesting).

LEFT The finished mandala outline before adding any details or shading.

WEDGE METHOD

Here is an example of creating a mandala with the wedge method. In this approach, begin by designing a single triangular section, or "wedge," of the mandala. This wedge represents one slice of the whole design and is created with careful attention to the patterns and elements as it will determine the final piece. Once this wedge is complete, the decision-making process is finished and you can start the process of repeating it around the mandala's circumference, filling in each area to gradually draw the full artwork.

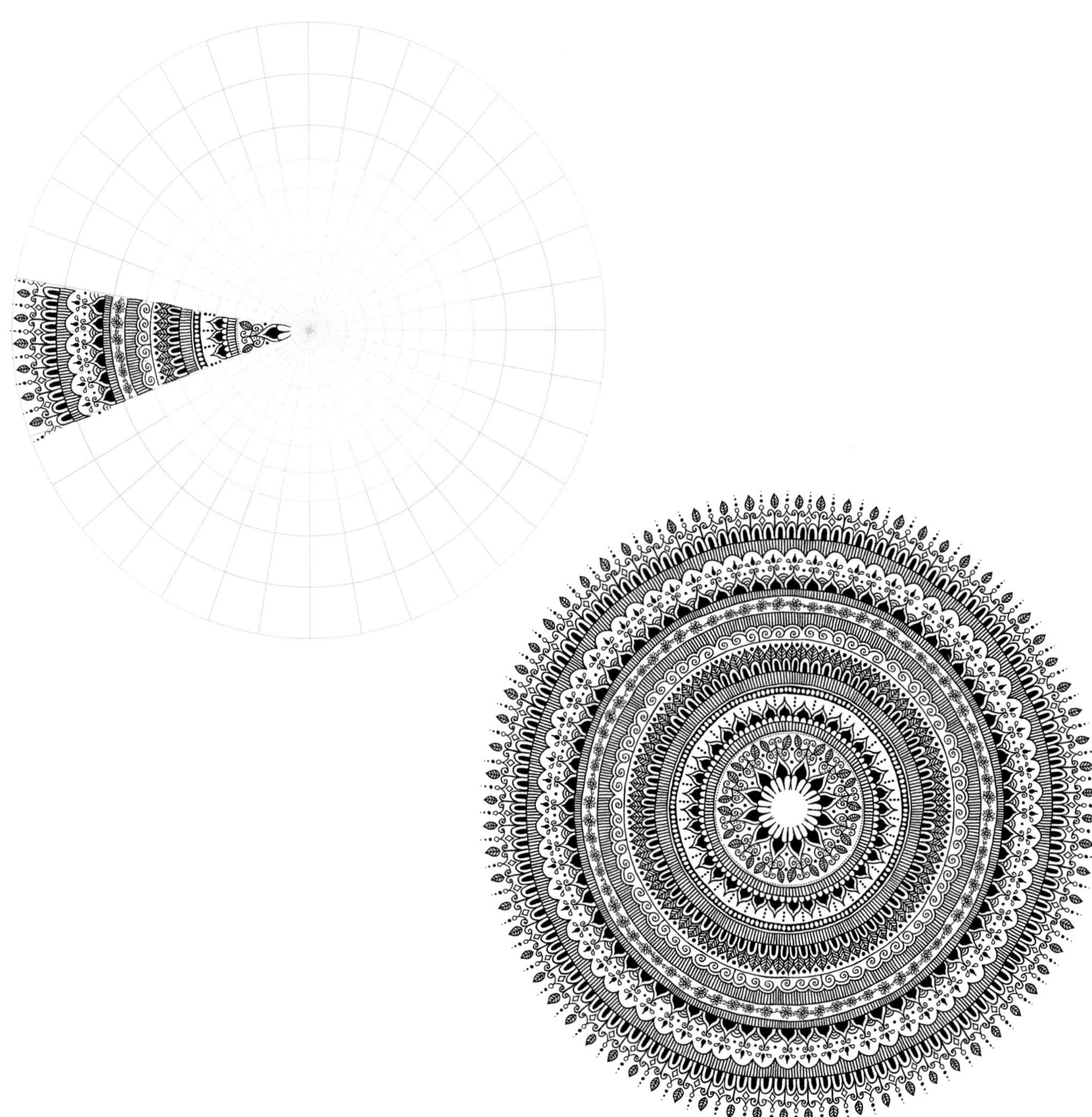

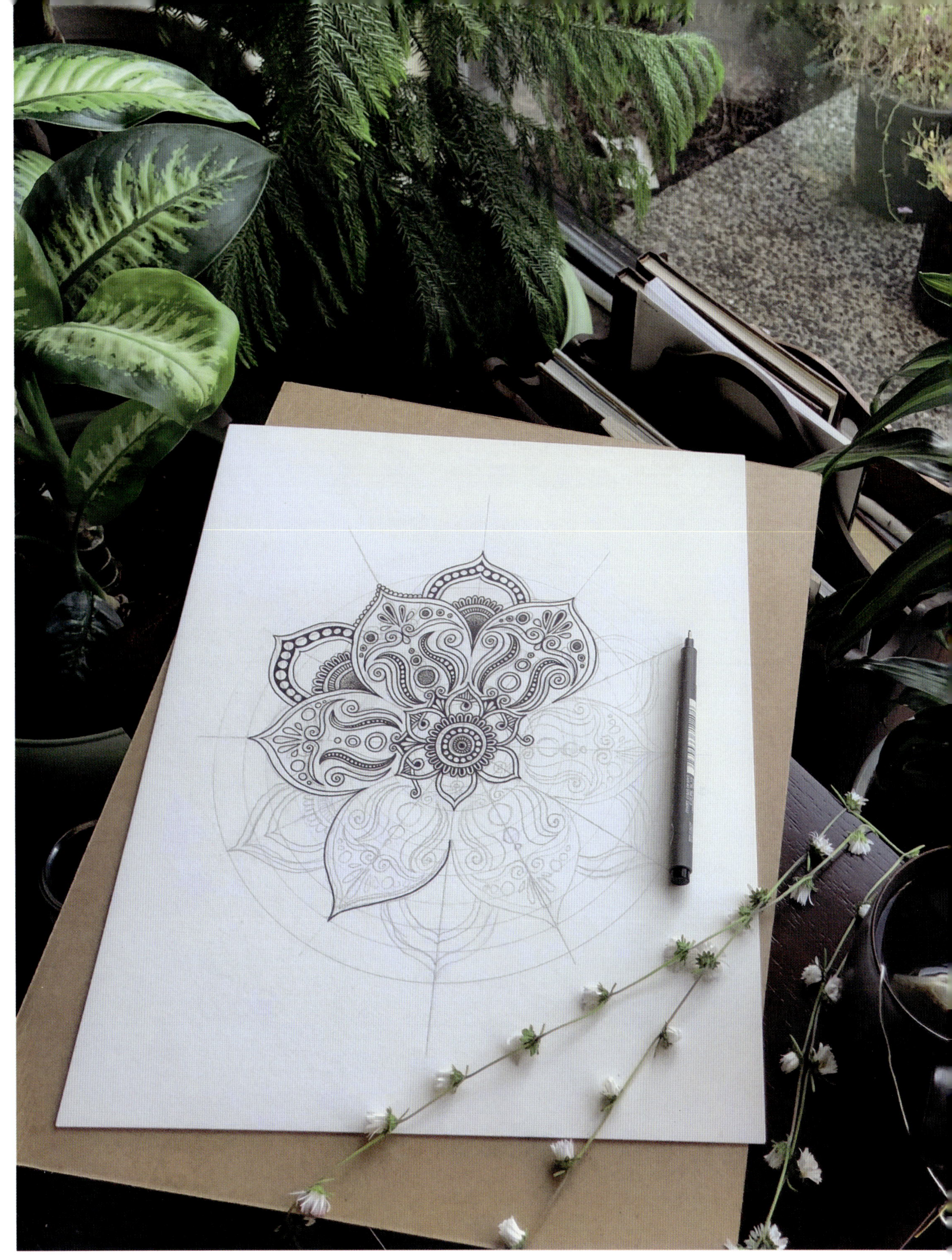

MOTIF PRACTICE

Below are some elements from my own artworks that you can practice drawing and incorporate into your mandala design. As you did before with the simple motifs—you can trace them, draw them freehand, and use them as inspiration for your own creations. Begin with a basic shape and gradually build upon it, allowing your design to evolve.

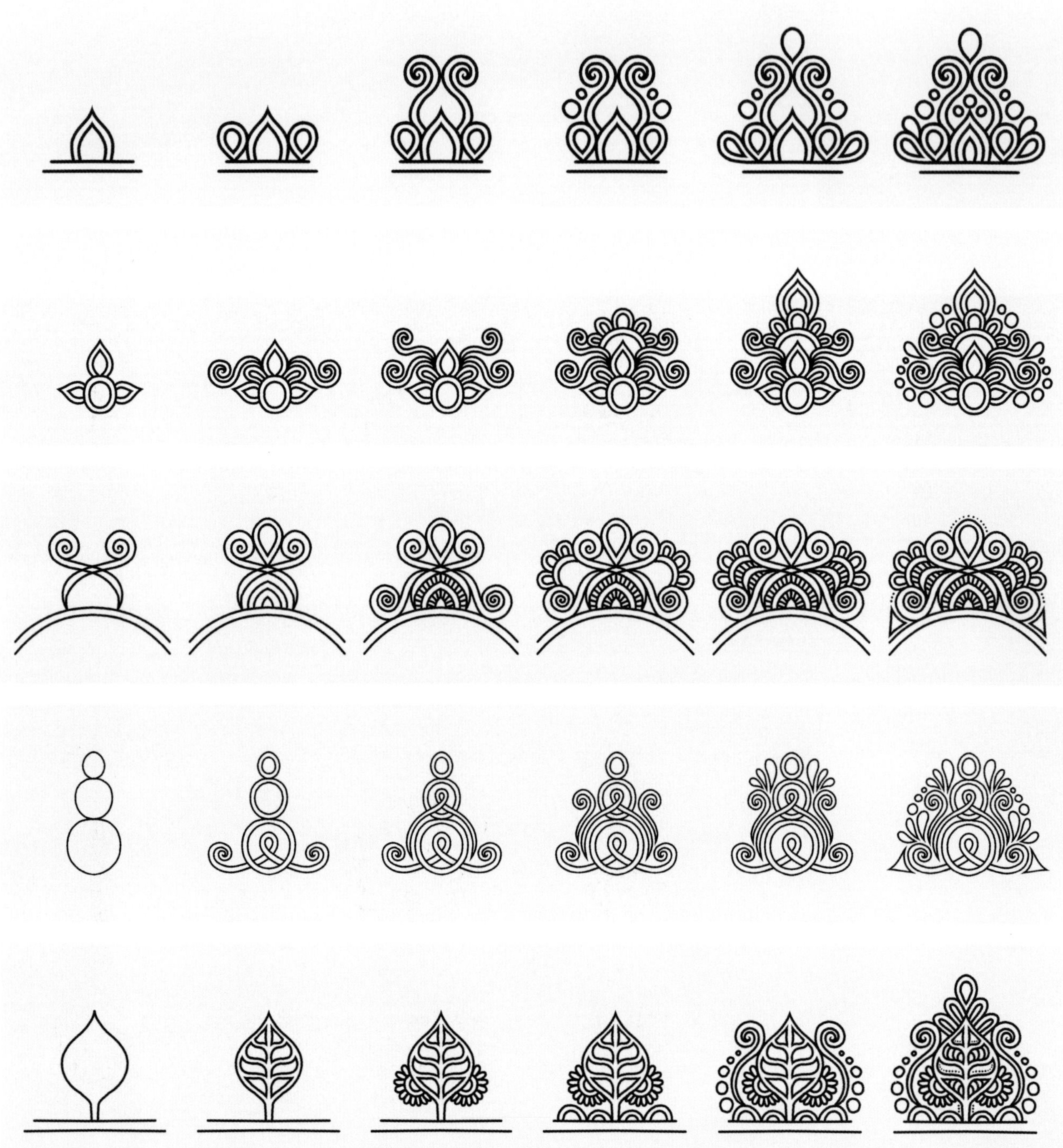

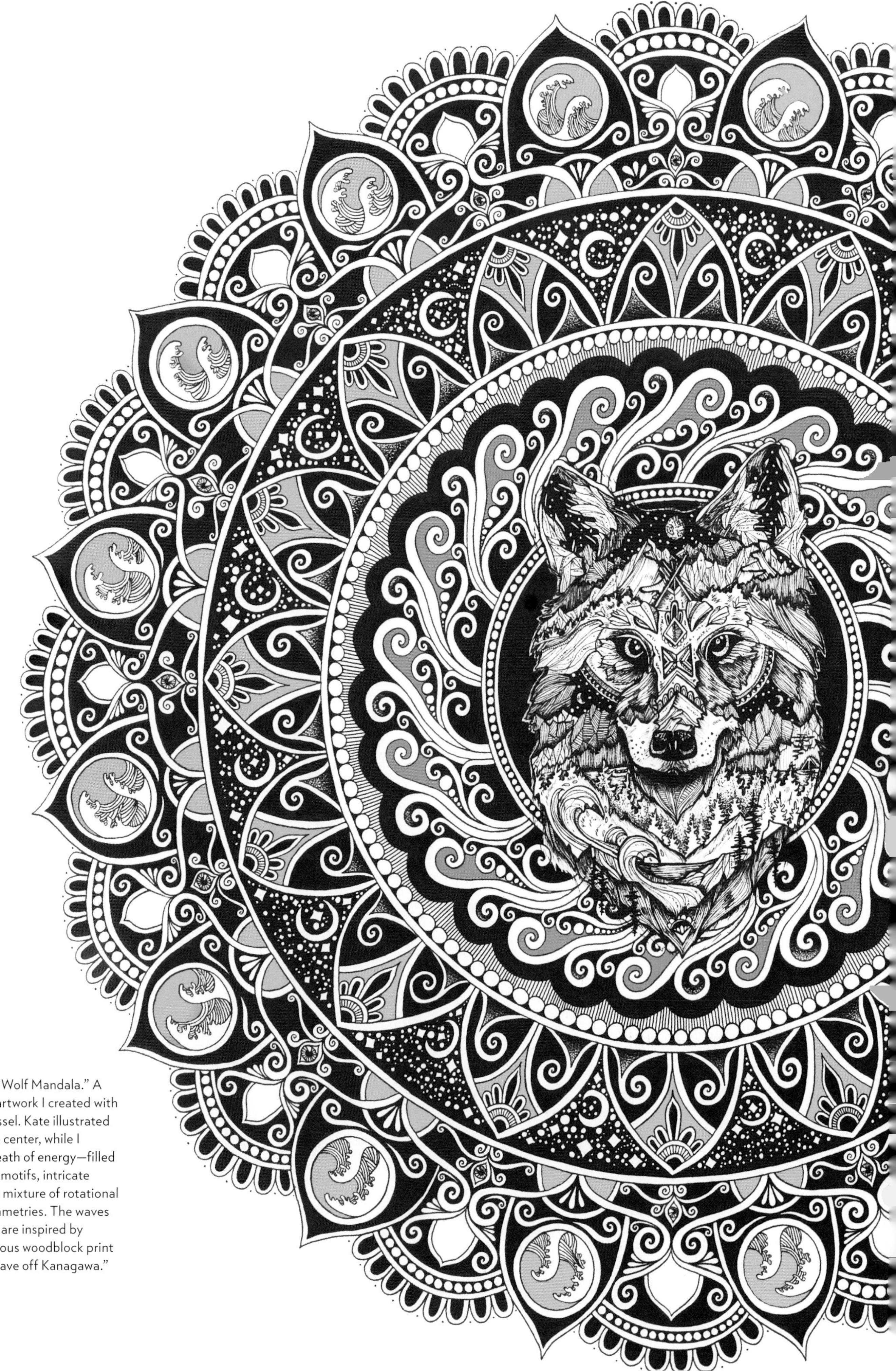

RIGHT: "The Wolf Mandala." A collaborative artwork I created with artist Kate Zessel. Kate illustrated the wolf at the center, while I created its wreath of energy—filled with patterns, motifs, intricate designs, and a mixture of rotational and radial symmetries. The waves in my drawing are inspired by Hokusai's famous woodblock print "The Great Wave off Kanagawa."

DIGITAL PRE-VISUALIZATION TECHNIQUES

Pairing your hand-drawn analog artwork with a tablet and stylus allows you to explore and refine your ideas digitally before committing ink to the physical piece. Incorporating this use of technology in your art enables you to visualize potential changes and see how they affect the overall aesthetic and harmony of your design.

TIP

I recommend Apple's iPad Pro and Apple Pencil Pro, paired with the drawing app called Procreate.

INSIGHT

Before I had my iPad, I had many artworks that didn't turn out so well because of adding elements that negatively affected the entire design. Incorporating technology in this way has definitely pushed my drawing skills further because I now can experiment freely without worrying it won't "work."

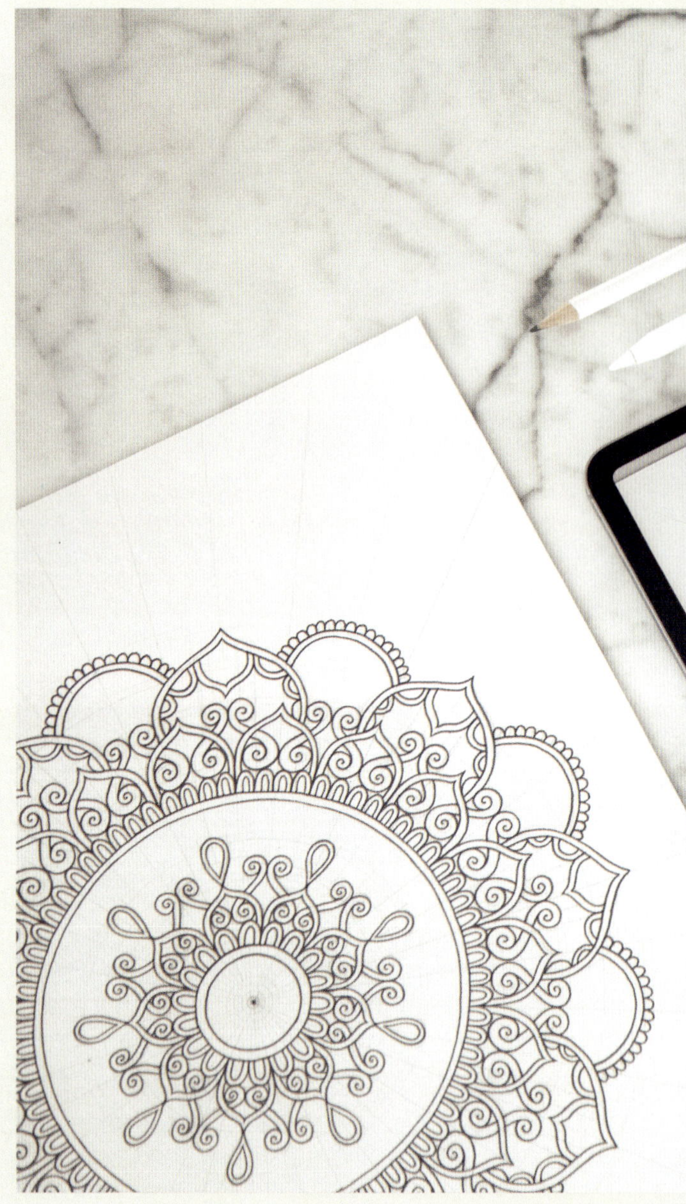

STEP 1
Take a photo of your drawing in its current state.

STEP 2
Open the photo in a drawing software app.

STEP 3
Add a new drawing layer on top of the imported image. (This allows you to draw and test different ideas without altering the original photo.)

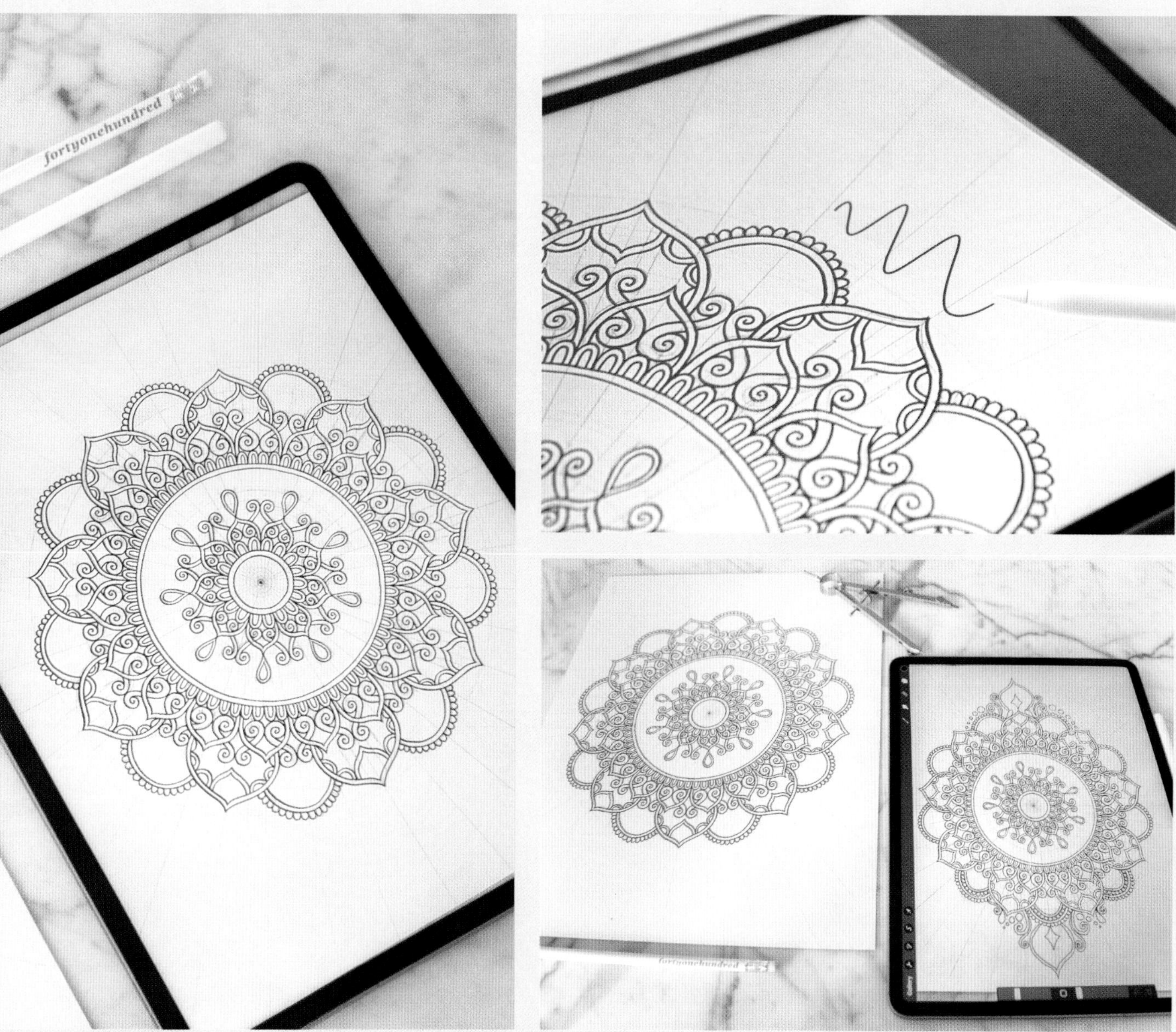

STEP 4

Use this new layer to try out different design options, such as extending new line work sections, adding colors, altering patterns, and testing new shapes.

STEP 5

Assess how the different elements look together in the digital format compared with the original artwork.

This process helps you identify what works best and make adjustments before making marks on your physical artwork. It provides the flexibility to explore various possibilities without the risk of ruining your original piece. It allows you to avoid potential issues that could arise from untested ideas and ensures that your final art aligns with your vision.

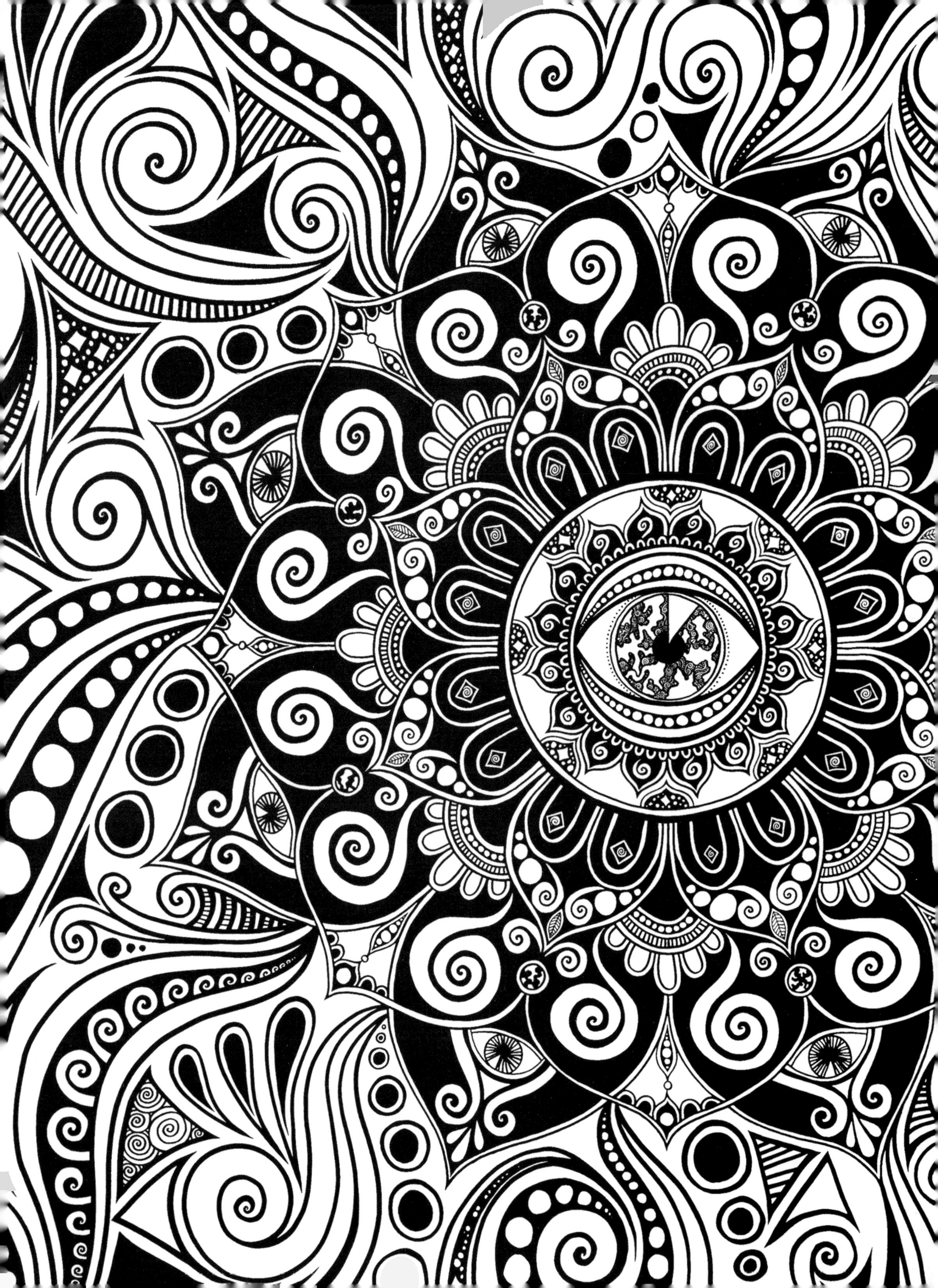

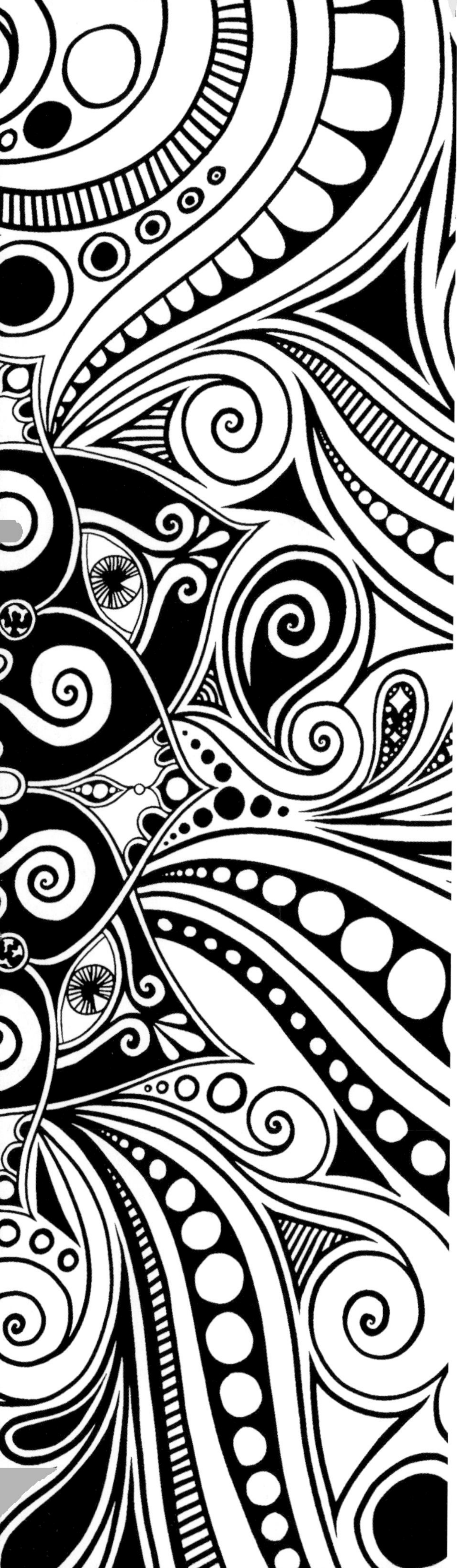

7

ADDING DEPTH + DETAILS

HAVING DRAWN OUR FREE-FLOWING patterns or mandala outline, our focus can now shift to adding depth and intricate details to elevate our artwork further. This stage transforms our artwork from being a creation of line work into a more dynamic piece.

We will enhance the existing lines and shapes with additional layers of shading, dots, lines, extra patterns, and perhaps touches of color too. Some of the techniques can be incredibly calming and immersive (especially the technique called stippling), helping to promote a meditative state of mind. These details will define the final appearance of our artwork. By enriching our design with these extra details, we breathe new life into our creation, unlocking its full potential. This transforms our artwork from a simple flat drawing to a piece of art that has multiple dimensions and varying design hierarchies.

DOTS, LINES, AND OTHER DETAILS

When adding details, it's essential to consider how these elements will interact with your overall composition. The more details you incorporate, the "darker" and more textured your art will appear. Therefore, it's crucial to choose the sections for adding details carefully to maintain a balanced arrangement. Some techniques include hatching, stippling, shading, block fill, negative space, and color.

Hatching

Hatching is drawing closely spaced parallel lines to create shading and texture. Varying the density and direction of the lines can produce different shades and effects.

Stippling

Stippling uses many small dots to create shading and gradients, placing dots closer together for darker areas and farther apart for lighter sections. It's time-consuming, but also very meditative and highly effective.

Shading

By varying the pressure on your pen or pencil you can create smooth gradients and shadows.

BELOW: Adding line work features and decorative details to the mandala.

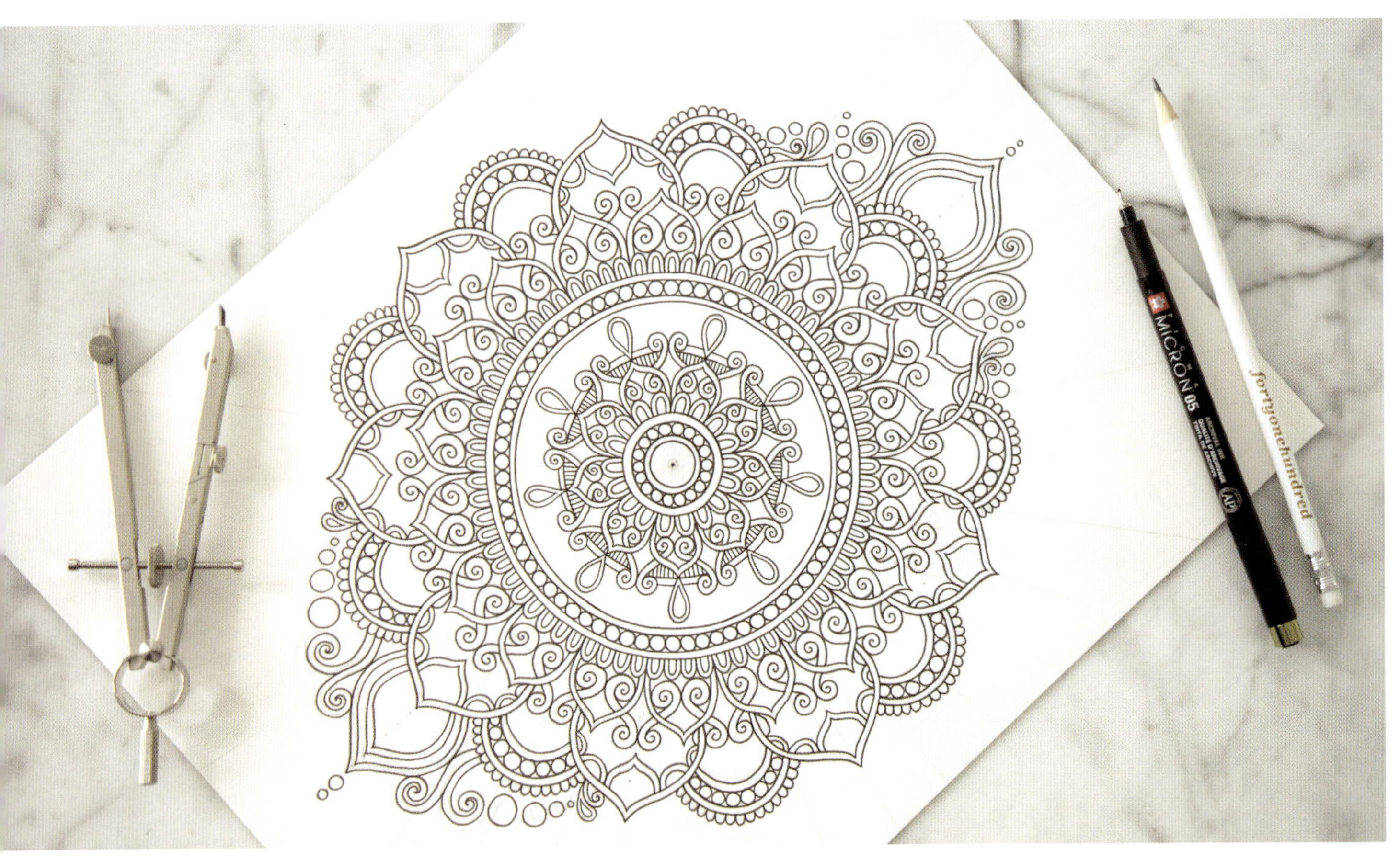

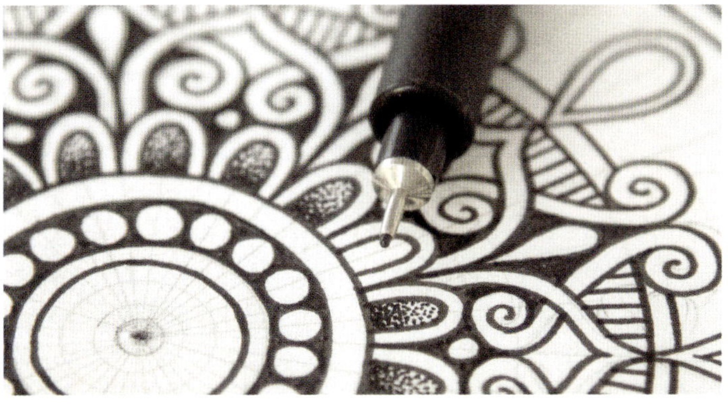

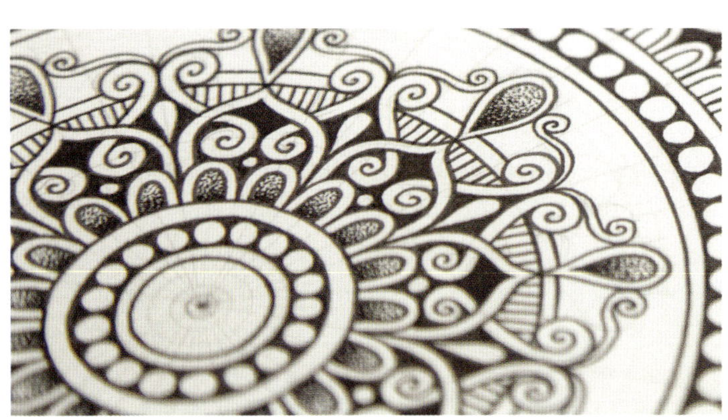

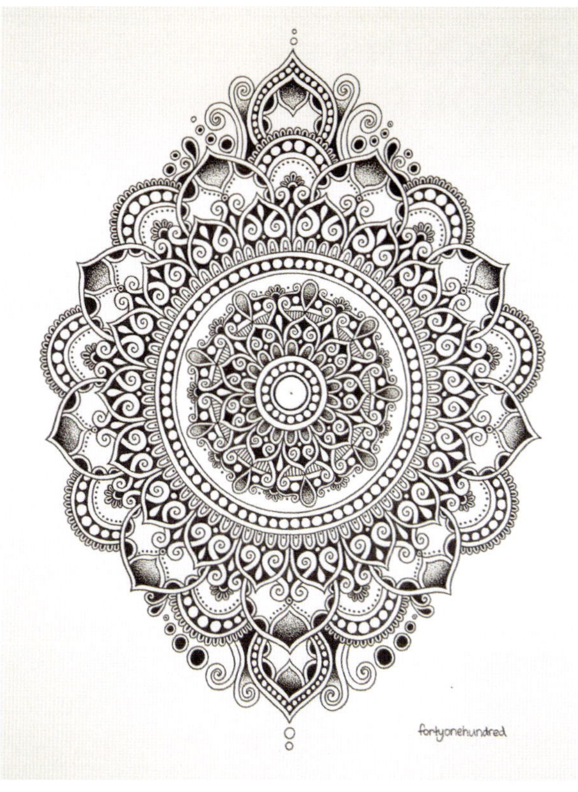

Block Fill

Completely filling in certain areas can create bold contrast and highlight specific parts of your design. This technique is particularly effective in making certain sections of your drawing pop.

Negative Space

Leaving parts of your design blank can be as impactful as adding details. Negative space can create a sense of balance and focus, drawing attention to the detailed areas of your artwork.

Adding Color

While we'll explore color more in the next section, incorporating color strategically into your line drawings can emphasize certain patterns and details, adding another layer of complexity to your design.

As you experiment with these techniques, you'll discover which ones best complement your style and the mood you want to convey in your artwork. Remember, the key to using dots, lines, and details effectively is to enhance your design without overwhelming it. Balancing these elements will result in a visually engaging and harmonious composition.

ABOVE, LEFT: Adding hatching, stippling, and block fill create incredible depth and interest.

ABOVE, RIGHT: The finished mandala.

TIP

Sometimes it's hard to see how your artwork is progressing. Is there enough detail or does it need more? Something I've found helpful is viewing my artwork in front of a mirror. This change in perspective provides a fresh look at my work and I can often better decide whether it's done or needs more refinement.

CHOOSING COLOR PALETTES

Color is a vibrant, dynamic, and invigorating medium for self-expression, and you should absolutely explore its use in your art if you feel inclined. I've had the pleasure of working closely with a designer named Olivia, who is a master with color. Watching her seamlessly blend and choose color combinations is truly inspiring.

Mandalas from different cultures and elements of nature are rich with color, so it's certainly not something to overlook. Perhaps I'm also reminding myself here, but exploring color is something we should all try. Online tools like Adobe Color and Pantone are great for finding captivating color palettes.

I love the purity of black and white; it feels raw and unembellished, allowing the forms to take center stage and placing the emphasis on the shapes and patterns. It's bold, classic, and striking. However, when I do incorporate color, it is lovely to see a whole new artwork take shape. What I enjoy most is adding touches of gold, which create a striking contrast against the black and white. I've experimented with other colors too, usually in neutral tones, but I mostly use black and white.

Photographing natural scenes and extracting their colors can be a very effective way to find a color palette. During my time in Canada, there was one particular spot where the forest parted onto the beach that always drew me in. As the sun dipped, it bathed the landscape in pink-gold hues, splayed out in gold rays through the warm olive green of the towering pine trees. The soft neutral tones of the sand and rocks balanced this intensity perfectly. It was a breathtaking mix of colors that inspired several artworks.

If you enjoy working with color, I wholeheartedly encourage you to try it and embrace it.

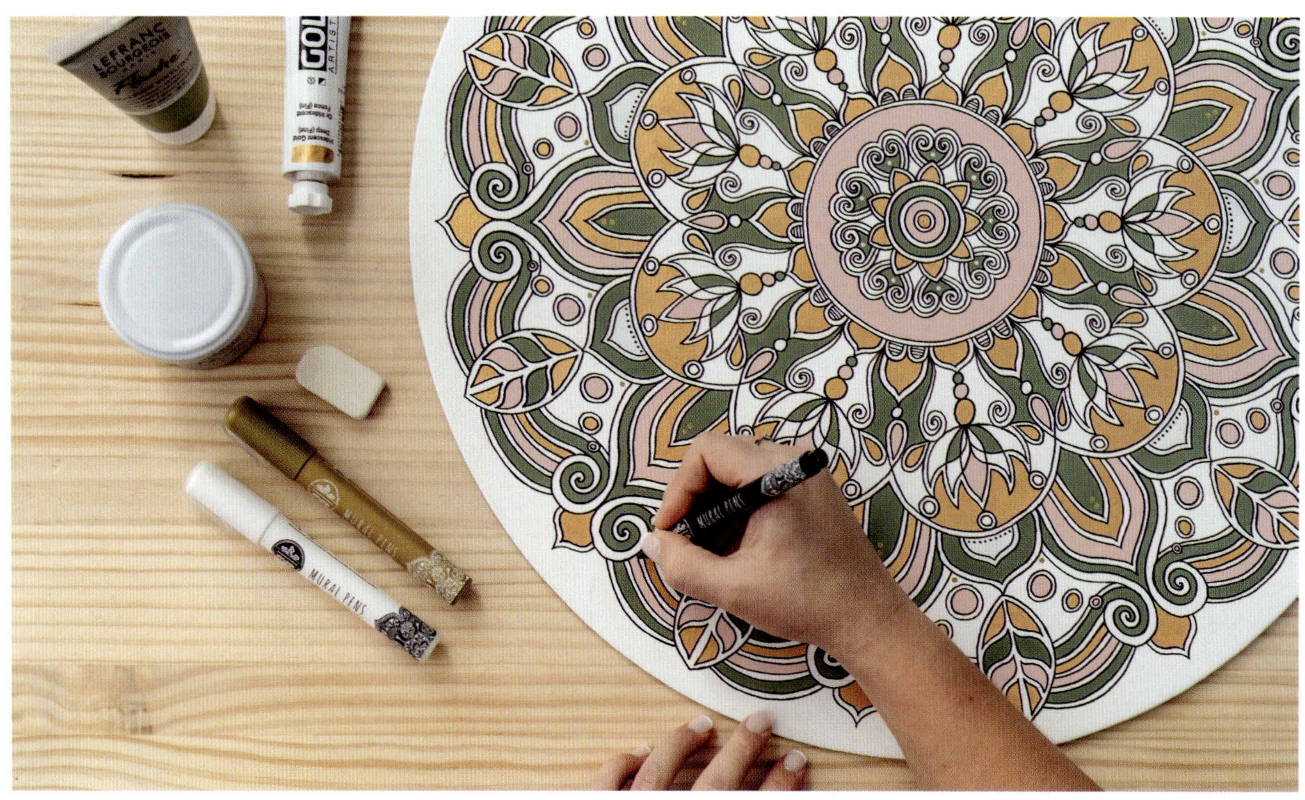

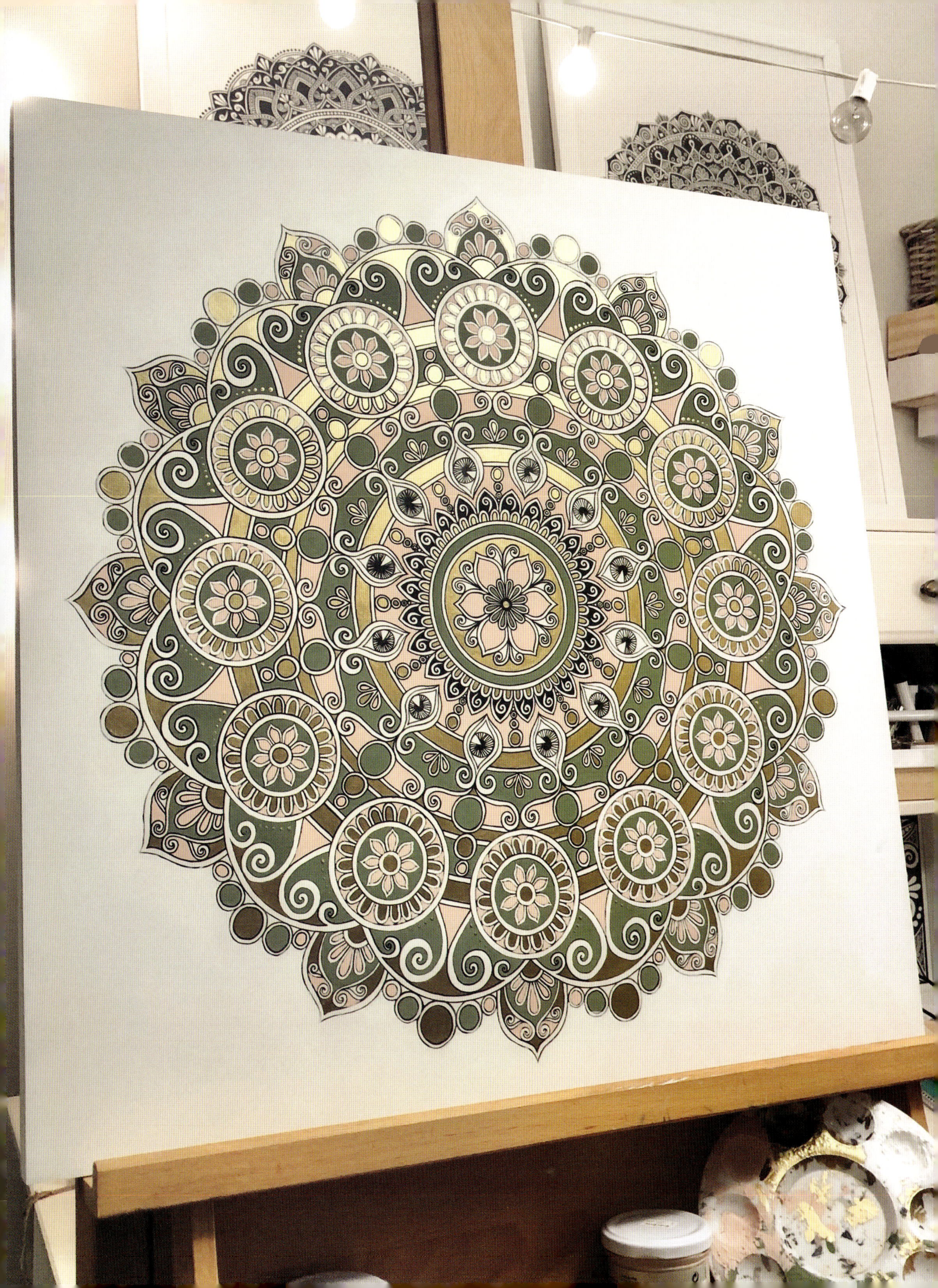

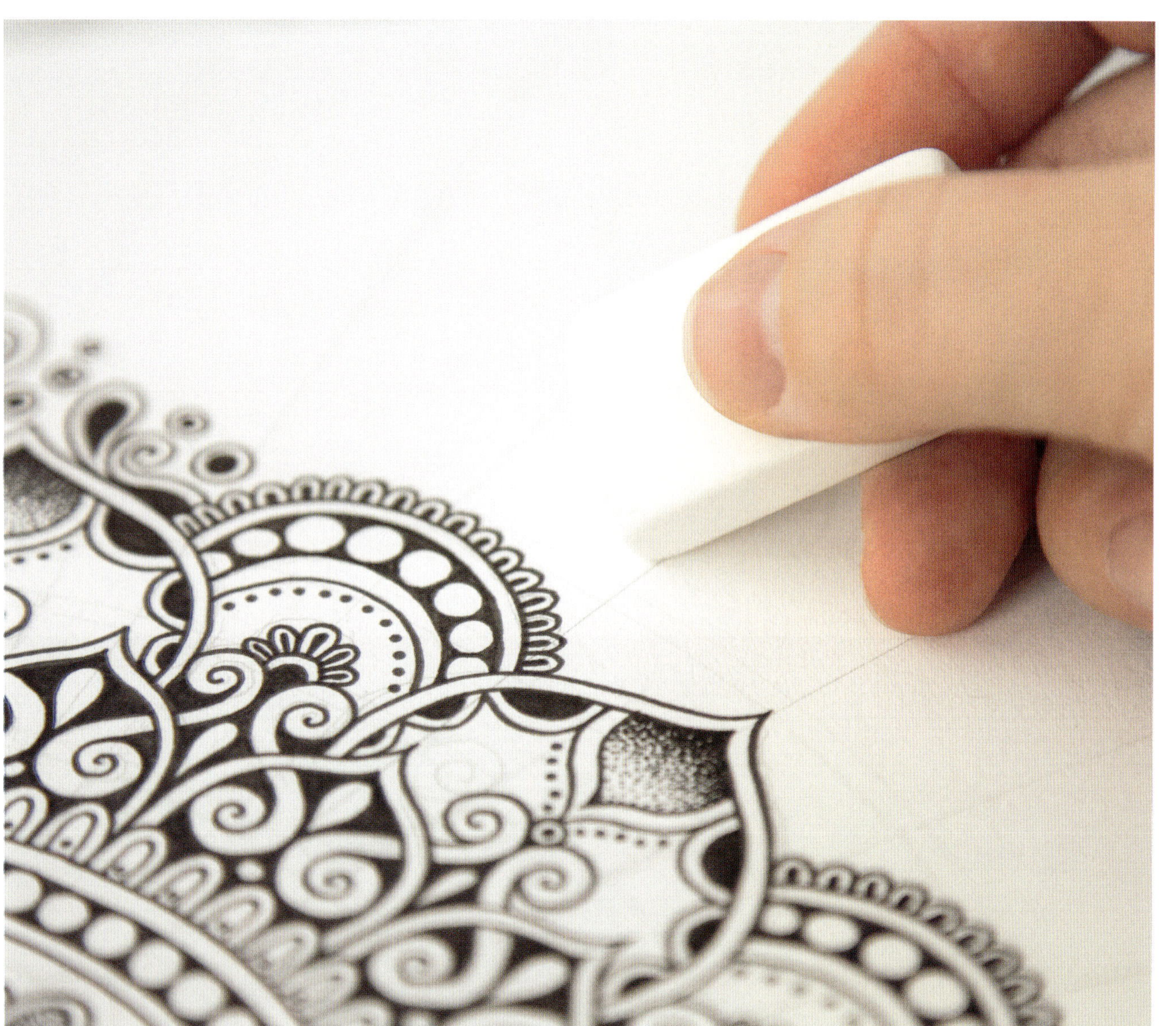

FINISHING TOUCHES

Completing your artwork with final steps truly brings it to life. Adding finishing touches, such as erasing pencil lines, refining details, and signing your art, offers a satisfying sense of completion—a true "full circle" moment.

Erase Pencil Lines

Work your way around the paper or canvas, erasing the pencil underneath the ink. You can damage the surface if you use a scrubbing motion with your eraser, so take care to erase gently and only touch the areas where there is pencil, instead of rubbing over the whole surface.

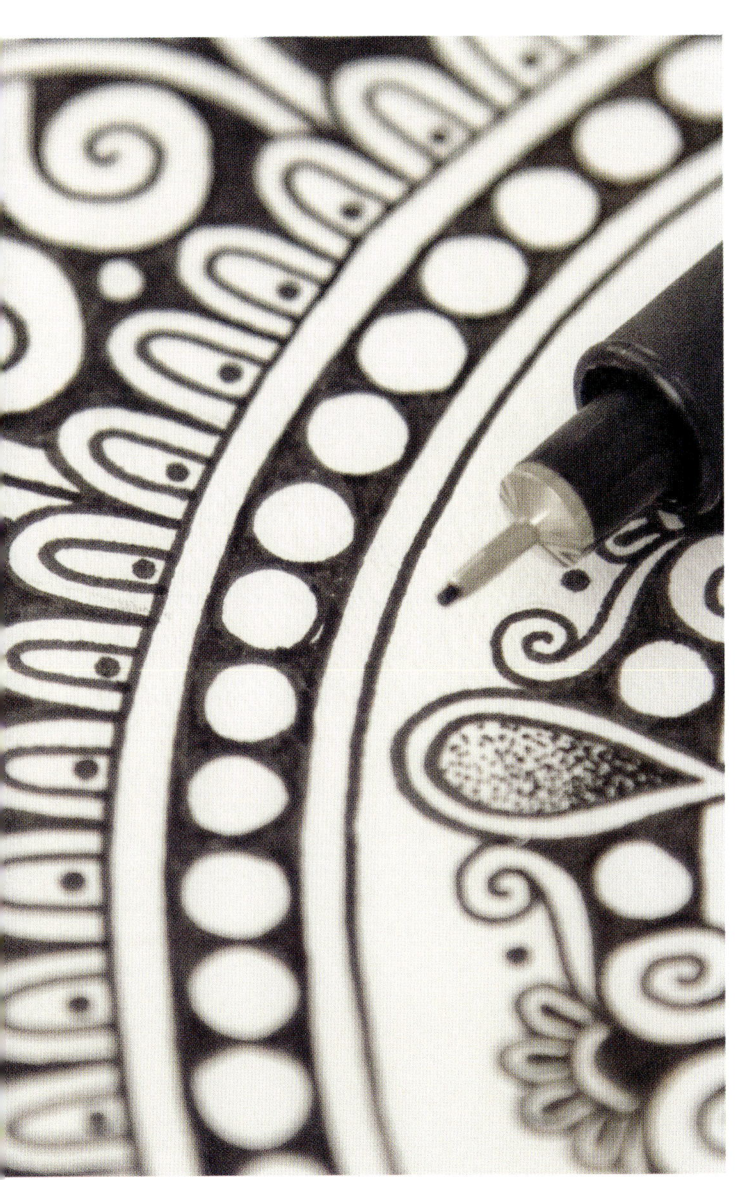

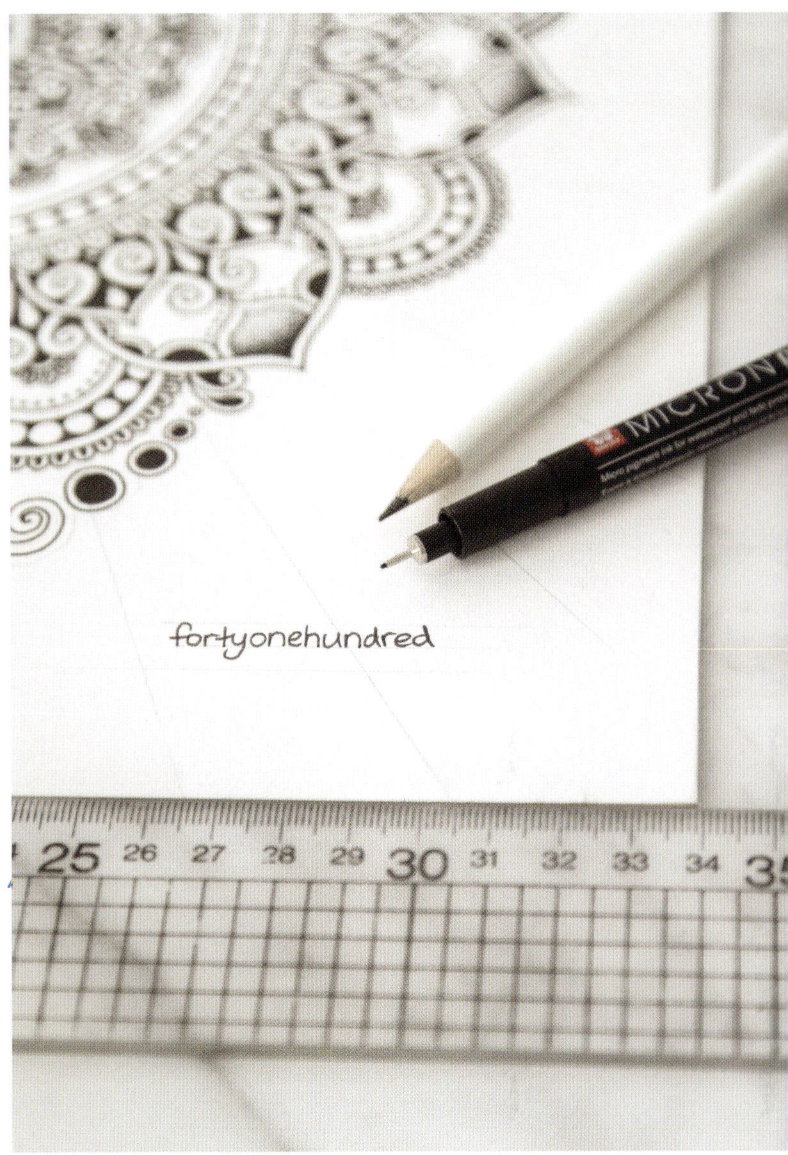

Touch-ups

Look closely at the artwork now that all the pencil has been erased. There may be patches without ink that you could revisit, or perhaps a section of shading you missed.

Sign Your Artwork

Signing your work marks the final step, bringing closure to the time and effort spent on your creation. I like to sign on the bottom right corner, which is the traditional art-signing convention, but you can choose any placement you prefer. I sign with my artist name, fortyonehundred. You could choose to sign with your real name, or an artist name, or even just your initials. You might want to add the date or year, title the artwork, or maybe even include a small quote.

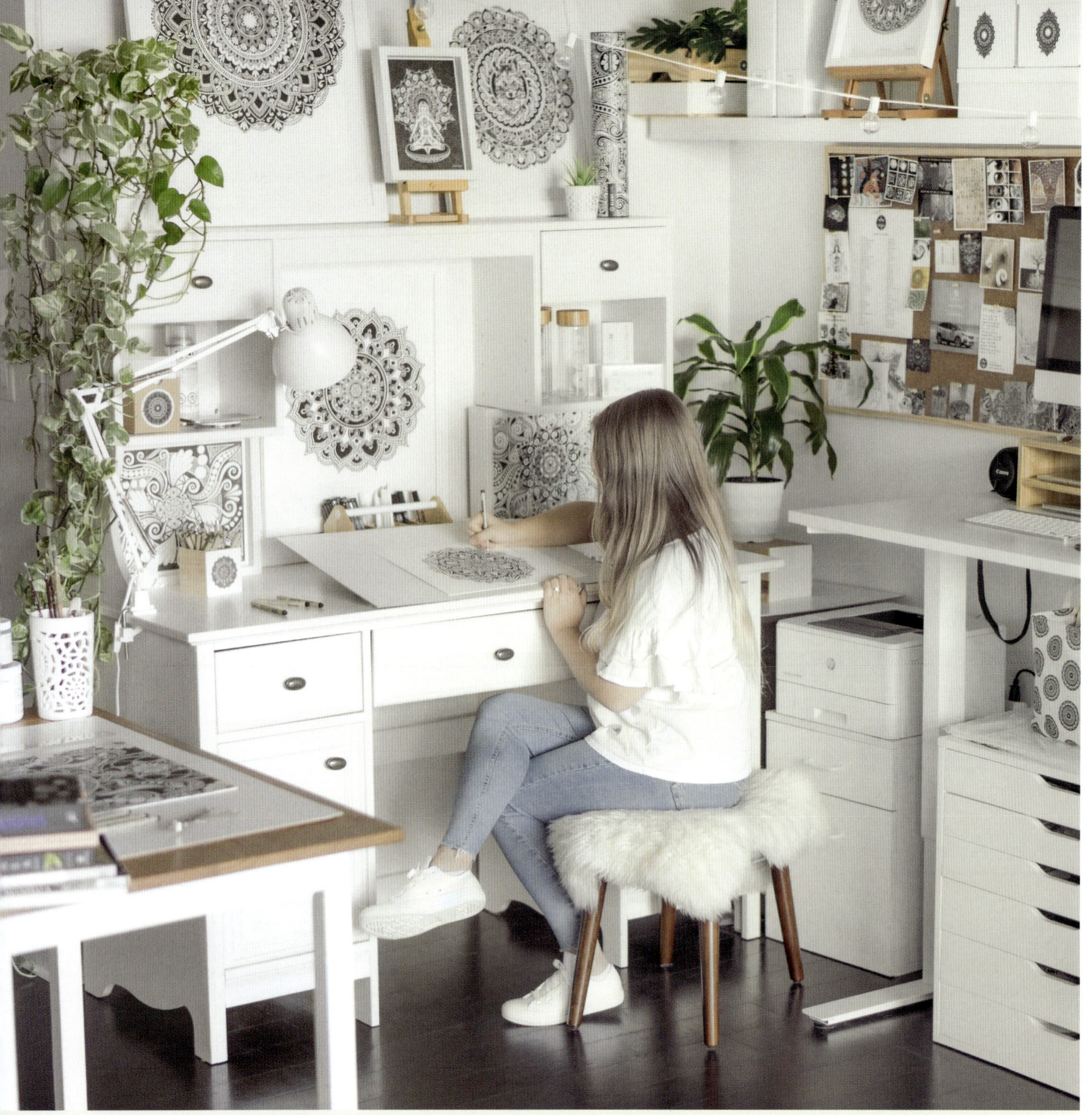

THE STORY BEHIND MY ARTIST NAME

When I began my artistic journey, I felt compelled to create under an artist name. After considering several options, I chose "fortyonehundred." This name combines "41," the latitude coordinate of Wellington, New Zealand, where my art journey began, and "100," to symbolize the themes of wholeness and completion in my artworks. I am inspired by the intersection of art, mathematics, science, human behavior, and nature, so this artist name resonated with the interconnected themes present in my artwork.

Document Your Creation

Documenting your art allows you to visualize your progression over time, offering a clear and motivating timeline of your artistic evolution. By photographing each piece, you can observe changes, pivotal moments, and improvements in your drawing skills and techniques. This visual record not only highlights your development but also encourages self-reflection, helping you see how your thoughts, emotions, and experiences may have manifested in your art along the way. Regular documentation helps bring a sense of achievement to your creations, reminding you of the dedication, effort, and time you've invested in your creative journey and mindful practice.

SHARING YOUR ARTWORK

In addition to the personal development and emotional insight, documenting your work is one of the first steps toward creating a coherent body of work, an art portfolio. You could build up to showcase your work to friends and family, be part of a group exhibition, start to grow a presence of your work online, or even present to galleries and potential collectors.

If you are thinking about sharing your work, taking high-quality photographs is essential. This topic is a big one, and I have lots of resources online if you'd like to learn more, including one of my online courses "Transform Your Art into Your Career," which you're welcome to explore if it sparks your interest.

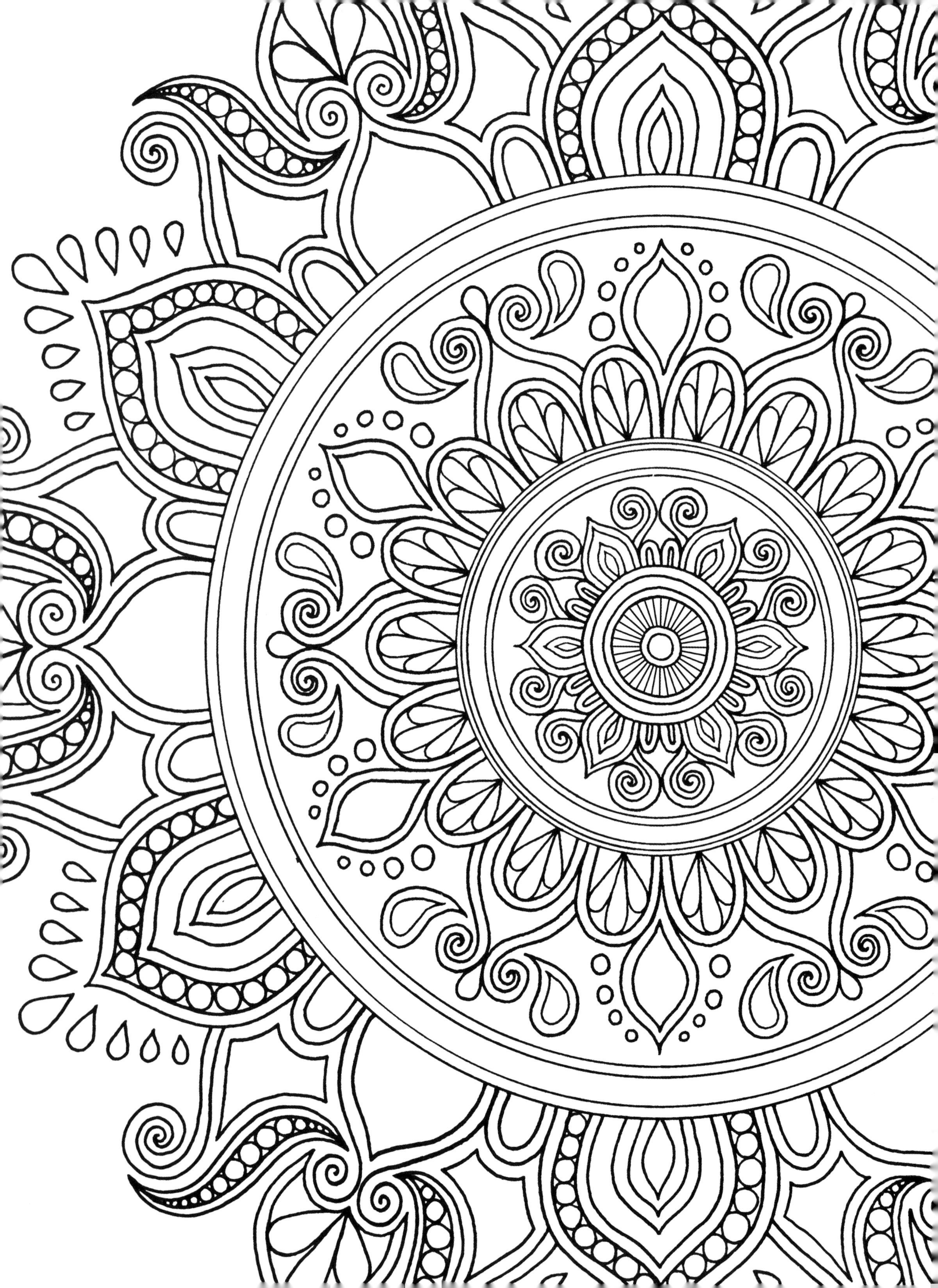

8

MAKE IT YOUR OWN

OVER THE NEXT PAGES, I have provided some of my line drawings, both of free-flowing designs and contemporary explorations of the mandala, for you to complete. Add your own design elements, experiment with color, or try different shading and detail techniques. Use these as practice templates or as an instant and accessible way to experience meditative drawing without starting from scratch. After the line drawings, I have also provided a blank mandala grid so you can study the structure and start the process of creating your own mandala.

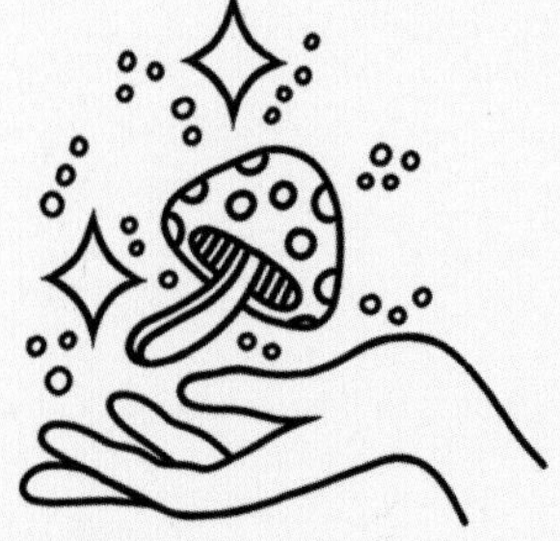

When practiced mindfully, drawing can deepen our connection with ourselves and the world around us.

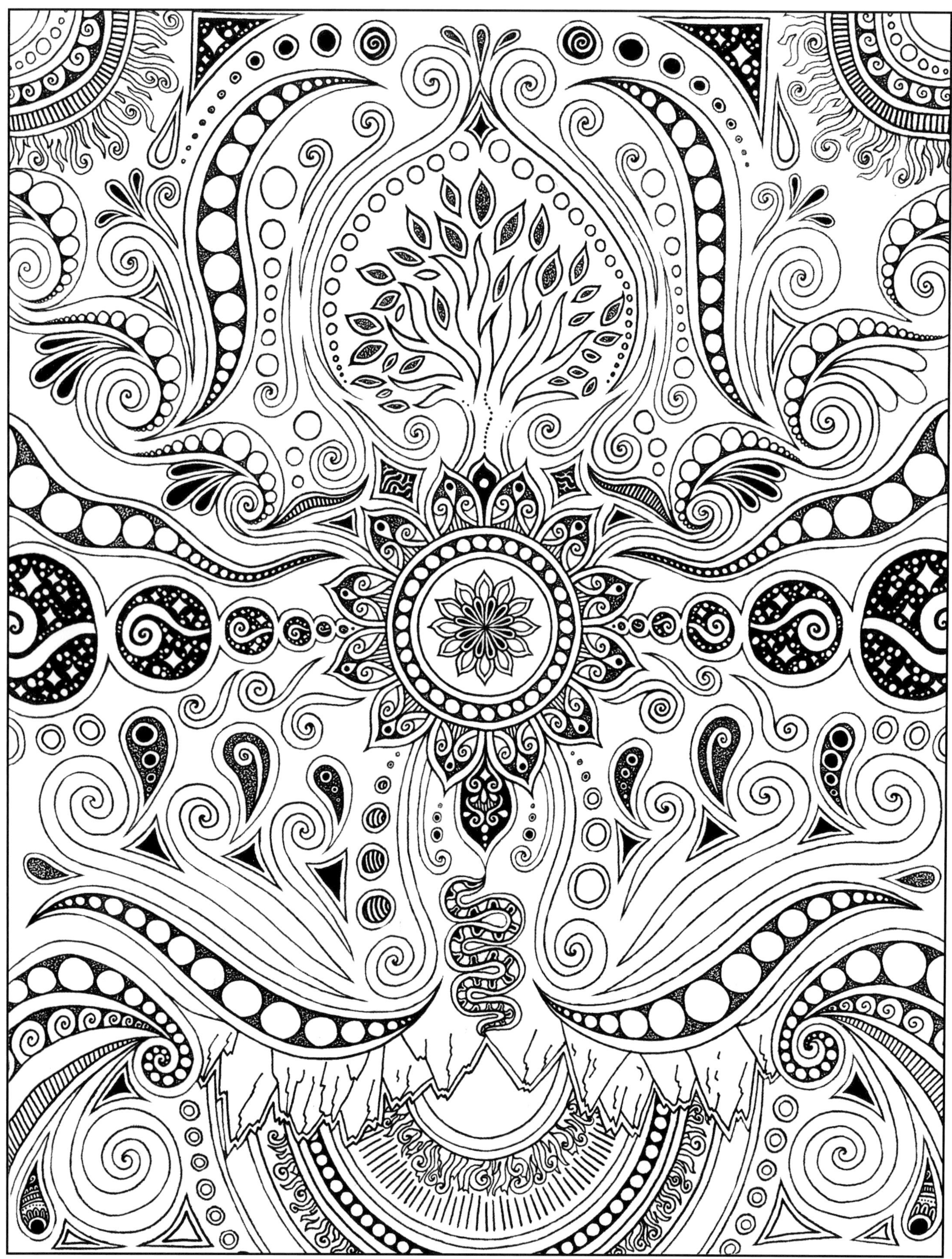

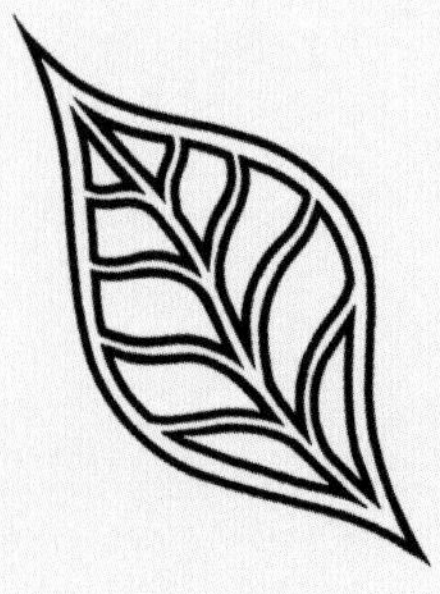

Drawing is a practice like anything else, and we get better through time, attention, and effort.

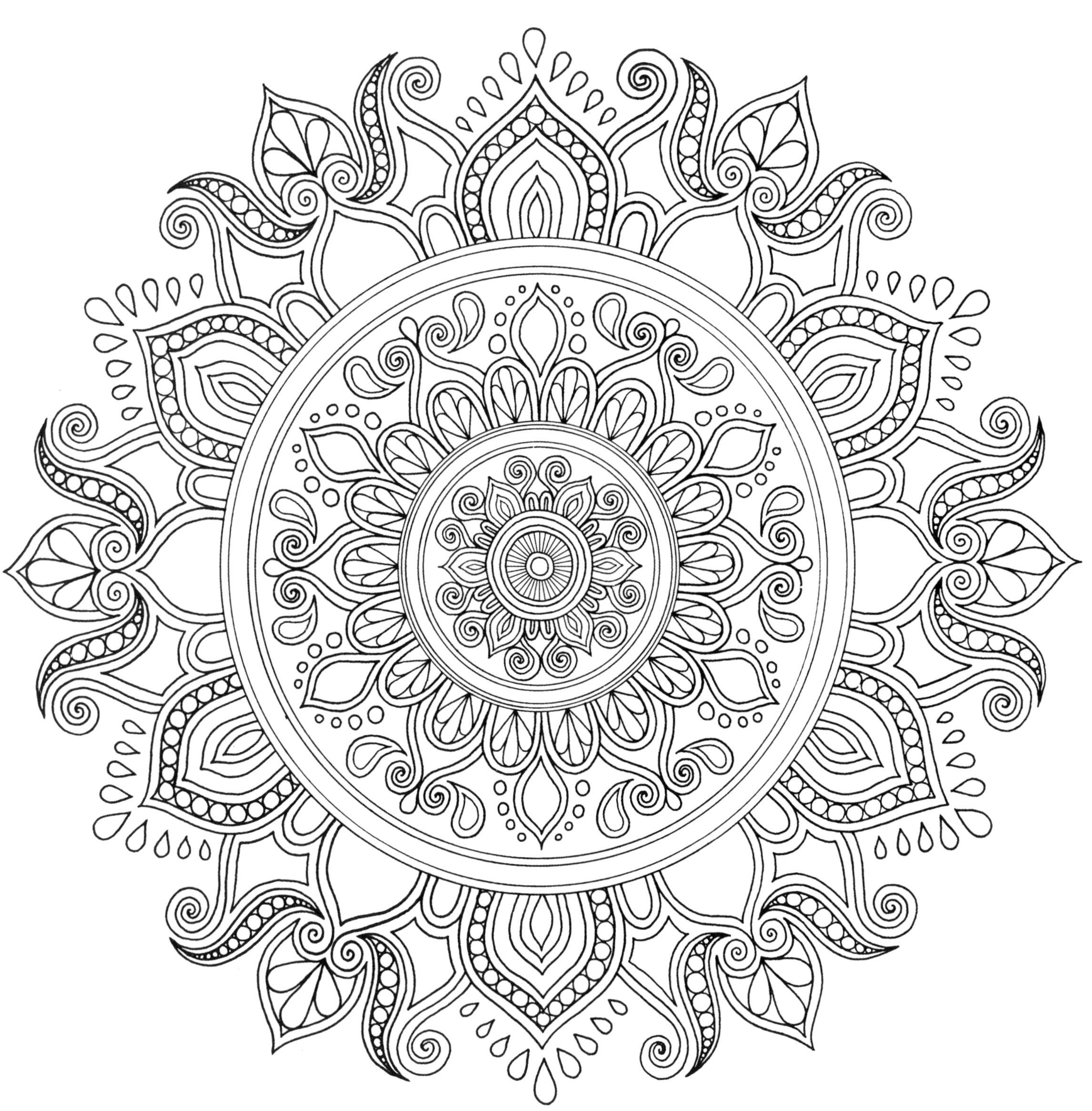

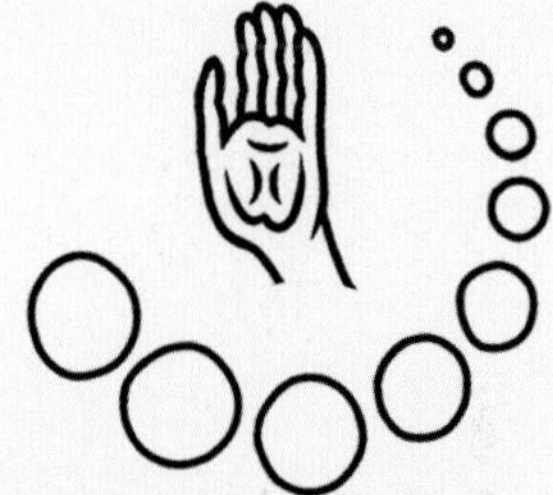

Give yourself permission and freedom to draw, to explore, and to tap into this practice that has been waiting for you at your fingertips.

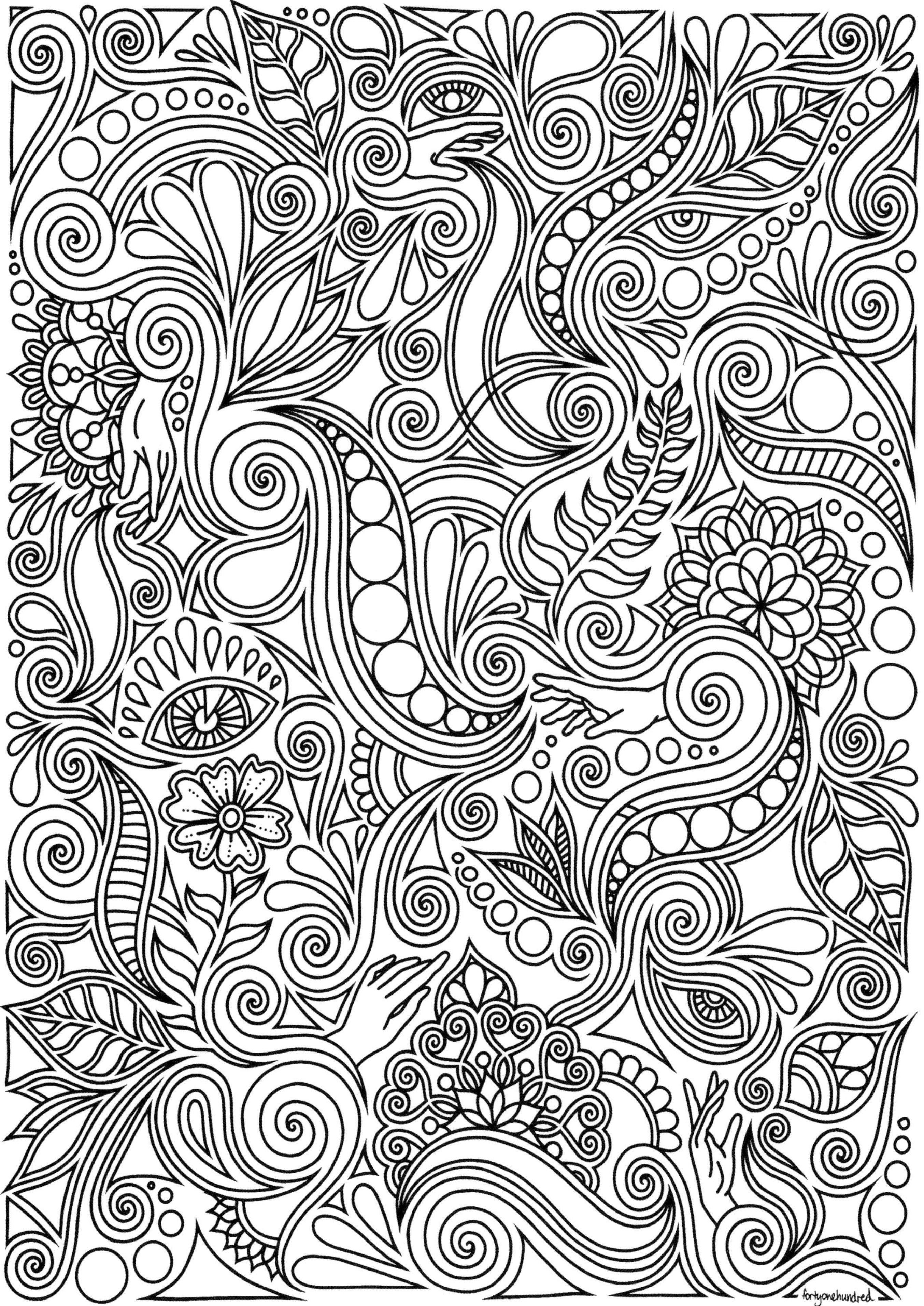
fortyonehundred

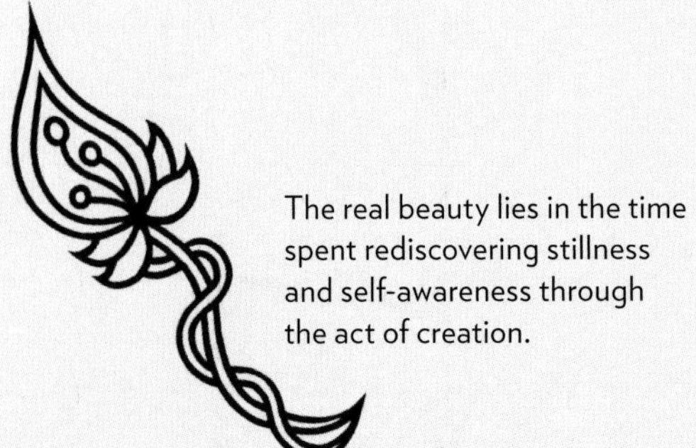

The real beauty lies in the time spent rediscovering stillness and self-awareness through the act of creation.

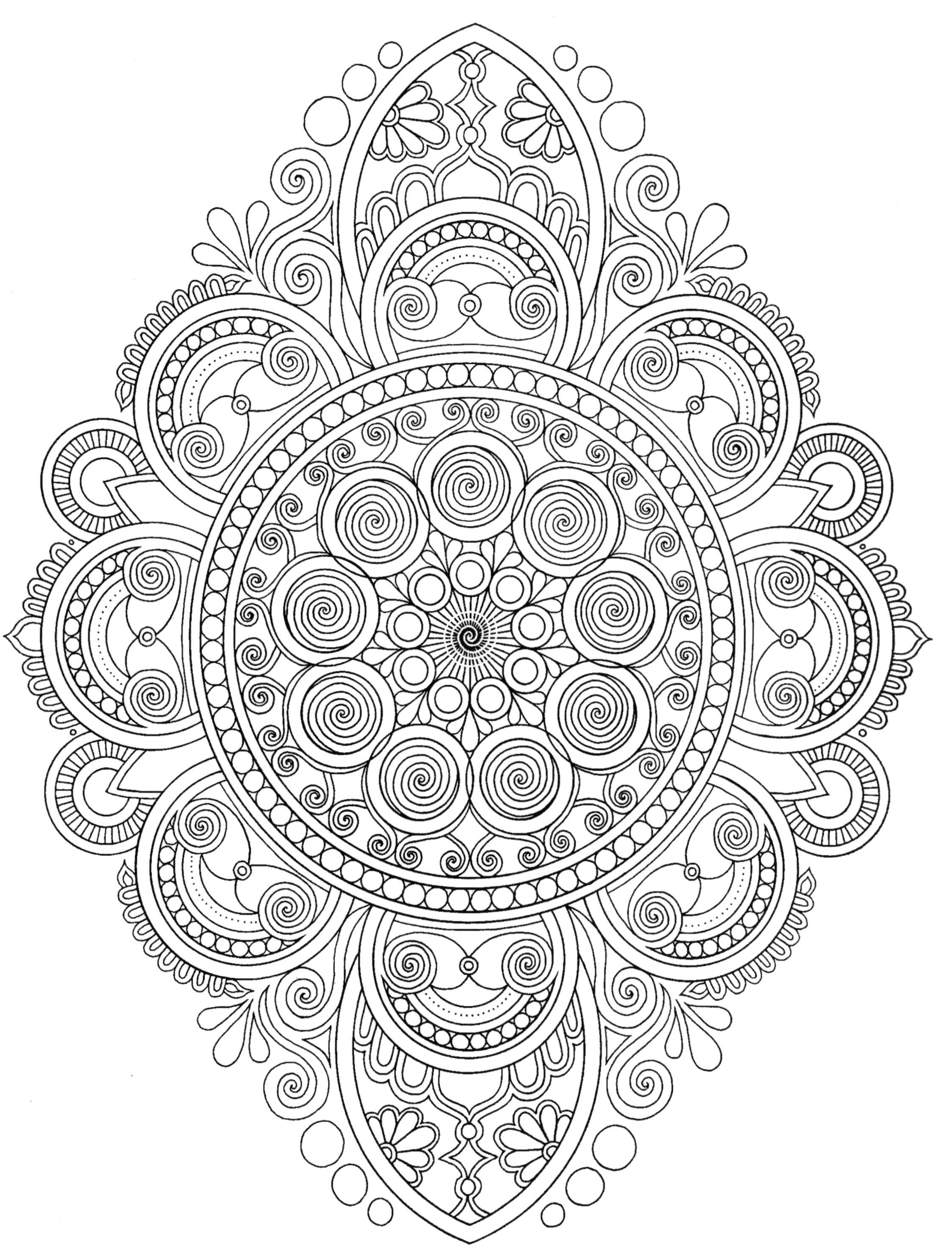

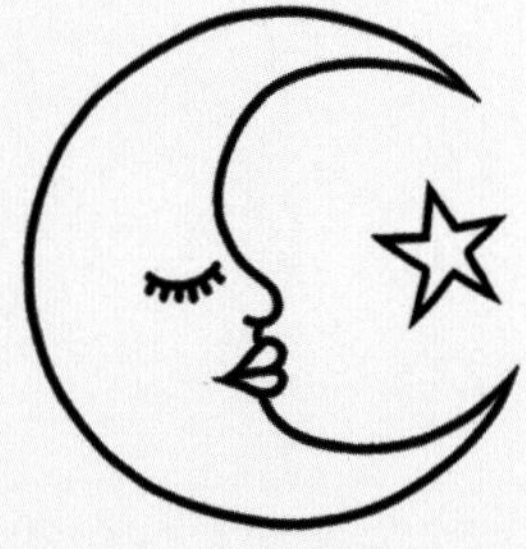

Let each touch of the pen or brush
become an act of meditation.

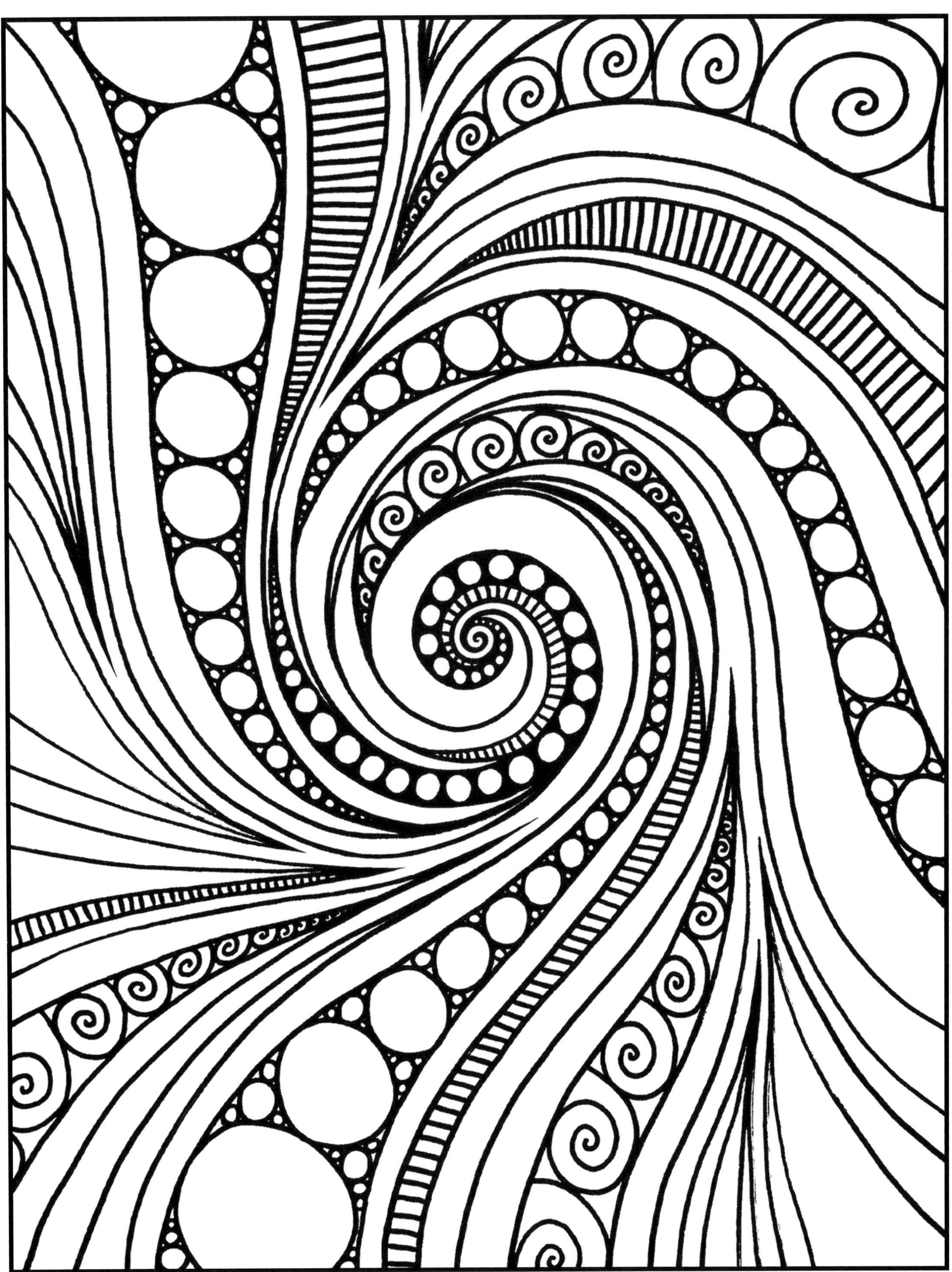

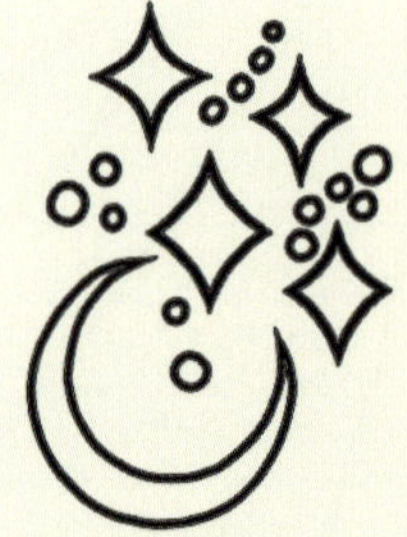

The practice of meditative drawing taps into our natural pull toward circular shapes and fractal patterns, promoting calmness and emotional well-being.

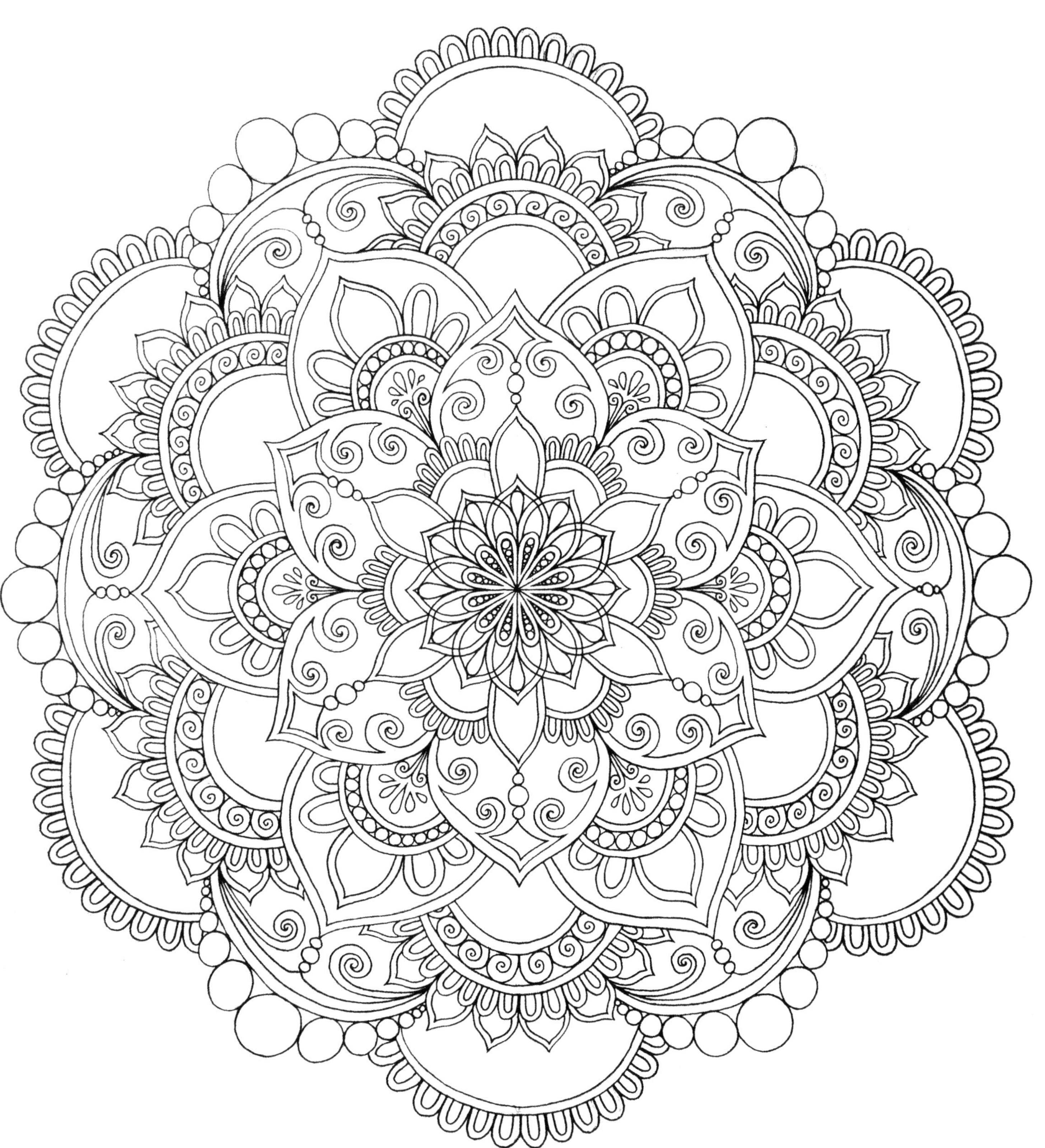

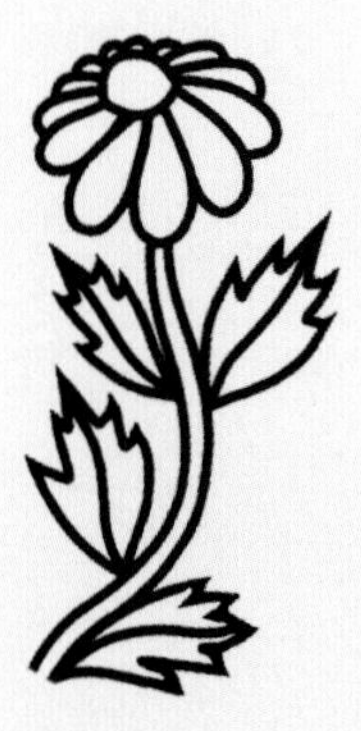

If you can draw a dot, then a line, then a dot and a line again—before you know it, you've created a pattern and the start of an artwork, and a beautiful one at that. You can draw.

MANDALA GRID

Here is a ready-made grid you can use to practice your own mandala designs.

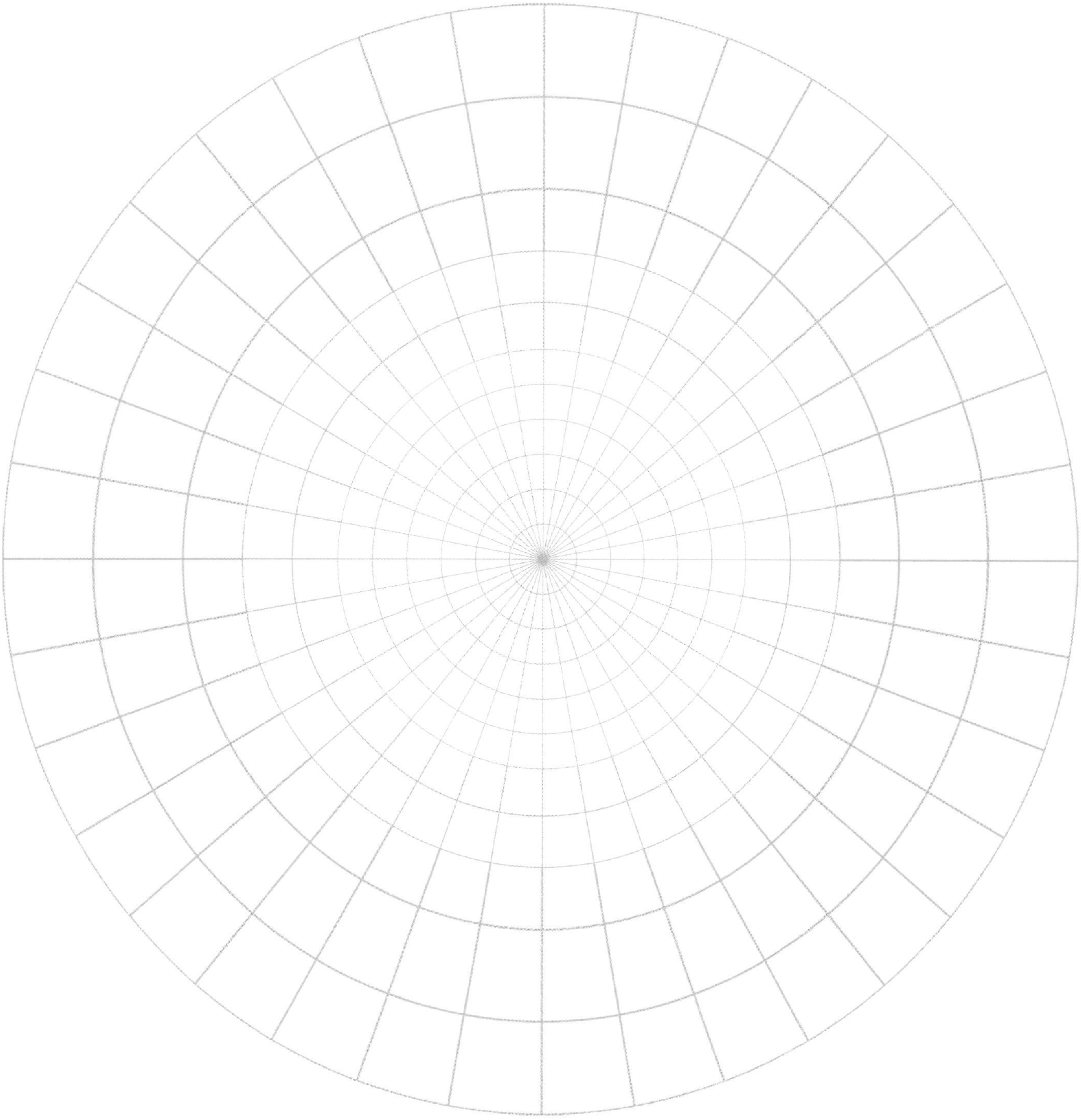

SCAN THIS CODE to download additional blank mandala grids.

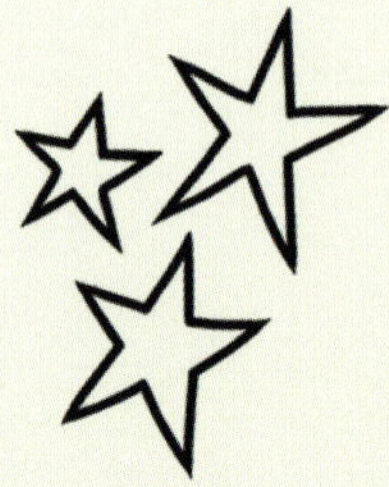

Being mindful and focused on the mark
being made encourages us to center ourselves
in the present moment.

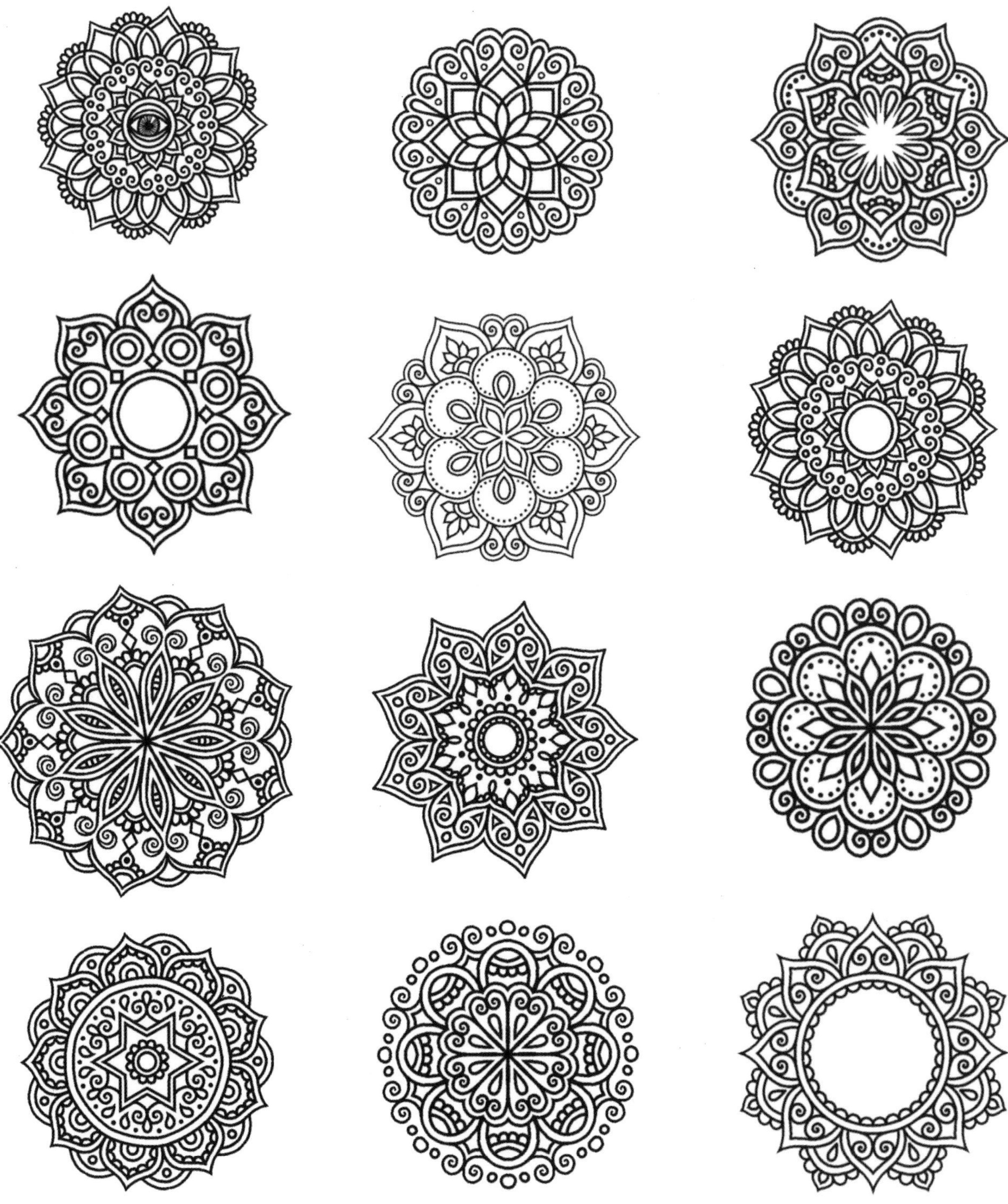

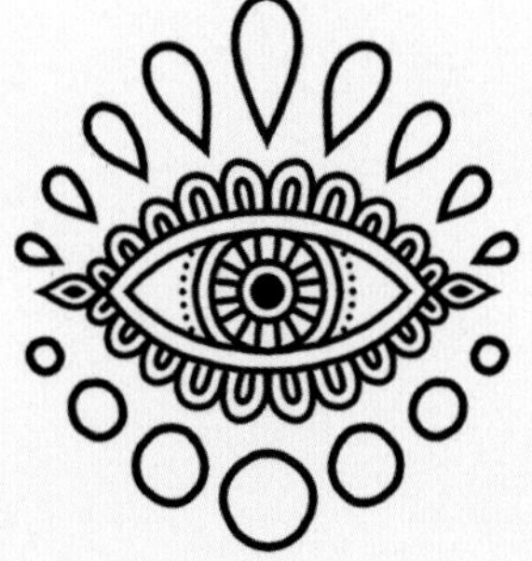

As we continue to draw, our skills evolve and new ideas emerge, leading us on a path of continual creative expansion.

CONCLUSION

Engaging in this practice of meditative drawing is not merely about the act of creating art; it is an invitation to explore and untap the creative energy that already lives within us.

As you immerse yourself in the repetition of drawing patterns, you may begin to notice subtle shifts in your mind and body. It's that same feeling you've experienced before—similar to the focus in yoga and the calmness of walking in nature.

Art has a unique capacity to serve as a bridge between our inner and outer worlds. These artworks can become a powerful tool for reflection, offering a lens through which we can examine our internal state, while contemplating the world around us.

This practice encourages us to strip away layers of self-doubt and external expectation, allowing us to access the infinite space of our imagination. After all, there's no pressure to share or present your drawings; it can simply be a private practice, between you and yourself.

Meditative drawing cultivates clarity, calm, and self-awareness, bringing a deeper sense of purpose and connection into your life. I hope you have enjoyed this book and that it encourages you to develop your own art practice.

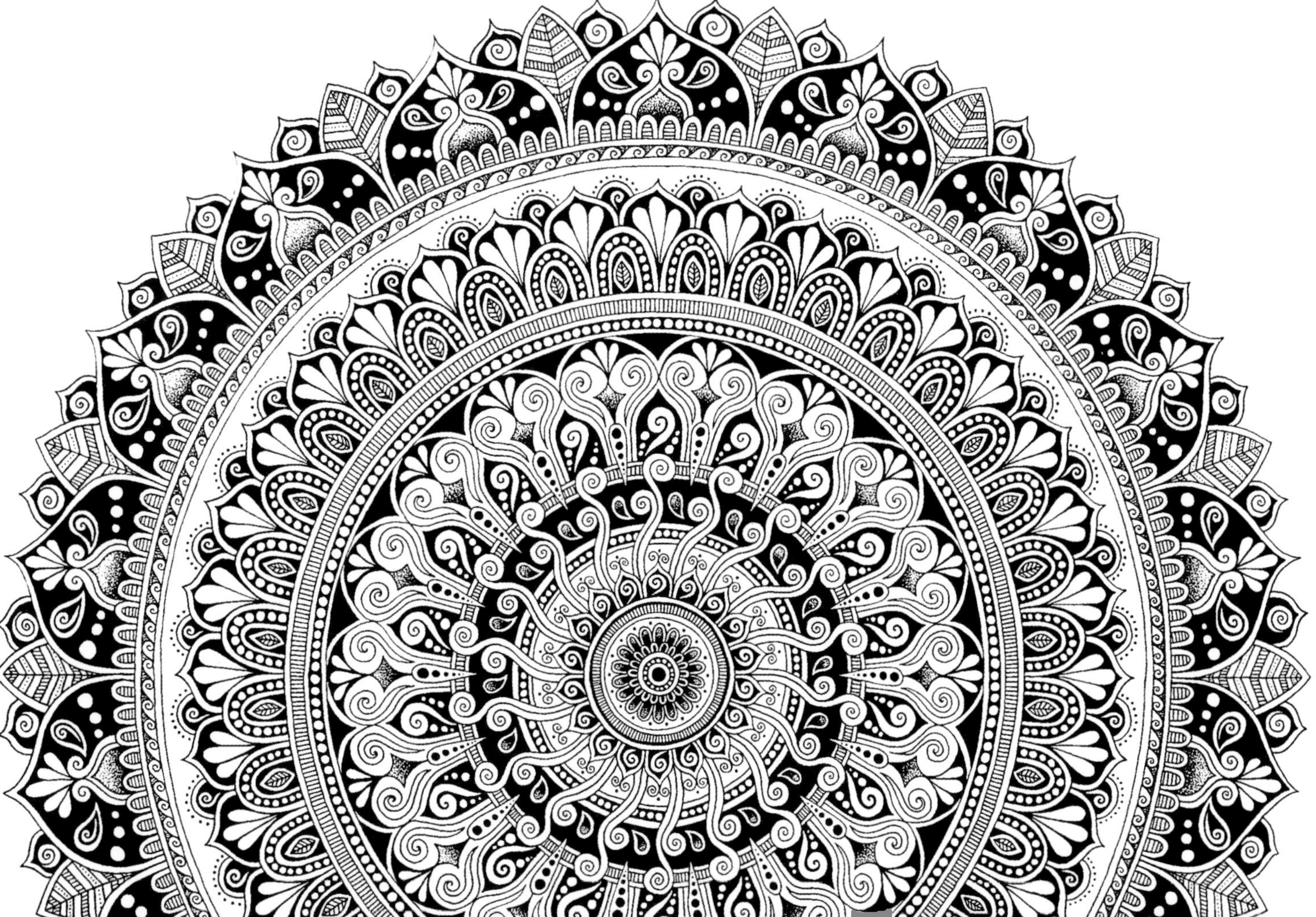

RESOURCES

For those interested in exploring mandalas, fractals, and mindfulness further, there is a wealth of reading and learning available. Below is a small selection of books and videos that offer valuable insights and inspiration on these topics. I've also included references to the studies mentioned throughout this book, providing a foundation for further academic exploration that can deepen your understanding and enrich your artistic practice.

Books

- *An Illustrated History of the Mandala: From Its Genesis to the Kalacakratantra*, Kimiaki Tanaka, Wisdom Publications, 2018.
- *Designa,* Adam Tetlow, Wooden Books, 2014.
- *Ernst Haeckel's Art Forms in Nature: A Visual Masterpiece of the Natural World,* Ernst Haeckel, Art Meets Science, 2023.
- *Fractals: On the Edge of Chaos,* Oliver Linton, Wooden Books, 2024.
- *Mandala: Journey to the Center,* Bailey Cunningham, DK, 2003.
- *Math for Mystics: From the Fibonacci Sequence to Luna's Labyrinth to the Golden Section and Other Secrets of Sacred Geometry*, Renna Shesso, Weiser Books, 2007.
- *Patterns in Nature: Why the Natural World Looks the Way It Does*, Philip Ball, University of Chicago Press, 2016.
- *Ruler and Compass: Practical Geometric Constructions*, Andrew Sutton, Wooden Books, 2022.
- *Sacred Geometry and Magical Symbols*, Iva Kenaz, Independently Published, 2018.
- *Sacred Geometry: Language of the Angels*, Richard Heath, Inner Traditions, 2021.
- *The Collected Works of C. G. Jung*, C. G. Jung, Princeton University Press.
- *The Golden Ratio: The Divine Beauty of Mathematics*, Gary B. Meisner, Race Point Publishing, 2018.
- *The Mandala Bible: The Definitive Guide to Using Sacred Shapes*, Madonna Gauding, Firefly Books, 2011.
- *The Mandala Book: Patterns of the Universe*, Lori Bailey Cunningham, Union Square & Co., 2020.
- *Mandala: The Architecture of Enlightenment*, Denise Patry Leidy, Asia Society Galleries Tibet House, 1998.

Videos

- *Abstract: The Art of Design* (Netflix)
- *Ai Weiwei: Never Sorry*
- *Fractals and the Art of Roughness*: Ted Talk by Benoit Mandelbrot
- *Fractals: Hunting the Hidden Dimension* (NOVA)
- *How Art Made the World* (BBC)
- *Sky Ladder* (Netflix)
- *The Code* (BBC)
- *The Secret Life of Chaos* (BBC)

Studies

Babouchkina, A., & Robbins, S. J. (2015a). Reducing negative mood through mandala creation: A randomized controlled trial. *Art Therapy*, 32(1), 34–39. https://doi.org/10.1080/07421656.2015.994428

Bühnemann, G. (2017). Modern mandala meditation: Some observations. *Contemporary Buddhism*, 18(2), 263–276. https://doi.org/10.1080/14639947.2017.1373434

Campenni, C. E., & Hartman, A. (2019). The effects of completing mandalas on mood, anxiety, and state mindfulness. *Art Therapy*, 37(1), 25–33. https://doi.org/10.1080/07421656.2019.1669980

Csikszentmihalyi, M. (1988). The flow experience and its significance for human psychology. *Optimal Experience*, 15-35. https://doi.org/10.1017/cbo9780511621956.002

Curry, N. A., & Kasser, T. (2005). Can coloring mandalas reduce anxiety? *Art Therapy*, 22(2), 81–85. https://doi.org/10.1080/07421656.2005.10129441

Greenhalgh, W. A. (2020). *Mindfulness & the Art of Drawing: A Creative Path to Awareness*. Brighton, UK: Leaping Hare Press.

Kellogg, J. (1978). *Mandala: Path of Beauty.* Lightfoot, VA: MARI.

Kellogg, J. (1992, July). Color from the perspective of the great round of mandala. *The Journal of Religion and Psychical Research*,15(23), 138–146.

Kellogg, J., & Di Leo, F. (1982, January). Archetypal stages of the great round of the mandala. *The Journal of Religion and Psychical Research*, 5(1), 38–48.

Kellogg, J., MacRae, M., Bonny, H., & Di Leo, F. (1977, July). The use of the mandala in psychological evaluation and treatment. *American Journal of Art Therapy*, 16, 123–130.

Robles, K. E., Liaw, N. A., Taylor, R. P., Baldwin, D. A., & Sereno, M. E. (2020). A shared fractal aesthetic across development. *Humanities and Social Sciences Communications*, 7(1). https://doi.org/10.1057/s41599-020-00648-y

Sabelli, H. (2000). Complement plots: Analyzing opposites reveals mandala-like patterns in human heart beats. *International Journal of General Systems*, 29(5), 799–830. https://doi.org/10.1080/03081070008960973

Sandmire, D. A., Gorham, S. R., Rankin, N. E., & Grimm, D. R. (2012). The influence of art making on anxiety: A pilot study. *Art Therapy*, 29(2), 68–73. https://doi.org/10.1080/07421656.2012.683748

Slegelis, M. H. (1987). A study of Jung's mandala and its relationship to art psychotherapy. *The Arts in Psychotherapy*, 14(4), 301–311. https://doi.org/10.1016/0197-4556(87)90018-9

Taylor, R. P., & Spehar, B. (2016). Fractal fluency: An intimate relationship between the brain and processing of fractal stimuli. *Springer Series in Computational Neuroscience*, 485–496. https://doi.org/10.1007/978-1-4939-3995-4_30

ACKNOWLEDGMENTS

I want to express my gratitude to everyone who has supported my creative venture over the past decade—whether through collecting my artworks, interest in this book and the online courses, being part of brand collaborations, engaging with my work online, or listening to me ramble on excitedly about fractals. All of it counts, and I couldn't have done it without you.

To my family, especially my amazing parents, Geraldine and Barry—for their constant support and providing a full life of education and unconditional love. To my friends, particularly Claudia—for her fun spirit, gentle guidance, writing retreats . . . and collaborative procrastination. And to my lovely little dog, George, who isn't here now but was a big part of my story.

Thanks also goes to a few people who may not know the impact they've had: My great-aunt Isabel, a thoughtful academic and fascinating person, has always been my supporter. One of my schoolteachers, Mr. Peters, originally inspired my interest in learning. My neighbors and family friends, Fiona and Graham, have always been kind and interested in my antics. My master's supervisor, Tonya, let me follow my own path while also somehow keeping me on track. My friend and fellow artist, Sean, helped me join a shared art studio in Wellington when I was just starting out. I feel very lucky to know and cross paths with these wonderful, intelligent people.

Thank you to the brands and business partnerships that have supported my work, especially Apple®—without which I couldn't create my work or have written this book.

I am very grateful for my book editors, Michelle Bredeson and Karen Julian, and the whole team at Quarry and Quarto Publishing for their belief in me (and their patience) throughout the process of bringing this book to fruition.

Thank you all for being part of this adventure. I'm excited to share the next chapter of my journey with you.

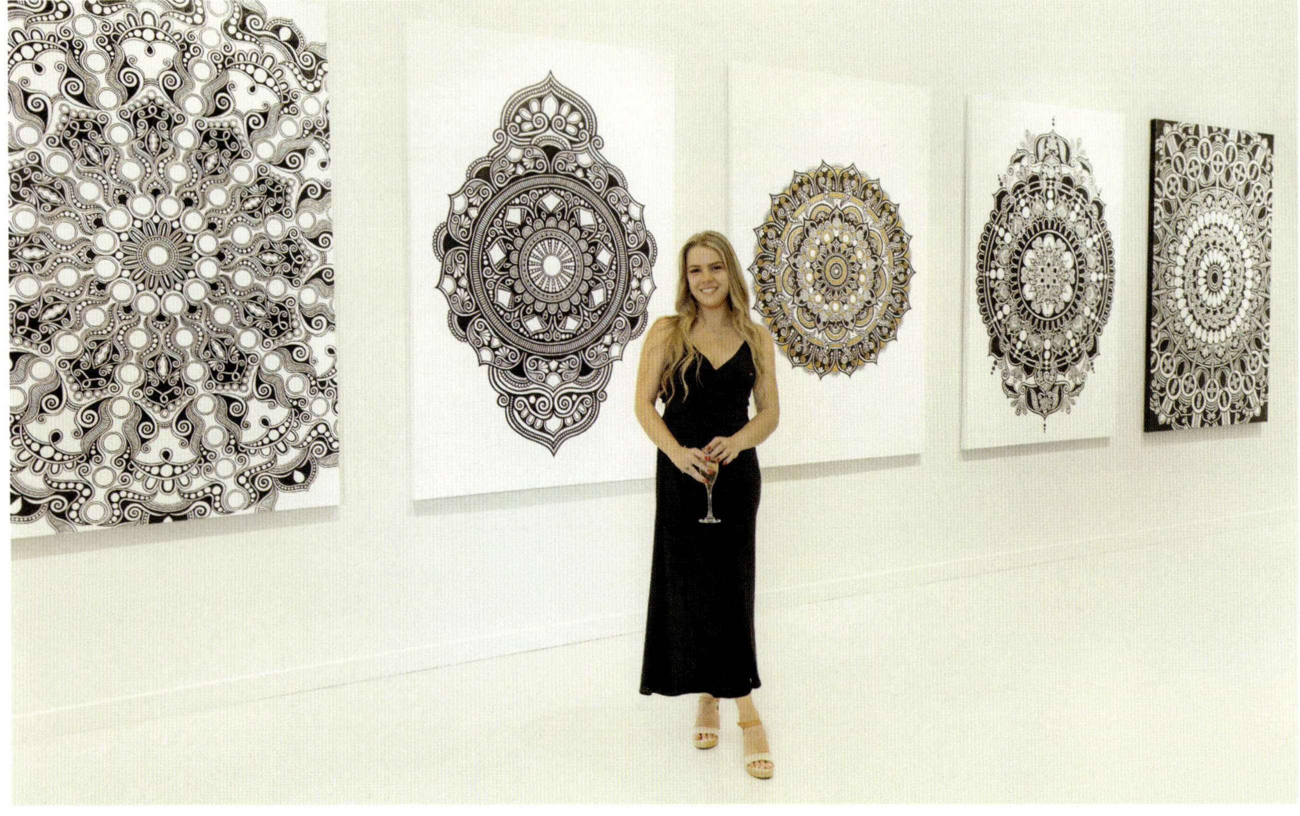

INDEX